MUSICOLOGY

Musicology: The Key Concepts provides a vital reference guide for students of contemporary musicology. Its clear and accessible entries cover a comprehensive range of terms, including:

- Aesthetics
- Canon
- Culture
- Deconstruction
- Ethnicity
- Identity
- Subjectivity
- Value
- Work

Fully cross-referenced and with suggestions for further reading, this is an essential resource for all students of music.

David Beard and **Kenneth Gloag** are Lecturers in Music at Cardiff University.

YOU MAY ALSO BE INTERESTED IN THE FOLLOWING ROUTLEDGE STUDENT REFERENCE TITLES:

MUSICOLOGY

The Key Concepts

David Beard and Kenneth Gloag

LONDON AND NEW YORK

First published 2005
by Routledge
2 Park Square, Milton Park, Abingdon, Oxon, OX14 4RN

Simultaneously published in the USA and Canada
by Routledge
270 Madison Ave, New York, NY 10016

Routledge is an imprint of the Taylor & Francis Group

© 2005 David Beard and Kenneth Gloag

Typeset in Bembo by Taylor & Francis Books
Printed and bound in Great Britain by
TJ International Ltd, Padstow, Cornwall

British Library Cataloguing in Publication Data
A catalogue record for this book is available from the British Library

Library of Congress Cataloging in Publication Data
Beard, David.
   Musicology: the key concepts / David Beard and Kenneth Gloag.
      p. cm.
   Includes bibliographical references (p.   ) and index.
   ISBN 0-415-31693-6 (hardback : alk. paper) -- ISBN 0-415-31692-8 (pbk. : alk. paper)
1. Musicology. I. Gloag, Kenneth. II. Title.
   ML3797.B35 2005
   780′.72--dc22

                                                                                    2004017044

ISBN: 0-415-31693-6 (hbk)
ISBN: 0-415-31692-8 (pbk)

CONTENTS

LIST OF KEY CONCEPTS

absolute
aesthetics
alterity
analysis
authenticity
autonomy
avant-garde

biography (life and work)
body

canon
class
cover version
critical musicology
critical theory
criticism
cultural studies
cultural theory
culture
culture industry

deconstruction
diegetic/nondiegetic
discourse

Enlightenment
ethnicity
ethnomusicology
expressionism

feminism
form
formalism

gay musicology
gender
genius
genre
globalization

hermeneutics
historical musicology
historicism
historiography
history
hybridity

identity
ideology
influence
interpretation
intertextuality

jazz

landscape
language
literary theory

Marxism
meaning

ACKNOWLEDGEMENTS

The idea for this book emerged through our experience of teaching students, both undergraduate and postgraduate, in music at Cardiff University and we would like to thank all who helped produce the positive atmosphere within which this book was conceived. More specifically, our ideas have been explored and developed through our MA programmes in Musicology and Music, Culture and Politics, and the supervision of research students, and we would like to acknowledge the importance of the exchange of idea and perspective between ourselves and numerous postgraduate students over recent years. In particular we would like to thank Natasha Page, Bryan Marshall, David Manning, Alana Lowe-Petraske, Sarah Hill, Frances Mitchell, Danijela Špirić and Carys Wyn Jones for their input.

A number of colleagues at Cardiff University provided valuable advice and comments and, particularly in the early stages, the presence of Peter Sedgwick was invaluable. We would also like to thank David Wyn Jones and Charles Wilson for their comments on this project from proposal to completion. Finally, this book would not have been possible without the support of Milon Nagi, Rosie Waters and their colleagues at Routledge, and we extend our thanks to them.

NOTE ON THE TEXT

The aim of this book is to make available a range of ideas for further consideration and discussion. We have therefore attempted as far as possible to use modern editions of texts that the reader is most likely to have access to. In some cases, this takes the form of anthologies and translations. For example, when we refer to Kant's *Critique of Judgement*, we base our references on the extracts translated and published by le Huray and Day in their superb collection titled *Music and Aesthetics in the Eighteenth and Early Nineteenth Centuries* (le Huray and Day 1981), which, although out of print at the time of writing, is more likely to be available in a music library than is Kant's complete text. We hope that this will form a first point of contact through which a path can be taken towards other complete texts and related concepts.

Bibliographical references are given throughout using the author date system. However, where we make passing reference to a year of publication without the author's name in parentheses, this is intended only to give a historical location and not to form part of the reference system. Dates of historical figures, such as composers and philosophers, are given in the name index, and all cross-references are indicated in bold.

INTRODUCTION

Music/musicology

Music and musicology are both separate and related constructs. Music, as a practical activity, has its own history, but musicology, as a process of study, inquiry and reflection, while it forms its own context and employs distinct concepts, is clearly dependent upon and reflective of music as its subject.

Music has a long history, while musicology has, by comparison, enjoyed a relatively short lifespan. Yet musicology, which can broadly be defined as the thinking about and study of music, could be argued to have been already present within the acts of composing and performing music. Music is an art form and context that has always invited theoretical speculation and critical reflection, and we can presume that composers, for example, have always thought about their own creative processes and that these processes are somehow informed by the study and experience of other, already existing, music. However, such reflection and interaction may be seen to stop short of a properly conceived musicology that could be understood to stand outside the creative process in order to provide a clearer perspective upon that process, its end product in the form of a musical **work** and, just as significant, the social and cultural contexts within which the process and product could be situated and interpreted. This broad conception of musicology is in contrast to the narrower focus of specific aspects of musicological activity. Although earlier figures such as Forkel and Fétis outlined programmes of what could be conceived of as an early musicology, it was Austrian musicologist Guido Adler who provided the first description of, effectively a prescription for, musicology. In an article titled 'Umfang, Methode und Ziel der Musikwissenschaft' (The scope, method and aim of musicology), published in 1885 in the first issue of *Vierteljahrsschrift für Musikwissenschaft* (Adler 1885; see also Bujić 1988, 348–55), Adler outlined a separation between the historical and systematic dimensions of music, with the rigour of the exercise reflected in the term *Musikwissenschaft* (science of music). He repeated this model in his *Methode der Musikgesichte*, published in 1919. For Adler, the historical field consisted of the organization of music history into epochs, periods and nations. In contrast, the systematic field was to consist of the internal properties and characteristics of music such as harmony and tonality. Clearly, a great deal of musicological activity after Adler could be seen to reflect this division, with the study of music history often reflecting large-scale categorization (see **historiography**) and the construction of a **canon** of the Western tradition of classical music. However, the systematic field could be seen to anticipate the development of music **analysis** and the emergence of specific theories of harmony, tonality and form (see **theory**). However, what is most revealing about Adler's project in general is its quasi-scientific nature, with the claim of the systematic reflecting the rationalizing and positivistic (see **positivism**) impulses and search for objectivity common to a number of musicological contexts. However one responds to Adler's division, the study of music remains a set of distinct areas, many of which might be significantly different from any other while also potentially informing each other. This difference is further extended in this book through the inclusion of areas such as ethnomusicology (see **ethnicity**), **jazz** and **popular music** studies, with musicology now understood as an all-embracing term for the study of music that embraces difference and respects the 'whole musical field' (Middleton 1990, 7), a project that is different from more traditional models of musicology, which had previously sought to exclude such music and ideas from its domain. We are not the first to make this claim of difference, and we see our enterprise as reflecting the current condition of the discipline (or disciplines?) of musicology.

A possible historical narrative for musicology could suggest that a point of origin could be situated within the reflections upon the nature, content and function of music that existed in the distant past of ancient Greece and the theories of Plato and the poetics of Aristotle (see Barker 1989). Later, but still distant, writings upon music took the form of medieval and **Renaissance** treatises and polemics. The **Enlightenment** of the eighteenth century witnessed the rationalization of knowledge and consequently further enhanced the position and status of music within an intellectual **discourse**. The Enlightenment also gave birth to the emergence of a new historical consciousness that would further develop during the nineteenth century. The eighteenth century also brought into focus the philosophical inquiry into the nature of music in the shape of an aesthetics of music. **Historicism** and aestheticism (see **aesthetics**) became central characteristics of the nineteenth century and the defining **Roman-ticism** of that time. Romanticism reflected the literary, linguistic dimensions of musical experience, which were simultaneously heightened and subverted by the impact of **modernism** in the early twentieth century, with the rationalization of modernity providing a context for the systematic study of music in the form of musicology.

The above synopsis of a historical development is persuasive and accurate in terms of a chronology and main developments, yet it also has its problems. It suggests a linear **narrative**, an onward progression and development through time, with one phase connecting to the next with a remarkable degree of continuity and inevitability, leading towards Adler's musicology and then the contexts and concept of modernism, suggesting a historical narrative that is ripe for **decon-struction**. In other words, it tells a certain history that is informative but that also simplifies, effectively ignoring the detours and disrup-tions, misinterpreting the ruptures and ripples and replacing difference with similarity. Paradoxically, it now demands a more complex per-spective. In dealing with the contemporary condition of musicology through its key concepts, we hope that we can provide the reader with the starting points from which the critical understandings of such paradoxes can begin to emerge.

In this book, we have taken the broad perspective, reflecting the diversity of our own musical experiences and interests, which we think also reflects the contemporary situation of both music and musicology. Therefore, references to **jazz**, or different aspects of **popular music**, for example, for us sit easily alongside our interests in aspects of the Western art music **tradition**. We see no contradiction, or tension, between interest in, and an ability to write about, the music of Bee-thoven, Birtwistle, Coltrane, Bill Frissell and Cornershop, and to engage with the writings of Barthes, Derrida, Dahlhaus and Kerman, among others. If this book then looks to a diversity of musical and intellectual interests, there is also, we hope, an underlying consistency as defined by the actual concepts identified as suitable for inclusion. Many concepts, such as **post-structuralism** and **postmodernism**, for example, both of which have come late to musicology, have a relevance and explanatory force for all musical contexts.

Clearly, there are problems in distinguishing between concept and context. We can conceptualize **style**, for example, as a set of issues that surround the use of this term in musical discourse and discuss the use of style as a subject and parameter of musicological inquiry. But this may ultimately be a different exercise from the writing of a detailed history of a specific style or stylistic period (see **periodization**), such as the Classical or Baroque style, an exercise that would involve a specific context. However, the process of inquiry may require the application of various different concepts. From this perspective, our selection of concepts is a reflection of a certain practice, in effect a keywords of musicology. These concepts can now be conceived of as forming part of the contemporary musicologist's toolbox.

Musicology has undergone dramatic changes since the 1980s. In writing this book we became highly aware of a before and after effect, in which a certain shift in musicological discourse became a recurrent feature. We try to avoid this as a recurrent model and perhaps also to avoid the temptation to over-interpret or over-dramatize this situation. Nevertheless, the essential fact is that what constitutes musicology now is very different from how it might have looked in the 1960s or 1970s. It is also important to reflect upon the fact that these shifts occur in parallel with the broadening of musical repertories that are seen as being available for musicology. But what came before and what came after? What is the dividing line, and is it real or imaginary?

In 1980, American musicologist Joseph Kerman published an article titled 'How We Got into Analysis, and How to Get Out' (Kerman 1994). Without doing a systematic musicological search, we guess that this is probably one of the most commonly cited texts in this book: it appears in relation to concepts such as analysis, **new musicology** and post-structuralism, among others, and it is clearly a polemical statement that has enjoyed a wide range of responses and reactions. In 1985, Kerman published a book titled *Contemplating Music* in America and *Musicology* in Britain (Kerman 1985) in which he outlines the divisions of musicology and presents a critique of what he perceives as the **formalism** and positivism that had come to define musicology. In the article, Kerman outlined the problems of analysis, its ideological nature (see **ideology**) and consequently the relationship between analysis and **organicism** as a 'ruling ideology' (Kerman 1994, 15). Kerman's critique is a persuasive one, highlighting the *a priori* assumptions that musical analysis can easily make about the unity of a musical work. However, for some, it may just as easily raise other problems. Kerman's plea for a more 'humane' form of criticism may be rather vague, and his discussion of Schumann's 'Aus meinen Thänen spriessen' from the song cycle *Dichterliebe* (1840) might just be the type of programmatic description that many musicologists will remain suspicious of. However, this article and the book that followed did make an impact, and much of the writing that comes after Kerman, some of which has been described as forming a new musicology, often acknowledges the power of Kerman's arguments. So, do

Kerman's polemics provide the dividing line between an old and a new musicology? With reference to Kerman's *Musicology*, Nicholas Cook and Mark Everist, in the preface to a collection of essays titled *Rethinking Music*, suggest that a 'before Kerman/after Kerman paradigm' may be a myth, yet, 'as myths go, this is quite a helpful one' (Cook and Everist 1999, viii). We would agree with this view. For some, musicology after Kerman may be marked by a sense of loss, a nostalgia for musicology past, while, for others, the current state of the discipline is better for the critical reflection inspired by Kerman. It also provides a reference point, a moment against which departures can be measured.

It is possible, therefore, that musicology becomes more critical and less positivistic, more concerned with interpretations and less with facts (see **interpretation**). It has also become more interdisciplinary as the boundaries between different types of music are partially erased and the search for new critical models pushes way beyond the limits of a traditional musicology. For some, this is something to be resisted (see Williams 2004) but, from our own vantage point, this is a good time to try to be a musicologist, with a seemingly endless range of music to study and the challenge of developing and extending our vision and vocabulary providing endless stimulus and motivation for current and future research. We hope this book will help.

Further reading: Bowman 1998; Korsyn 2003; Shuker 1998; Stevens 1980; Williams 2001

MUSICOLOGY

The Key Concepts

ABSOLUTE

The concept absolute music emerged during the **Romanticism** of the nineteenth century and was first articulated in the writings of philosophers such as Herder and critics such as E.T.A. Hoffmann (see **criticism**). Paradoxically, however, it was given musical and philosophical representation in the writings of Richard Wagner, who coined the term (Dahlhaus 1989a, 18). It refers to purely instrumental music that appears to exist without reference to anything beyond itself and was often seen as the opposite of programme music, or music with a descriptive content. It therefore featured in the polemics of the Viennese critic Eduard Hanslick (see **aesthetics**, **criticism**, **meaning**), who attacked the extra-musical dimensions of Wagner's work and, through the understanding of a pure, absolute music, led to the claim of an aesthetic **autonomy** and a formalist account of music (see **formalism**).

E.T.A. Hoffmann's writings on Beethoven had raised the importance of instrumental music and located it within the context of Romanticism. In his famous review of Beethoven's Fifth Symphony (1807–8), Hoffmann declares:

> When music is spoken of as an independent art the term can properly apply only to instrumental music, which scorns all aid, all admixture of other arts, and gives pure expression to its own particular nature. It is the most romantic of all arts – one might say the only one that is *purely* romantic.
>
> (Charlton 1989, 236)

This suggestion of an 'independent art', by implication an absolute music, elevates instrumental music and ascribes a high aesthetic **value** through the formation of a **canon** of great works, processes that were most clearly defined through the context of the symphony (see **genre**).

For Wagner, absolute music was an object of criticism from his own perspective of the music-drama, which sought to embrace the widest possible musical and extra-musical world. However, through reference to the Ninth Symphony of Beethoven (1822–4), Wagner proposes a sense of transition, or emergence. Referring to the instrumental recitative of the fourth movement, Wagner states: 'Already almost breaking the bounds of absolute music, it stems the tumult of the other instruments with its virile eloquence, pressing toward decision, and passes at last into a song like-theme' (Dahlhaus 1989a, 18). Clearly,

Beethoven's Ninth Symphony, with its incorporation of text and voice, was an important work for Wagner, which he interpreted as a model for his own synthesis of music and **language**. The music that Wagner describes as absolute is music that becomes absolute through its lack, or absence, of certain features, but, for supporters of an absolute music, these absences were its strength. German musicologist Carl Dahlhaus, in his definitive study of absolute music, states:

> The idea of 'absolute music' – as we may henceforth call independent instrumental music...consists of the conviction that instrumental music purely and clearly expresses the true nature of music by the very lack of concept, object, and purpose.
>
> (*ibid.*, 7)

In other words, music was seen to achieve a certain purity around its lack of a fixed concept or function, claims that echo the 'art for art's sake' ethos of the period. For Dahlhaus, this absolute music now became paradigmatic: 'the idea of absolute music – gradually and against resistance – became the [a]esthetic paradigm of German musical culture in the nineteenth century' (*ibid.*). The establishment of this paradigm posed problems for the **reception** of other genres, such as the lied, which depended upon a text for its nature and identity. The debates generated around the claim towards an absolute music also cast a shadow over **modernism** during the twentieth century through its own utopian aspirations towards an aesthetic purity and autonomy.

Further reading: Chua 1999; Dahlhaus 1983a, 1989b; Grey 1995; Hoeckner 2002

AESTHETICS

'Aesthetics' is a general term that was coined to describe philosophical reflection on the arts, including music. An aesthetics of music, therefore, asks some fundamental questions about the subject, such as what is its nature? What does music mean? Individual positions and beliefs can be described as aesthetic. It is also associated with **ideology** in that specific sets of beliefs situate specific aesthetic responses and interpretations (see, for example, **Marxism**) and can also dictate the nature of the questions asked of music.

While the philosophical scrutiny of music has a long history, beginning with Plato and Aristotle (see Barker 1989), the origin of the term is generally associated with Baumgarten, who used it in his *Meditationes philosophicae de nonnullis ad poema pertinentibus* of 1735 (le Huray and Day 1981, 214; Baumgarten 1954). Baumgarten was concerned with the distinction between knowledge and perception and their respective faculties, superior and lower: '*Things known*, then, are those known by the superior faculty; they come within the ambit of logic. *Things perceived* come within the ambit of the science of perception and are the object of the lower faculty. These may be termed *aesthetic*' (le Huray and Day 1981, 214). On this account, aesthetics is concerned with perception, how we see art, read literature and listen to music. All these acts require us to interpret what we see, read and hear, therefore it is possible to understand aesthetics in relation to **interpretation** (see **hermeneutics**). Baumgarten's distinction between things known and things perceived also relates to the opposition between rationalism and empiricism (between what we know and what we experience) that was a recurring feature of the period (see **Enlightenment**).

One of the foundational texts of aesthetics is Immanuel Kant's *Critique of Judgement* (*Kritik der Urteilskraft*, 1790; see Kant 1987), who was one of the leading German philosophers of the period. It is therefore logical that his ideas have been given a certain prominence. Much of Kant's thought emerges through the tension between empiricism and rationalism, with his distinctive contribution being the forging of a synthesis between these two large-scale poles. In the critique, Kant is concerned with how an aesthetic quality such as beauty may be both perceived and rationalized. Musicologist Wayne Bowman, in his book *Philosophical Perspectives on Music* (Bowman 1998), provides a neat summary:

> Kant explores the distinctive characteristics and grounds for judgements of beauty from four perspectives, or four 'moments': their quality, their quantity, their relation, and their modality. The quality of aesthetic judgements is, he says, *disinterested*. Their quantity is, though *conceptless*, *universal*. Their relation is *purposive* (while strictly speaking, *purposeless*). And their modality is *exemplary*.
>
> (Bowman 1998, 77)

What does it mean to describe a judgement as disinterested? For Kant, we need a certain sense of detachment, an aesthetic purity, which leads us to avoid the temptation of seeking to prove or establish a pre-determined outcome. If, for example, we approach a painting with the expectation that it is beautiful, then it is likely that the expectation will be fulfilled. For Kant, this is not an aesthetic judgement. Rather, if we are disinterested then we are more likely to allow ourselves to achieve a truer perception of whether the art work is beautiful or not. However, in order for it to be a judgement, it has to be grounded in something more than mere personal preference. For some, this disinterestedness, by implication a detachment, leads not only to a certain aesthetic purity but also to a disengagement with the real world and the reality of art works. It could also ignore the contexts, circumstances and beliefs that may conspire to influence our perception.

Kant's reference to the universal provides a step from individual perception to a more general, collective understanding. In other words, if we perceive the art work to be beautiful, others should be able to experience the same qualities. This universality shifts the act of judgement away from a pure **subjectivity**, and this distinguishes Kant's view from Baumgarten's 'lower faculty'. Kant also raises the question of the purpose of the art work, the third of the four perspectives summarized by Bowman, and it is this perspective that looks towards **formalism**. For Kant, aesthetic judgements are grounded in the work itself, its patterns, structures and what he defines as its 'formal finality'. In other words, how the work is recognized as a complete entity, a unified object, reflects a process of judgement. Finally, Bowman refers to a modality that is exemplary. The aesthetic judgement defines a condition that is set as an example, it becomes a model for others, a view that looks towards the establishment of a condition of **value** (see **canon**). This summary of Kant's thought outlines a series of issues that recur throughout the history of aesthetics.

Kant was also concerned with the comparison of different art forms, including music, and considered their relative aesthetic merits:

As far as charm and stimulation go, I should place after poetry that art which comes closer to it than any of the other arts of eloquence and which can thus very naturally be combined with it: music. For although it communicates by means of mere sensations without concepts, and therefore does not, like poetry, leave anything to reflect on, it nevertheless moves us in more ways and with greater intensity than poetry does, even if its effect is more transient.

(le Huray and Day 1981, 221)

For Kant, music, in comparison with poetry, moves us with great intensity, but it is essentially transient in nature, therefore, as music passes through time its mode of communication is such that it can only suggest ('mere sensations') without articulating recognizable concepts. This can be conceived as music's weakness, its inability to articulate precise **meaning**. However, it is equally possible to counter this interpretation with an alternative perspective that grasps music's suggestiveness and ambiguity as virtues not flaws.

G.W.F. Hegel, a later, highly influential German philosopher, also reflected upon the nature of music and used comparison with other arts as a discursive strategy. For Hegel, in contrast to Kant, music's transience is, in the words of Bowman, 'not the impediment Kant believed...but an invaluable instrument of self-realization' (Bowman 1998, 104). Hegel saw the process of aesthetic judgement differently from Kant. For Hegel, art works could also portray beauty as an intrinsic, objective quality. Music, and the arts in general, also assumed wider significance within Hegel's philosophy, serving 'the deepest interests of humanity, and the most comprehensive truths of the mind. It is in works of art that nations have deposited the profoundest intuitions and ideas of their heart' (*ibid.*, 97).

Throughout the nineteenth century, the philosophical reflection on music, and the aestheticization of music, intensified. Nietzsche and Schopenhauer, both post-Hegelian German philosophers of the period, captured, in different ways, the heightened subjectivity and intensification of meaning evident in the music of their time. For example, in his *Die Welt als Wille und Vorstellung* (The World as Will and Idea) of 1819 (Schopenhauer 1995), Schopenhauer saw music as an art of great significance, that which comes nearest to representing his philosophical concept of the Will:

> It [music] stands quite apart from all the others. In it, we do not perceive an imitation or a copy of some idea of the things that exist in the world. Even so, it is such a great and eminently splendid art, it creates such a powerful reaction in man's inmost depths, it is so thoroughly and profoundly understood by him as a uniquely universal language, even exceeding in clarity that of the phenomenal world itself.
>
> (le Huray and Day 1981, 324)

The debates about the nature and significance of music continued throughout the twentieth century and, under the impact of

modernism, intensified. The emergence of a **critical theory** also had implications for the aesthetic understanding of music.

In recent years, the **new musicology**, through its critique of a formalist understanding of music, has also extended the discussions around issues and perspectives that can be defined as aesthetic. For example, the recent work of Lawrence Kramer has revisited the recurring aesthetic question of the meaning of music, or, what music means. His book *Musical Meaning: Toward a Critical History* (Kramer 2002) revisits this debate but gives it a contemporary dimension. The range of music covered in this book is also of significance: it includes the Marx brothers, John Coltrane and Shostakovich as well as the expected starting point of nineteenth-century **Romanticism**. This diversity of musical repertoire provides a challenge for any contemporary aesthetics of music. Is it possible to construct strategies of interpretation that can find common ground across a wide range of musical contexts? Or do different types of music pose different questions that demand different aesthetic responses?

See also: **autonomy**, **genius**, **language**, **postmodernism**, **sublime**

Further reading: Adorno 1997; Bowie 1993; Cook 2001; Dahlhaus 1982; Hegel 1993; Kivy 2002; Lippman 1992; Scruton 1999

ALTERITY

Alterity refers to difference or otherness and is often used interchangeably with these terms. However, its origins lie in a shift of focus in **cultural studies** away from the philosophical sense of self established by the seventeenth-century French philosopher René Descartes – who based his understanding of the other always in relation to the self – towards a cultural and historical approach that focuses more specific attention on understanding the Other in its own right. As this sentence shows, a shift in emphasis is often illustrated by the use of the capitalized form of the term; for example this form is used by the psychoanalytical theorist Jacques Lacan following his interest in desire and the work of G.W.F. Hegel (see **identity**). In cultural studies, alterity is related to greater concern for differences of **race**, **ethnicity**, **gender** and **class**. In post-colonial studies (see **post-colonial/ postcolonialism**), for example, the concept of the subaltern was adopted from Italian Marxist cultural critic Antonio Gramsci (see Gramsci 1971). The subaltern group is one that is defined by its difference from a ruling elite, and in the context of post-colonial theory it applies to non-ruling indigenous societies and their cultures.

In cultural terms, alterity concerns those sections of post-**Renaissance** European society that are forbidden but desired: women, exotics, bohemians, primitives and peasants, for example. In this context, the use of minuets followed by waltzes in Classical period concert music may be understood as 'enabling the rational bourgeois to deal with the disturbing fascination of the degenerate aristocracy on the one hand, the earthy peasantry on the other' (Middleton 2000a, 63). By extension, sonata form (see **analysis**) was conducive to depicting difference, the second theme routinely being described as 'feminine' in contrast to the 'masculine' first theme (see **gender**). Key schemes could also reflect difference: famously, Mozart carefully considered his choice of key when depicting the rage of the Turkish character Osmin in *Die Entführung aus dem Serail* (1785–86) (Kivy 1988).

The discipline that perhaps most obviously pertains to alterity, at least from a Western perspective, is ethnomusicology. Philip Bohlman has outlined how through the 1950s ethnomusicology began to shift away from considering non-Western music as Other towards a new perspective that:

> insisted that the hermeneutic [see **hermeneutics**] potential of a music must lie in that music's uniqueness, in its bearing no relation whatsoever to any other music, least of all to Western music. . . . A canonic reversal therefore occurred, in which the true music of the Other was Western art music. . . . This was less a matter of rebelling against the **canon** of Western art music than of turning to the rather more numerous and more enticing canons of non-Western music.
>
> (Bohlman 1992, 121)

This quotation points to the fact that recognition of difference and the exclusion of others is central to the construction of musical canons. According to Bohlman, the discipline of musicology 'covers up the racism, colonialism, and sexism that underlie many of the singular canons of the West. . . . Canons formed from "Great Men" and "Great Music" forged virtually unassailable categories of self and Other, one to discipline and reduce to singularity, the other to belittle and impugn' (*ibid.*, 198).

British musicologist Richard Middleton has developed this idea, in particular the sense of popular music as Other to Western classical forms. He has done so by developing Paul Gilroy's concept of the 'Black Atlantic' – the black Other considered in terms of its role in the development of **modernism**. Middleton extends this idea to one of the 'Low Atlantic', which juxtaposes popular against elite and considers how, within that, 'low' and black relate to each other. Middleton proposes two approaches to alterity in music. One, illustrated by Wagner's setting of Nordic myths, is assimilation, bringing difference into a stylistically integrated musical language (see **style**). The other is resistance and projection, where the Other 'is externalized in a sphere of apparent social difference':

> It is this strategy which explains the attractions of the many thousands of 'peasant dances', 'Volkslieder', 'bohemian rhapsodies', 'Scottish' or 'Slavic' character pieces, 'plantation melodies', and so forth which throng the nineteenth-century repertory... the aim of both assimilation and projection strategies is to manage the threat posed by potentially infinite difference to the authority of the bourgeois self, by reducing such difference to a stable hierarchy.
>
> (Middleton 2000a, 62)

Middleton goes on to note how in Mozart's opera *Die Zauberflöte* (1791), the high characters are balanced by a range of low others: 'women; blacks, in the persons of the "mooris" Monostatos and the slaves; and plebeians, in the form of the comic birdcatcher, Papageno' (*ibid.*, 64). Throughout the opera, a hierarchy of social groups and individuals is established, although it also illustrates the humanizing desire of the **Enlightenment**, its aspirations and its limits. He also explores Duke Ellington's cultivation of a 'jungle style' in jazz, which 'coupled an exotic appeal to captivated whites... [with] an urban-jungle subculturalism, rooted in black popular tastes but routed toward the hip, hybrid modernistic art of bebop' (*ibid.*, 73). Bernard Gendron has further explored ways in which discourses (see **discourse**) concerning alterity have helped to construct *avant-garde* expressions in **jazz** and **popular music** (Gendron 2002).

Consideration of the significance of categories of difference in Western music has most commonly arisen in the work of new musicologists (see **new musicology**). Some of these scholars have examined ways in which nineteenth-century composers marked areas of their music as structurally different through tonal, expressive or thematic means. American feminist musicologist Ruth Solie suggests that the important question for musicologists is: 'How do social life and culture construct the differences that all of us understand and enact in daily life?' (Solie 1993, 10). One example of this line of thinking is Susan McClary's consideration of **narrative** agendas in Brahms's Third Symphony (1883). McClary refers to 'Other' keys that register dissonances, 'stand in the way of unitary identity' and must 'finally be subdued for the sake of narrative closure' (McClary 1993b, 330). McClary associates the increased use of dissonant keys during the nineteenth century with 'the prevalent anti-authoritarianism of **Romanticism**' (*ibid.*, 334), and the piece as a whole she summarizes as 'a document that speaks of heroism, adventure, conflict, conquest, the constitution of the self, the threat of the Other, and late nineteenth-century pessimism' (*ibid.*, 343).

In some instances, alterity is implied through differences in style or musical **language**, or an artist's **reception**. This has led to various scholars asking if composers such as Handel and Schubert were gay (see Thomas 1994; McClary 1994; see also **gay musicology**). In certain well-documented instances, composers may have felt different from other artists and society – Philip Brett has produced much invaluable work that follows from Benjamin Britten's lifelong sense of alienation (Brett 1993). Composers living in exile will inevitably experience a sense of difference, and Peter Franklin has explored the exceptional dynamics of Los Angeles around 1940, when the city was home to composers as diverse as Stravinsky, Schoenberg, Rachmaninov and Korngold (Franklin 2000). This study reveals a fascinating mix of prewar European musical values (see **value**) as they are enacted and related to a foreign setting, and the sense of difference felt by Korngold as a composer of film music (see **place**).

All composers and musicians who have felt themselves to be at the periphery of musical practice may seek to destabilize the barriers surrounding them – a point that applies as much to women composers in the twentieth century as it does to Hispanic musicians in New York. It may even extend to composers now perceived to be at the centre who, at times in their own lives, considered themselves to lie outside it, such as Wagner, Elgar and Mahler. Importantly, ideas about what is central or peripheral will change throughout history.

Further reading: McClary 1992; Street 2000

ANALYSIS

Analysis is a sub-discipline within musicology that is concerned with a search for internal coherence within a musical **work**. It therefore takes the musical text – usually a score, although also potentially a **sketch** or other form of manuscript with musical notation – as the primary, autonomous object of study (see **autonomy**), focusing on an examination of a work's internal structure (see **structuralism**). Analytical practice frequently involves the application of ideologically guided decisions and choices (see **ideology**), which are applied in order to divide a musical structure into smaller constituent elements (see Kerman 1994). These elements are then considered in isolation, in relation to one another, in relation to the work as a whole, or in relation to a number of other works. It can be seen that evaluation and selection are crucial to analysis. In these terms, the concept of analysis has become synonymous with a search for unity in musical structure. However, this idea has come under significant criticism from both analysts and non-analysts (see Street 1989; Cohn and Dempster 1992).

An important stimulus to the development of music analysis can be found in certain eighteenth-century philosophical thought, for example Lord Shaftesbury's notion of 'disinterested attention' – in which the act of contemplation is valued in and for itself – and the concept of **aesthetics** developed by Alexander Baumgarten (see Bent and Drabkin 1987, 12). There are now many different forms of music analysis, and often they can be mutually exclusive. At the simplest level, analysis provides a set of vocabularies or symbols for discussing and describing the basic elements of music, its harmonies, scales and metric schemes. Examples of this include figured-bass notation, which has been in use since the eighteenth century, and the use of roman numerals to designate chord types, introduced in a four-volume theoretical work by Gottfried Weber published between 1817 and 1821. Analysis has also developed in relation to musical form, **style** and **genre**, all of which examine musical content according to technical and formal considerations that have been associated with particular historical periods (see **periodization**). Johann Forkel's biography of Bach, published in 1802, contained the seeds of stylistic classification and sketch study (see **biography**), while J.A.P. Spitta's *Johann Sebastian Bach* presented formal analyses of individual works (Spitta 1884). Spitta's work also contains attempts at symbolic interpretations of Bach's music, an approach that was paralleled in the pictorial **language** of the analyses of E.T.A. Hoffman (see **hermeneutics**, **criticism**). Following the influence of linguistic theory, analytical methods that attempt to interpret music in terms of **meaning** subsequently developed in the more theoretical context of semiotic analysis (see **semiotics**; see also Nattiez 1990b; Samuels 1995; Tarasti 1994) as well as methods influenced by **narrative** theory (see Hatten 1994; Karl 1997).

As this discussion has indicated, analysis often engages in evaluation of abstract, conceptual levels in music, describing features that are not obvious in a score but arise from consideration of theoretical ideas that have been developed in specific historical and cultural contexts. According to Roger Parker and Carolyn Abbate:

> The analysis that merely describes musical events is like the translation that passes over all meaning, that passes over the 'truly poetic'. To go beyond mechanical conversions of musical notation into written words, analysis must uncover something beyond or behind the mere sonic surface.
>
> (Parker and Abbate 1989, 1–2)

The authors of this quotation have subsequently become associated with a desire to move beyond analysis itself. In particular, they are conscious that, although it does not always reveal itself, analysis is the result of an interaction between the music itself, music **theory**, aesthetics and history.

Analysis is always preceded by some form of music theory that has either been developed in isolation from specific pieces or has arisen from a direct response to patterns that emerge in existing works. An example of this is the composition teaching of German music theorist Johann Christian Lobe, which was influenced by Lobe's admiration for, and analyses of, the music of Beethoven (see Bent 1984). Other important theorists whose analyses of music influenced their theoretical work include German music theorists Heinrich Christoph Koch and Hugo Riemann, who developed theories of rhythm and phrase structure.

Throughout history, analytical methods and questions have shifted according to the prevailing cultural and aesthetic preoccupations of the time. In the early nineteenth century, analysts were concerned with demonstrating what made a work 'great' (see **genius**). Seventeenth- and eighteenth-century analytical approaches reflect the study of modal systems and an interest in rhetoric (see **language**), while later nineteenth- and twentieth-century analysis is heavily influenced by **organicism** – this is demonstrated by the prevalence of metaphors of growth in analytical accounts, such those of Austrian music theorist Heinrich Schenker, as well as the analytical publications of Rudolph Réti and Arnold Schoenberg. In the case of Schenker, it is the product of the last ten years of his life, the late 1920s and early 1930s, that subsequently captured the imaginations of mostly American theorists in the 1970s and 1980s. Consequently, it is Schenker's concept of a fundamental structure (*Ursatz*) as the basis of all tonal music, his exposition of the laws of organic coherence and his move towards a reductive, purely graphic form of analysis that subsequently formed the impetus for what is now called Schenkerian analysis, rather than his imaginative verbal interpretations and insistence on the relevance of autograph studies to analysis (see Dunsby and Whittall 1988; Schenker 1921–4, 1979). Joseph Kerman, for one, has noticed how organicism and the search for unity in musical composition became synonymous with music analysis (Kerman 1994, 15).

The principal claim made against analysis is that it measures existing works against normalized structures observed and codified in music theory. One result of this is that a work may be valued more highly if it closely matches a theoretical model, whereas a work that does not relate closely to a preconceived theoretical model may be valued less highly. This quasi-scientific measuring of music against factual, theoretical knowledge in order to validate a musical work (see **value**) represents a positivistic view of the world (see **positivism**). This view has come under considerable criticism in recent years, notably by Joseph Kerman (Kerman 1985, 12) and has led to a shift in musicological practice since the mid-1980s (see **critical musicology**, **new musicology**). According to Nicholas Cook:

> Schenkerian analysis . . . didn't . . . ask whether the music of Bach, Beethoven, and Brahms was of value. It *assumed* the music was of value, and tried to demonstrate this by showing how the music really was coherent, provided you dug down deep enough. It was, in short, an apologetic discipline, in the sense of being designed to defend a valued repertory, to underwrite its canonic [see **canon**] status.
>
> (Cook 1998a, 95)

One of the most systematic approaches to music analysis is Allen Forte's development and application of mathematical set theory to musical notation. In his book *The Structure of Atonal Music* (Forte 1973), he presents a method of accounting for pitch organization in atonal music. He not only provides a highly useful means of labelling collections of pitches, he also established a means of revealing and relating pitch collections as they are inverted or transposed – what Schoenberg described as *Grundgestalt* ('basic shape'). The spur to developing this analytical method was the apparently irrational musical procedures of freely atonal music, by composers such as Schoenberg and Webern, especially works dating from the first two decades of the twentieth century. In 1978, Forte applied his analytical method to a comprehensive analysis of Stravinsky's *The Rite of Spring* (1913), examining the possibility that the pitch material for the whole work was generated from a small number of pitch sets (Forte 1978). Subsequent criticism of Forte's method has focused on the apparently subjective criteria adopted for dividing a work (segmentation) – an apparently arbitrary selection process that does not always reflect the phrasing of the music – and the neglect of features such as rhythm, texture and timbre (see Taruskin 1986).

With the rise of highly individualistic compositional practices and new ways of rationalizing pitch space, there has been a corresponding growth of new analytical methodologies. These include attempts by a significant number of analysts to revise and adapt Schenkerian theory in order to apply it to medieval and **Renaissance** music (Judd 1998; Leach, 2003), late Romantic composers such as Bruckner, Tchaikovsky, Sibelius and Scriabin (Beach 1983; Baker 1986; Jackson and Hawkshaw 1997; Jackson 1995, 2001), early modernists such as Stravinsky (Straus 1990), and even explorations of its possible use in ethnomusicology (Stock 1993). Reassessment of music analysis has also extended to a reconsideration of music theory and theorists (see Bent 1996a; Clark and Rehding 2001; Dale 2003, Rehding 2003). However, reassessment has also prompted a number of defensive responses from music theorists and analysts. Pieter van den Toorn, for example, has asked:

> why should we trust a facility with words, poetic expression, or sociopolitical comment rather than the methods of music theory and analysis, methods presumably more germane to the matter at hand? . . . why should we judge the former to be warmly human or 'humanistic', the latter coldly 'technical', specialist, or formalistic in its appeal?
>
> (van den Toorn 1995, 1)

Similarly, American music theorist Kofi Agawu has argued that new musicologists (see **new musicology**) need to beware of reproducing the kind of 'bad' analysis they have been critical of, a problem that arises whenever musicologists engage with a musical text. Agawu also notes that 'academic discourse is surely not racing toward a single finishing line' (Agawu 1997, 307). In other words, there should be space, in a pluralistic discipline such as musicology, for the development of new analytical and theoretical discourses. Even Kerman stated that 'I do not actually think we need to get out of analysis . . . only out from under' (Kerman 1994, 30). What has come under scrutiny following the influence of postmodern (see **postmodernism**) thought on musicology is the analytical model of a series of dialectics, between motif and elaboration, part and whole, coherence and incoherence. The traditional supremacy of an authorial voice, which analysis tends to uphold, is increasingly being located in a discursive network (see Kramer 1993b, 2001), and analytical discourse is searching for ways of being more self-reflective (see Guck 1994). As Adam Krims notes, criticisms of theory and analysis are:

> disturbing not because they are unfair, but precisely because they frequently are true: the characterizations must be taken seriously, as they raise the question of the very possibility of attempting music theory in the late twentieth century; and the response needs to be informed by postmodern theory and ground itself within the contemporary environments of the humanities.
>
> (Krims 1998a, 2)

One other important sign of a reassessment of analysis is a growing interest in analyzing popular music. The origins of such attempts can be traced back to the work of Philip Tagg (Tagg 2000) and a set of pioneering articles that appeared in the 1970s and 1980s by Walter Everett that consider a number of songs by the Beatles in Schenkerian terms (Everett 1985). This work, together with a range of other approaches to analysing popular music, was subsequently assessed in Richard Middleton's seminal overview *Studying Popular Music* (Middleton 1990). This was followed by Allen Moore's monograph on the Beatles' *Sergeant Pepper's Lonely Hearts Club Band* album (1967), which also adapts Schenkerian methodology (Moore 1997).

Owing to its complexity, progressive rock has attracted a range of motivic and harmonic analyses (see Covach 1997, 2000; Moore 2001a). It is interesting to note that a number of music theorists have 'crossed over' into popular music, bringing rigorous theoretical methodologies to their considerations of the genre. An example of this is Matthew Brown's Schenkerian analysis of Jimi Hendrix's 'Little Wing' (1967), in which the music is valued as 'a successful search through a tonal problem space' (Brown 1997, 165; see also Forte 1996; Bernard 2000). This work implies a familial relation between concert and popular music. By extension, Philip Tagg has adapted semiotic analysis to popular music following his identification of a number of characteristics that are common to melodies throughout all styles and genres. However, some musicologists have argued that analysis of popular music, as well as analysis of film and television music, requires new approaches rather than methods developed for analysing concert music. However, it is here, at the intersection between traditional models of analysis and forms of musical expression, which have previously been considered the property of cultural and social studies, that analysis holds some of the most significant and exciting potential.

Further reading: Adorno 1994; Bent and Drabkin 1987; Dahlhaus 1983b; Gloag 1998; Middleton 2000c; Moore 2003

AUTHENTICITY

Authenticity is invoked in different musical and musicological contexts, but generally it indicates some notion of truth and sincerity. It most commonly appears in relation to performance, but it also operates within **critical theory** and in relation to **popular music**.

The trend towards a 'historically informed' or period performance has often mistakenly been described as 'authentic'. Such a performance may be one that seeks to use some or all of the following factors: the instruments of the composer's time; an awareness of playing techniques of the period through reference to documentary evidence such as treatises and descriptive accounts; and the composer's intentions as evident from the original manuscript and related material such as amendments and corrections (see **historical musicology**).

The search for a historically aware, perhaps 'authentic' performance originates in the nineteenth century and reflects the general historical consciousness of that period. However, the attention given to documentary evidence is a reflection of the positivistic nature of musicology as it developed through the twentieth century (see **positivism**). The aspiration towards authenticity can also be seen as a consequence of the twentieth century's preoccupation with the past and as such it can be viewed in relationship to **modernism** and, more specifically, with the neoclassicism that emerged in the 1920s. This point is made with great clarity and conviction by American musicologist Richard Taruskin (Taruskin 1995, 90–154). Taruskin also claims that the relationship between 'historical' as 'authentic' performance and 'modern' performance is confused:

I hold that discussions of authentistic performance typically proceed from false premises. The split that is usually drawn between 'modern performance' on the one hand and 'historical performance' on the other is often quite topsy-turvy. It is the latter that is truly modern performance – or rather, if you like, the avant-garde wing or cutting edge of modern performance – while the former represents the progressively weakening survival of an earlier style inherited from the nineteenth century, one that is fast becoming historical.

(*ibid.*, 140)

In other words, what has been thought of as 'modern' performance has a long history, reflecting the romantic **subjectivity** of the nineteenth century (see **Romanticism**), while 'authentic' performance, rather than recreating the past, states its own sense of the contemporary through its current perspective on the past. Taruskin revisits this paradox through comparison of recordings of Beethoven's Ninth Symphony (1822–4) by Wilhelm Furtwängler, a conductor who reflected the influence and legacy of Wagner, and Roger Norrington, a specialist in period performance practice. Taruskin concludes by describing Norrington as a 'truly authentic voice of the late twentieth century' (*ibid.*, 260).

Clearly, the desire to recreate the sounds and gestures of the period within which a musical work was composed is highly laudable, and the rise of specialist performance ensembles has resulted in many fine performances and recordings (see **recording**). However, given that such musical activity takes place within a modern, perhaps postmodern, (see **postmodernism**) context, it is difficult to describe accurately any such performance as authentic, particularly given the increased commodity status of classical music and the profoundly inauthentic process of recording and marketing music (see **culture industry**). According to Richard Taruskin:

Do we really want to talk about 'authenticity' any more? I had hoped a consensus was forming that to use the word in connection with the performance of music – and especially to define a particular style, manner, or philosophy of performance – is neither description nor critique, but commercial propaganda, the stock-in-trade of press agents and promoters.

(*ibid.*, 90)

Since Taruskin made this statement in 1988 (in Kenyon 1988), the term 'authentic performance' seems to have fallen increasingly into disuse in this context.

Authenticity is also invoked in the critical theory of influential German theorist Theodor Adorno. Adorno's use of the term is, not surprisingly, complex. For Adorno, following the demise of the legitimizing framework of a common musical **language** and practice, the authenticity of the art work is located in its consistency of material and internal logic. While recognizing that material is always marked by past conventions, these conventions are now stripped of their original functions and meanings (see **meaning**). The resulting sense of loss conspires with a truth to itself. This truth is also a recognition of reality, a reality that for Adorno was defined by the horror of Auschwitz: 'The authentic artists of the present are those in whose works there shudders the aftershock of the most extreme terror' (Paddison 1993, 56). In other words, truth and reality are reflected in the work's forms and materials, but this does not suggest that the music should attempt a programmatic description of such factors, or that a reconciliation between **work** and world is possible.

Given the references to historical performance practice and the critical theory of Adorno, the introduction of authenticity in relation to popular music may seem paradoxical, but popular music and its study resonate with issues of truth, integrity and sincerity and therefore directly raise issues of authenticity. Clearly, the relationship between popular musician and fan can form an **identity** around a certain truth, and the intensity and expression of the popular music experience is often one of sincerity. This is most clearly evident in the role of singer-songwriter, within which we hear and feel a direct line of communication from songwriter through performance or recording to listener. This is clearly defined in the music of Bob Dylan, for example. The raw intensity of the voice indicates a personal experience and a depth of meaning that conveys an aura of authenticity. However, the fact that Dylan's music is contained within a culture industry and is marketed as a consumer commodity simultaneously questions this aura.

The complexity of this situation has been touched upon recently by several popular music scholars. American cultural theorist and commentator on popular music Lawrence Grossberg identifies three specific formations of authenticity (Grossberg 1993). These are neatly summarized by Johan Fornäs, whose background is quite explicitly in **cultural studies**, in his book *Cultural Theory and Late Modernity* (Fornäs 1995b): 'Grossberg distinguishes three forms of authenticity in rock discourses [see **discourse**]. The most common is associated with hard rock and folk rock, and builds on the romantic **ideology** of rock as a construction by and expression of a magically dense community. In more dance-oriented and black genres authenticity is instead localized in the construction of a rhythmical and sexual body. A third form appears in postmodernist self-conscious pop and avant-garde rock [see **postmodernism**], which plays with styles, well understanding that they are always artificially constructed, but through this very cynical self-knowledge shows a kind of realistic honesty' (*ibid.*, 276). Grossberg's categories, and Fornäs's summary and development, are useful and insightful. So-called hard rock portrays its own sense of intensity and sincerity and usually involves the performance of original material, but it also conveys a recognizable, audible trace of its own origins. For example, we can hear the rock music of Led Zeppelin, one of the definitive instances of rock music, in relation to its precursors, rhythm 'n' blues and rock 'n' roll. However, the example of Led Zeppelin is interesting because, although it articulates a sense of truth and integrity, it has been shown that their dependence on these precedents bordered on plagiarism (see Headlam 1995). The example of Led Zeppelin can therefore also be seen to look towards Grossberg's suggestion of the authentic celebration of the inauthentic, a condition that captures the problematics of thinking authenticity within the postmodern celebration of the inauthentic.

Further reading: Lawson and Stowell 1999; Mazullo 1999; Moore 2001a, 2002

AUTONOMY

Music's alleged autonomy is often constructed as the antithesis of its **meaning**. The belief that music functions as an autonomous entity is reflected through **formalism** and is given a practical representation through the act of **analysis**. To understand music as autonomous is to conceive it as a separate, self-contained construction. The work of German philosopher Immanuel Kant, particularly his *Critique of Judgement* of 1790 (le Huray and Day 1981, 214–29; Kant 1987), provided a defining reference point for consideration of autonomy within aesthetics. In the *Critique of Judgement*, Kant put forward the idea of the disinterested, which means that aesthetic responses are 'free' and distinct from other, more common, responses and desires. Kant also raised the view that the purpose of art works is to be without purpose. In other words, they are an end in themselves (see **aesthetics**)

The most direct use of a concept of autonomy in relation to music was to describe music's separation (its autonomy) from **language** with the emergence of a purely instrumental music since the eighteenth century, effectively liberating music from the constraints of both the written word and social function, such as liturgical and ceremonial contexts (see **absolute**). The separation from word and language would lead German philosopher G.W.F. Hegel, in his lectures on aesthetics given during the early nineteenth century, to describe a 'self-sufficient music':

> Accompanimental music exists to express something outside itself. Its expression relates to something that does not belong to music as such but to an alien art: poetry. Now if music is intended to be purely musical, it must eschew and eradicate this alien element. Only then can it fully liberate itself from the constraints of verbal precision.
>
> (le Huray and Day 1981, 351)

Kant's absence of purpose (function) was to be echoed in the nineteenth-century notion of 'art for art's sake' and reflected Romanticism's preoccupation with its own forms of expression (see **Romanticism**). However, it ignores the importance of the relationship between music and word in the nineteenth century, as symbolized by the song cycles of Schubert and Schumann, among others, and the music dramas of Wagner.

A model of musical autonomy was most clearly articulated by the Viennese music critic Eduard Hanslick in his *Vom Musickalisch-Schönen* (On the Musically Beautiful), first published in 1854. According to Hanslick:

> If now we ask what it is that should be expressed by means of this tone-material, the answer is musical ideas. But a musical idea brought into complete manifestation in appearance is already self-subsistent beauty; it is an end in itself, and it is in no way primarily a medium or material for the representation of feelings or conceptions. The content of music is tonally moving forms.
>
> (Hanslick 1986, 28–9)

On this account, music is about itself, its beauty an internal phenomenon, and it does not exist to express or represent anything beyond itself. The actual content of music is the details, themes and forms, which move through time and result in a **work** that is an end in itself. For Hanslick, the high point of what was then contemporary music came in the instrumental music, both orchestral and chamber, of Brahms. This music was presented by Hanslick as the autonomous alternative to Wagner's preoccupation with meaning through an 'extra-musical' dimension.

This view of an autonomous music reflects a certain formalism, one that was subject to critical scrutiny both in Hanslick's own time and since. However, there is a long legacy that flows from Hanslick. Much of the aesthetic identity of **modernism** reflects a belief in music's autonomous character. This reflection is given musical substance in the work of both Schoenberg and Stravinsky, and the problematics of the autonomy of music within modernism is critically theorized by German critical theorist Theodor Adorno (see **critical theory**). For Adorno, the relationship between the musical work and its context cannot be reduced to a direct parallel between the two domains, but that the musical content, its material, bears the immanent trace of the antagonisms and problematics of the world (see **authenticity**). This model of autonomy is given musical representation through the music of Beethoven:

> The kinship with that bourgeois libertarianism which rings all through Beethoven's music is a kinship of the dynamically unfolding totality. It is in fitting together under their own law, as becoming, negating, confirming themselves and the whole without looking outward that his themes come to resemble the world whose forces move them; they do not do it by imitating that world.
>
> (Adorno 1976, 209)

According to this version, music achieves a certain aesthetic autonomy, the musical materials look to themselves ('without looking outward'), but it is through this process that a resemblance to the real world reveals itself and not through any process of 'imitating the world'. It could be argued that this account of musical autonomy, a highly complex and sophisticated one, can be traced through the history of musical modernism, which, for Adorno, has its origins in the late works of Beethoven. It is a version of autonomy that allows the musical work to establish its own identity, but it also accounts for resemblances between that identity and its context.

The view of music as somehow autonomous has been subjected to intense critical scrutiny in recent years, with much of the **new musicology** seeking to reposition music in relation to context and meaning and the determination of any position in relation to the question of autonomy reflecting its own ideological orientation (see **ideology**).

See also: **analysis, post-structuralism, structuralism**

Further reading: Chua 1999; Dahlhaus 1989a

AVANT-GARDE

A French term originally used in military circles to describe an advanced guard of soldiers, *avant-garde* is a concept that gained currency in the nineteenth century as a term to describe progressive, pioneering tendencies in all the arts that were hostile to mass **culture** and designed to shock. The concept, which may apply to artists, composers, producers, directors or critics, although sometimes used as a term of abuse, more commonly values (see **value**) such notions as **autonomy**, experimentalism and innovation over, and in opposition to, **tradition**. In common usage, it locates these tendencies within so-called high art forms, such as poetry, painting, concert music and the novel, in which it has been associated with a 'concentration on the mental processes of the artist' (Butler 1980, 5) as represented in works such as James Joyce's *Finnegans Wake* (1939) and Jean-Paul Sartre's *Le Nausée* (1938).

The concept has existed at least since the early nineteenth century, and in music it found early expression in the polemical writing of Schumann, Wagner and the New German School, although embryonic forms of *avant-garde* expression may be found much earlier, for example in the innovative musical notation of the fourteenth-century French composer Phillipe de Vitry, Bach's controversially experimental organ music, and the late **style** of Beethoven. The concept accrued more specific meaning in the twentieth century, when it became attached to such artistic movements as futurism, dadaism and surrealism in the 1920s and, in the 1940s and 1950s, integral serialism in music and American abstract expressionist painting.

One of the most important contributions to theorization of the *avant-garde* was published by German critical theorist (see **critical theory**) Peter Bürger (Bürger 1984). Bürger's approach is historical: in his view, as artists gained more autonomy from patrons they became more frustrated by the social ineffectiveness of their art, which led to more radical confrontations between artists and society. Jochen Schulte-Sasse, in his foreword to Bürger's book, states:

> The development from the autonomy of art in the eighteenth century to the Aestheticism of the late nineteenth and early twentieth centuries is in Bürger's perspective an intensification of art's separation from bourgeois society.... He insists that the tendency inherent in art's autonomous status drove both the individual work and the institution 'art' to increasingly extreme declarations of their autonomy [as reflected in] an increasing

consciousness on the part of the artist of writing techniques, how material is applied, and its potential for effect.... Bürger sees this development as logical and necessary, yet as negative, since it led toward a state in which art works are characterised by semantic atrophy.

(Schulte-Sasse 1984, xiii)

In other words, *avant-garde* art rejects the autonomous role allotted to it by society while recognizing an awareness of the futility of its greater freedom of expression. This realization leads to attacks on the institution of art itself, on its role in creating a function for art, on the mechanisms that produce art, and on the **reception** of art. The concept of eliminating art as an institution is neatly captured in Pierre Boulez's call for the opera houses of Europe to be burned down (Boulez 1968). Questioning artistic institutions also necessitates greater reflection on the concept of the **work** of art, since this is the mechanism by which society consumes and institutionalizes music. Again, Boulez offers a useful example, as his tendency to keep works in progress resists the notion of music as fixed and autonomous; similarly chance techniques, as used by Boulez and John Cage, also belong to this concept (see Boulez 1993). However, in other ways, composers such as Boulez and Stockhausen re-institutionalized the *avant-garde*, establishing new musical orthodoxies supported by broadcasters, music festivals and universities. Bürger notes that *avant-garde* movements transcend period styles, observing that 'there is no such thing as a Dadaist style or a Surrealist style' (Bürger 1984, 18) and that in certain senses *avant-garde* art might be interpreted as anti-organicist (see **organicism**), although this would be debatable within the context of serial music. He also notes that 'the revival of art as an institution and the revival of the category "work" suggest that today, the avant–garde is already historical' (*ibid.*, 57), a view that would be supported by late twentieth–century artists more interested in a pluralism of styles (see **postmodernism**).

A number of musicologists, including Ulrich Dibelius (Dibelius 1966, 1988), Reginald Smith Brindle (Brindle 1975), Gianmario Borio (Borio 1993) and Paul Griffiths (Griffiths 1995), have provided important accounts of *avant-garde* practice in music since 1945. However, although Smith Brindle opens his book by drawing attention to world historical events, such as the invention of the atomic bomb and the first manned landing on the moon, by way of associating musical developments with science, experimentation and extremity, his study – and others like it – consists primarily of an account of the musical techniques of *avant-garde* composers. In this sense, it can be seen to reinforce a discourse of objectivity, progress, abstraction and liberation from bourgeois constraints that was established by composers such as Arnold Schoenberg and Milton Babbitt. One scholar who has called on this approach to be revised is American musicologist Susan McClary. In an article published in 1989, she outlined an apparent 'siege mentality' on the part of certain composers, who seemed to regard their audience as irrelevant and commercial success as positively undesirable (see McClary 1989; Babbitt 1984).

While composers such as Babbitt advocate the continued support of universities for composers of 'serious' music and the denial of any kind of extra-musical **meaning** in their work, McClary argues that much would be gained from considering the 'human (i.e. expressive, social, political etc.) dimension of [*avant-garde*] music' and that this 'need not qualify as retreating into anti-intellectualism as Babbitt repeatedly suggests' (McClary 1989, 65). Such efforts, she hopes, would help to 'lose the mystique of difficulty, which might well be replaced with an acknowledgement of human vulnerability' (*ibid.*, 66). She rejects the opposition of *avant-garde* and mass culture advocated by critical theorists such as Theodor Adorno and emphasizes that *avant-garde* music should not be studied exclusively in accordance with 'the autonomous terms it has tried to enforce' (*ibid.*, 76). She suggests a number of forms of inquiry, including consideration of misogyny and homophobia in *avant-garde* music, and the formation of the communities and institutions that support such music.

Following on from McClary, a number of studies have explored the concept of the *avant-garde* in relation to commercial music. Bernard Gendron, in his seminal book on **popular music**, **jazz** and the *avant-garde*, states:

> I use the term 'avant-garde' roughly to denote any high-cultural production of a modernist [see **modernism**] or postmodernist kind, in opposition to traditional high culture. . . . In France I situate the birth of the modernist avant-garde sometime in the middle of the nineteenth century, best codified by Baudelaire's 'Painter of Modern Life', though one could with plausibility go back to the second-generation romantics [see **Romanticism**] (Gautier, Nerval) in the 1830s and their invention of 'art for art's sake'. Not by chance the rise of the avant-garde coincides with the rise of mass culture – mass newspapers, poster advertisements, the professionalization of popular song – and begins in subtle ways immediately to interact with it. This was not by

chance, because the restricted market of the avant-garde, driven by fashion and constant turnover in symbolic value, mirrored the mass market better than any other restricted cultural market (e.g., the traditionlists [*sic*] market).

(Gendron 2002, 16)

A number of important points emerge from this definition. First, the association of the *avant-garde* with the idea of 'art for art's sake', a Romantic aesthetic that was raised to an even higher status by Wagner, especially in his opera *Tristan und Isolde* (1859) and his colossal operatic cycle *Der Ring des Nibelungen* (1851–9). Second, it raises the more radical idea that the *avant-garde* is related to fashion and mass marketing. Gendron explores, for example, the link between a fashionable Parisian interest in African art and the rise of artists such as Picasso and Cocteau, who adapted methods used in mass marketing to promote their own work. Third, citing critical and journalistic **discourse** on the Beatles, bebop (see **jazz**) and new wave, Gendron investigates how a sense of hierarchy operates in jazz and popular music and how a **language** develops that is closely linked to *avant-garde* conceptions dating from the nineteenth century. Other areas that have recently received closer attention include examinations of the political and social institutions that have supported *avant-garde* music (see Born 1995; Carroll 2003) and consideration of the **aesthetics** of *avant-garde* music (see Grant 2001).

Further reading: Martin 2002; Nyman 1999

BIOGRAPHY (LIFE AND WORK)

The writing of the biography of composers and musicians has been a standard dimension of musicology since its inception, with 'Bio-graphistik' highlighted by Adler in his original schematic prescription for musicology (see **Introduction**). Musical biography forms a literary **genre** based around the ordering of facts relating to the life of the composer and the relationship to context in terms of other people and specific places (see **place**). However, many biographies extend beyond the consideration of biographical information to embrace the assumed relationships between life and **work**. Within this exercise, the biography now provides a context through which the work can be both situated and interpreted (see **interpretation**).

Biographical studies of composers have a long history, but the writing of composer biography as a distinct literary genre was defined during the early nineteenth century in works such as Forkel's study of Bach and further extended through the emergence of biographical writing on Beethoven. The biographical writings of both Ferdinand Reis and Anton Schindler around the mid-point of the century helped to focus attention on the suggested importance of life for an understanding of the musical work. The later nineteenth century witnessed a general rise in historical consciousness (see **historiography**), and this was reflected in the construction of monumental studies of recognizably great composers, a process that was complicit in the consolidation of the **canon**. This trend was evident in works such as Jahn's extensive biography of Mozart (Jahn 1891) in conjunction with the representation of the composer as **genius**. The attempt to construct a comprehensive account of the life and work of a great composer found a parallel in the collating, dating and editing of musical works that was to become the central concern of a **historical musicology**.

The music of J.S. Bach enjoyed a revival of interest during the nineteenth century, and this was reflected in the biography written by Philip Spitta (Spitta 1884). Spitta's work is subtitled 'His Work and Influence on the Music of Germany, 1685–1750' and consists of three extensive volumes. The first volume begins with the family history and background, an obvious starting point in most biographical narratives (see **narrative**), considers the young composer's education and early influences (see **influence**) and discusses the early works under the subtitle of 'The first ten years of Bach's "Mastership"'. The narrative constructed by Spitta is one of emergence to mastery, and it is one that is central to most biographical writings.

However, Spitta also considers the music that was constructed by this life, often in detail, and this life and work approach as defined by Spitta has been sustained since then and often presented in a more compressed manner. This was standardized by publications such as Dent's *Master Musicians* series, which has its origins in the late nineteenth century. The general title of this series constructs an overtly canonical and gendered perspective (see **gender**). However, such publications did provide a great deal of information and interpretation in a recognizable format and accessible manner, thus providing a connection between a professional musicology and a wider listening and reading public. Representative of this approach is Malcolm Boyd's study of J.S. Bach (Boyd 1983). This book is written within the generic history of the series, a history of which Boyd is fully aware, and it reflects the image of the composer at that time and the then current state of research. The book is sectionalized on the basis of location, a recurrent and logical model in the case of J.S. Bach, with the composer's residence in specific places – Weimar, Cöthen, Leipzig – providing a framework within which works in specific musical genres (see **genre**) are discussed.

Under the impact of **structuralism**, music **analysis** reflected the claim of a musical **autonomy**, within which the musical work was seen to be a self-sufficient object, free of the constraints of contextual factors such as biography (see **formalism**). However, this merely resulted in a new set of constraints that demanded critical scrutiny. The **new musicology** sought to regain both the **subjectivity** and contextualization that had apparently disappeared from musical **discourse**. One way in which both subjectivity and context can be brought back into focus is through the restatement of biography and the re-examination of life and work through a more contemporary lens. The primary site for such a reconsideration comes through the interrelated concepts of gender and sexuality. Clearly, the consideration of any composer's life demands consideration of his or her sexuality, yet most standard biographies resist, perhaps suppress, this demand. Recently, a number of important studies have raised such issues and provoked much debate, the most notable being American musicologist Maynard Solomon's consideration of Schubert's sexuality titled 'Franz Schubert and the Peacocks of Benvenuto Cellini' (Solomon 1989). This article considers aspects of Schubert's biography and certain documentation, such as letters and diaries, all of which look towards the suggestion of a homosexual **identity**. Such a process of inquiry reflects a certain absence in standard biographical narratives:

> Schubert's nature has for too long remained hazy, shadowy, and unfocused. Thus far, biographers have not been able to provide even a provisionally convincing portrait of his personality, to delineate his obsessions, to understand his familial and intimate relationships and ultimately to glimpse some of the driving forces of his creativity.
>
> (*ibid.*, 206)

For Solomon, exploring the sexuality of Schubert opens up the prospect of a new understanding of Schubert's life and work. However, how such exploration can lead to even just a glimpse of the creative process remains open to debate (see Agawu 1993b).

Interest has always been shown in the life of composers, and it would seem that such interest will continue to encourage biographical research and writing. The ongoing series of composer biographies published by Cambridge University Press, titled *Musical Lives*, high-lights this continuing interest. According to the publisher's definition:

> The books in this series will each provide an account of the life of a major composer, considering both the private and the public figure. The main thread will be biographical and discussion of the music will be integral to the narrative. Each book thus presents an organic view of the composer, the music and the circumstances in which it was written.

This series has already produced a number of interesting books, many of which shed new light on their chosen composer and, in some cases, the problems of writing biography (see Franklin 1997a). The description of the series as outlined above would seem to suggest that it covers similar ground to the earlier *Master Musicians* books, the difference being that the *Musical Lives* series avoids technical discussion of the actual music. Also notable are the composers thus far chosen for the series: they include Beethoven, Berlioz, Debussy, Mozart, Strauss and Webern. Clearly, there is a great deal of variation in terms of chronology and **style**, as well as biographical and musicological methodology, but they are all contained within the Western art music tradition, they are all men, and even if in some instances their position in relation to the canon is debatable, they do all sustain some form of relationship to that concept.

Further reading: McClary 1993a; Solomon 1982; Steblin 1993

BODY

The body may be considered in several different ways. There is the body's influence upon thought, which was a concern of Scottish philosopher David Hume, and later German philosopher Martin Heidegger, who in response to Descartes's central dictum, 'I think, therefore I am' (see **Enlightenment**), emphasized the body's crucial influence on human understanding of the world. There is also the body as represented in **discourse** and visual images – the way the body is (culturally) perceived and represented or written about. Bound up with these two forms is the body as a source and producer of lived experience, for example through singing, speaking, dancing or musical performance.

French literary theorist Roland Barthes made some notable attempts to write about this aspect of the body. His essay 'The Grain of the Voice' (Barthes 1977) is directed specifically at song, in which the voice 'has us hear a body which has no civil identity, no "personality", but which is nevertheless a separate body' (*ibid.*, 182). 'The "grain" is the body in the voice as it sings' (*ibid.*, 188). Following the work of Julia Kristeva, Barthes distinguishes between the materiality of the voice (the *geno-song* – sounds produced through interaction with the body) and the grammar of the music and language being sung (the *pheno-song*). He thereby attaches importance to the disruptive role of the 'grain' of the voice in its necessary dialectic with the rule-bound elements of music, those structured and sanctioned by society. To demonstrate this, he develops a critique of German tenor Dietrich Fischer-Dieskau, in whose voice is only to be heard 'the lungs, never the tongue, the glottis, the teeth, the mucous membranes, the nose' (*ibid.*, 183). Barthes further comments: 'His art – expressive, dramatic, *sentimentally clear*, borne by a voice lacking in any "grain", in signifying weight, fits well with the demands of an *average* culture' (*ibid.*, 185). These final remarks point to public unease when it comes to matters of the body, and a popular association between high art and the mind, ideas that Barthes seeks to revise.

Barthes has also written about his conception of the composer's body present in music. In his essay 'Rasch' (Barthes 1985), he examines Schumann's *Kreisleriana* (1838), locating within its musical phrases, gestures and tempo changes signs of the composer's own body beating, indicating movement or the intention to speak (*quasi parlando*). This restless patchwork of ebb and flow Barthes summarizes as 'the body in a state of music' (*ibid.*, 312).

Barthes's ideas have been applied to a wide range of vocal music. One such example is the study by Raymond Leppert and George Lipsitz of the country singer Hank Williams, who gained wide success despite his haggard and gaunt appearance (Leppert and Lipsitz 2000). It is argued that Williams's body stood as a **metaphor** for his songs and the time in which they were written, features matched by the subdued doubtfulness of his vocal delivery. And in the field of opera study, Carolyn Abbate has adapted Barthes's work, developing the idea of the disembodied voice (see Abbate 1993).

Another central issue that the concept of the body raises is that of the male gaze. Nineteenth-century painting often reveals an institutionalized privilege of men to scrutinize women's bodies (Williams 2001, 66–7). This idea is further developed in cinema studies, most notably by Laura Mulvey, reflecting the dominance of male film directors and cameramen whose work translates women in film into objects and men into subjects (see Mulvey 1975). Lawrence Kramer is one musicologist who has developed this idea, particularly in relation to nineteenth-century music, including Liszt's *Faust* Symphony (1861) and Richard Strauss's operas *Salome* (1905) and *Elektra* (1909) (see Kramer 1993b, 1990, 1993c, respectively). He notes that:

> For nineteenth-century men, the sexual pleasure of looking, scopophilia, can plausibly be said to rival physical penetration as the chief means of satisfying sexual desire.
>
> (Kramer 1990, 273)

Kramer and others (see Gilman 1988) have indicated how in *Salome* and *Elektra* the orchestra is at times used to represent the patriarchal gaze. They also reveal how the music may illustrate the central female characters subverting that gaze, while at other times they are punished by brutal characterization:

> as a dance the music is grotesque, its movement heavy-footed lurching, its orchestral texture a suffocating mass. The music on which Elektra stakes her identity is a projection of her myster-iously heavy body: the repellent, engulfing, degenerative body prescribed by the culture of *fin-de-siècle* misogyny.
>
> (Kramer 1993c, 147)

However, both in this opera and other works (for example, Schubert's 'Trout' quintet (1819); see Kramer 1998), a range of subject positions (see **subject position**) are explored, and interpretations (see **interpretation**) like those of Kramer and Gilman are especially effective at revealing the complexities of composers' relations to their audience and the bodies, or subjects, represented in the music. The idea of the male gaze also has relevance to **popular music**; for example, Nicola Dibben has explored voyeurism in the music of Pulp (Dibben 2001).

However, the concept of the male gaze may be criticized on the grounds of its emphasis on biological difference (see **alterity**). **Post-modernism** has done much to interrogate discourses that appear to make simplistic links between culture and the body. While a person's physical characteristics (**race**, **gender**, age) will inevitably inform his or her actions, feelings and expressions, this can lead to stereotyping and other extreme forms of essentialist discourse. For example, although some writers have developed effective studies based on characterizations of black music (see Brackett 2000 on James Brown; Maultsby 1990 on Africanisms), Philip Tagg has questioned the ease with which music is labelled 'white' or 'black', in particular the dichotomy commonly drawn between 'black' or 'Afro-American music' and 'European music' (Tagg 1989). He questions the kind of assumptions that not only lead some to expect stereotyped behaviour from black artists, 'like constant arse wiggling, pelvic grinding and jive talk' (*ibid.*, 295), but also a stereotyped musical **language**. Tagg's concern is not necessarily to deny the common existence of certain features in the music of black artists but to question the naive assumption that these are the original and exclusive property of black musicians, pointing out, for example, that blues notes 'also occurred on a regular basis in folk music from Scandinavia . . . [and from] Britain at the time of the main colonisation of the New World' (*ibid.*, 288).

Musicology has been slow to develop an interest in the body, although it is increasingly a concern of scholars working on popular music, opera, song and nineteenth-century instrumental music. Some of the earliest examples can be found in the work of sociologists studying body language, gender and **feminism** in popular music. Dick Hebdige has investigated the body as a site of cultural resistance or protest, as a means of expressing **identity** or belonging, and as a vehicle for **style** expression in popular culture (Hebdige 1979). Simon Frith and Angela McRobbie have pioneered inquiry into sexuality in rock (Frith and McRobbie 1990) developing the term 'cock rock' to describe certain lead guitar performance styles. Investigations of the impact of the body in dance music include Barbara Bradby's study of the cyborg, a technological amalgam of one female singer's voice with another's body (Bradby 1993), and Stephen Amico's consideration of masculine signification in house music (Amico 2001).

Further reading: Butler 1993; Frith 1996; McRobbie 1994; Scott 2000; Walser 1993; Whiteley 2000

CANON

Canon is a term that is used to describe a body of musical works (see **work**) and composers accredited with a high level of **value** and greatness. The origins of the term are in ecclesiastical and theological contexts, referring to those sources considered most worthy of pre-servation and propagation. Most cultures and cultural contexts reflect the presence of a canon and canonical values, but it is most clearly defined and active within the Western art music **tradition**. There is a common belief that a canon first emerged through the **Romanticism** of the nineteenth century and its fascination with great composers of the past (principally, the music of Haydn, Mozart and Beethoven but also the 'revival' of J.S. Bach). But, as American musicologist William Weber points out, there are many other canonical formations prior to Romanticism (Weber 1999).

Weber suggests that there are three basic types of musical canon: scholarly, pedagogical and performance. The scholarly reflects directly the activity of musicology and music **historiography**, while the pedagogical involves the teaching of music and as such has a long history and tradition. But it is the suggestion of performance that is most interesting. The formation of repertoires and, on the most basic level, the thinking that shapes concert programmes and recordings (see **recording**), can reflect the presence, perhaps pressure, of the canon. For Weber, 'performance is ultimately the most significant and critical aspect of musical canon' (*ibid.*, 340). Performance assumes this significance because, in contrast to musicological scholarship, it forms part of the public face of music.

Clearly, the notion of a canon is inextricably linked with aesthetic value (see **aesthetics**). The works that are considered to belong to the canon do so because they embody what for some constitute eternal qualities and transcendent dimensions. This is often most clearly situated in writing on literature. Harold Bloom, for example, in his survey of *The Western Canon* (Bloom 1995) identifies twenty-six 'great' authors, with Shakespeare at the centre.

Similar canonical values are also implicitly active in shaping writing on music. For example, Charles Rosen's *The Classical Style* (Rosen 1971) is one of the most perceptive studies of the music of Haydn, Mozart and Beethoven, and his exclusive focus on this triumvirate of composers clearly centres them within the canon. However, it could also be seen as a text that marginalizes the many other, less well-known composers who also contributed to the formation of a 'Classical style'. This process of exclusion highlights the reality that the canon acts as a source of cultural power and as such it becomes a mechanism through which non-canonical music is excluded from the public domain.

It is significant that Bloom begins his survey of his nominated literary canon with a distinctly nostalgic tone for the certainties of the past, but he also focuses on authority: 'This book studies twenty-six writers, necessarily with a certain nostalgia, since I seek to isolate the qualities that made these authors canonical, that is, authoritative in our culture' (Bloom 1995, 1). Works included in the canon then assume an authority; they are seen to exemplify certain qualities and values.

Recent writing on the topic has emphasized this negative dimension of the canon and posited alternatives, often focusing on 'marginalized' types of music and counter-canonical strategies (see Bergeron and Bohlman 1992). However, within specific musical areas that are outside the range of the canon of Western art music, there are still canonical pressures and tendencies. For example, in the context of popular music (itself clearly excluded from the collection of 'great works' that is the canon), the emphasis in its history on 'classic' popular music such as the Beatles and Bob Dylan reflects this situation.

See also: **alterity**, **discourse**, **gender**, **reception**, **work**

Further reading: Citron 1993; Goehr 1992; Weber 1992

CLASS

The concept of class refers to specific groupings of people defined through economic status and reflected in certain attitudes and identities (see **identity**). The classical economic understanding of class comes from **Marxism**, which defines classes in relation to the ownership of production and views history through the conflicts that result from the competing interests of distinct classes. However, for some, the Marxist understanding of class may be unnecessarily rigid and economically determined, factors that are undermined by contemporary contexts and processes such as social mobility and educational opportunity. But the idea of a core value and identity as defined through economic position and power remains compelling.

The presence of class in music and musicology is evident through the relationships between musicology and higher education, with related issues of access to knowledge and its association with power susceptible to a class-based perspective. Access is also an issue in relation to the arts and **culture** in general, in which economic position may act as a barrier while, for some, culture erroneously becomes an image of class status. In a recent polemical and somewhat humorous article, Dai Griffiths relates music and class through educational experience, that of the selective process of the British grammar school system of the postwar era, suggesting that there is a sense of musical **value**, perhaps a **genre**, that reflects this class-based educational context: 'Grammar schoolboy music is tough and gritty. The classic exponents of grammar schoolboy music were the New Manchester School and its acolytes' (Griffiths 2000, 143). The musical reference here is to the **modernism** of Harrison Birtwistle, Peter Maxwell

Davies and Alexander Goehr (referred to as the New Manchester School on the basis of a shared educational experience), and Griffiths goes on to suggest that this genre exists in opposition to the egalitarian spirit of popular music: 'Grammar schoolboy music loathed one thing in particular: pop music. Not jazz: pop music' (*ibid.*, 144).

The most significant direct references to class generally occurs in relation to **popular music**, in which it forms a background that is often articulated through an essentially sociological perspective. This is evident in the writing of sociologist Dick Hebdige in his classic account of subculture (see **culture**). He makes reference to class, specifically working-class youth, in relation to David Bowie and the glam rock of the early 1970s, which is defined as part of a retreat, or escape, from class: 'Bowie's meta-message was escape – from class, from personality, from obvious commitment – into a fantasy past or a science fiction future' (Hebdige 1979, 61). In other words, popular music formed an escape from class as reality into music as fantasy. However, in contrast to glam, punk rock was often constructed as a reflection of the reality of working-class youth, a construction that was not always an accurate reflection and one that did not always recognize the active presence of the **culture industry** (see Savage 1991).

The British popular music scholar Richard Middleton provides an outline of music history for the last two hundred years that uses class as a reference point and identifies 'three "moments" of radical structural change' (Middleton 1990, 12), the third and final of which 'begins sometime after the Second World War – most strikingly with the advent of rock 'n' roll – and can be termed the moment of "pop culture"' (*ibid.*, 14). The first of these three structural changes 'is the moment of the "bourgeois revolution", marked by complex and overt class struggle within cultural fields, by the spread of the market system through almost all musical activities, and by the development and eventual predominance of new musical types associated with the new ruling class' (*ibid.*, 13). This statement draws attention to the political relationships of class and culture and the presence of the market as well as the rise of a specific class, the bourgeoisie, through a period from the eighteenth century to the mid-nineteenth century. Middleton relates this political context to 'conflicts between different musical techniques', and, perhaps more significantly, he refers to 'immense struggles over what form music should take and what role it should play'. These conflicts and struggles relate to different musical spheres and contexts: 'this is evident in pub, school and street as, on another level, in orchestral concert music, opera, the fashion for virtuoso piano music and the work of the avant-garde composers of the Romantic movement [see **Romanticism**]' (*ibid.*, 13).

Middleton continues: 'By the 1890s, the start of a second major situational fracture can be seen. This is the moment of "mass culture", characterized by the development of monopoly-capitalist structures' (*ibid.*, 13). The production of a mass culture reflected the process of industrialization and the increasingly homogeneous nature of class relations, as evident from the economically and culturally consistent nature of an industrial proletariat and the further polarization of class relationships. Middleton refers to the emergence of a specifically American hegemony and relates this to specific popular styles such as ragtime, jazz and Tin Pan Alley that involve a 'drive towards "one-way communication" in homogeneous markets' (*ibid.*, 13–14).

For German critical theorist Theodor Adorno (see **critical theory**), the rise of a mass culture and 'one-way communication' would involve the ideological force (see **ideology**) that constructs the pacification of the proletariat, blinding members of the class to their true needs and interests (see **culture industry**). However, the suggested hegemony of class relations is most effectively theorized by Italian Marxist Antonio Gramsci, for whom the dominant class exerts power through persuasion and the normalization of the political process, culture being one of the main contexts for this and reflecting a new level of subtlety in the relationship between classes.

These issues of class resonate beyond Middleton's 'second situational fracture' and continue through the 'moment of pop culture' to the present. The certainties of a class-based political response to culture, including music, may have been somewhat displaced through the new subjectivities of contemporary critical contexts (see **subjectivity**), but the active presence of the market and the related notion of a culture industry in all spheres of cultural activity point to the continuing relevance of underlying economic conditions, a situation that is available for new scrutiny by future critical musicologists (see **critical musicology, new musicology**).

Further reading: Bottomore 1991; Day 2001; Scott 1989

COVER VERSION

Cover version is a term used in both everyday language and, increasingly, in popular music studies to describe the **popular music**

practice of a **recording** by performers other than those responsible for
the original version (see **work**).

Clearly, popular music has always depended upon songwriters to
produce songs for others to perform, a good example being Neil
Diamond's 'I'm a Believer' (1966), which was specifically written for
the Monkees, a band with no initial claim towards originality. But
cover versions tend to relate to songs already familiar and therefore
available for either revisiting and/or reworking. A process of transformation or translation can be evident. For example, in 2001 Atomic
Kitten had a hit with 'The Tide is High', which had been recorded by
Blondie in 1980 after its original manifestation as a ska/reggae sound
produced by the Paragons on the Trojan label during the 1960s. This
example produces a network of meanings and implications (see **meaning**). The song effectively changes **gender**, from the male **identity** of
the Paragons to the female voices of both Debbie Harry and Atomic
Kitten. It also involves a shift in ethnic identity (see **ethnicity, race**)
from the black sound and context of Jamaica to the white Anglo-
American context of both Blondie and Atomic Kitten. It also suggests
a process through which popular music passes through time to become a
historicized subject. The shift of ethnicity has a long history in popular
music, the appropriation of black rhythm 'n' blues sounds into a white
economic and cultural mainstream being a key process in the formation
of 1950s rock 'n' roll (see Gillett 1983; Palmer 1996). In contrast,
discussion of the gender implications has still to be fully recognized.

However, such issues have recently begun to be more fully theorized within an emergent musicological context. Dai Griffiths, in a
chapter titled 'Cover Versions and the Sound of Identity in Motion'
(Griffiths 2002), brings issues of gender, sexuality and race into focus
alongside the importance of **place**. Griffiths references a wide range of
recordings, from different periods and styles, concluding that 'cover
versions can supply case studies for the textual illustration and
mounting of discussion around questions of identity and political
power' (*ibid.*, 61). This suggests a new-found importance in the
practice of cover versions and their **interpretation**. While, for some,
the recycling nature of this process may look towards the superficiality
of popular music, in effect it becomes one of the ways in which
meaning can be both constructed and articulated through music. The
discourse that has now begun to evolve from this musical process and
context suggests that it has much potential for further consideration in
the study of popular music.

Further reading: Coyle 2002

CRITICAL MUSICOLOGY

Despite the more self-critical, reflexive relationship that musicology, at least since the mid-1980s, has developed with its subject, as seen in the rise of the **new musicology** and the resultant burgeoning of topics now taught in music departments, such as film, television and **popular music**, ethnomusicology (see **ethnicity**), cultural theory (see **cultural studies**), music **psychology**, music therapy, and performance **analysis**, for some there remains a sense in which most of these new efforts to change musicology are still too focused on central figures of the Western classical **canon**.

Embedded in a potential critical musicology is the idea of continually rethinking music to avoid establishing new orthodoxies or grand narratives (see **narrative**; see also Cook and Everist 1999), although, in general, it remains concerned with finding some kind of synthesis between **analysis** and a consideration of social **meaning**. One forum of such discussion has been *Critical Musicology: A Transdisciplinary Journal Online*, which defined itself as: '1. A form of musicology which applies aspects of Critical Theory as practiced within other humanities disciplines to music. 2. A form of musicology which involves the theoretical critique of previous musicological traditions' (www.leeds.ac.uk/music/info/critmus/). The purpose of this forum was to encourage an ever greater number of approaches to the study of music and respond to work that had not yet been seen to be fully aligned to the emergent new musicology. These included a more critical and philosophical understanding of the musical **work** (see Goehr 1992); a rejection of the fetishizing of music as text and an associated scepticism towards **sketch** and other source-based study (Griffiths 1997); less emphasis on the division of music into parent genres (see **genre**), such as classical, folk and pop (Moore 2001b; Griffiths 1999); consideration of the role of the **body** in the performance and experience of music (see Leppert 1988; Bohlman 1993); a shift to performer- and listener-centred inquiry and an associated interest in **subject position** (Clarke 1999; Dibben 2001); inquiry into the social conditions that affect how musicians learn to play (Green 2001); and a concern with music education, how it is taught, and how that may best relate to the different musical experiences that young people bring to the subject (McCann 1996; Green 1997).

Critical musicology has been very concerned with the production and consumption of music, for example the economics of popular music (see Wicke 1990). Of particular interest for critical musicologists in this regard is Jacques Attali's *Noise: The Political Economy of Music* (Attali 1985), in which attention is drawn to the power held by those who produce and market music so that 'Listening becomes an essential means of surveillance and social control' (ibid., 122). Another potential model for a critical musicology is provided by American ethnomusicologist Philip Bohlman's concern to draw attention to musicology itself as a political act while simultaneously warning against limiting revisionary methodologies to canonical works and composers:

> The arguments for resistance, **post-colonial** discourse, and sub-altern voices are already in the musics that surround us, and we ignore them only by not listening to them. . . . Musicology's crisis, therefore, confronts it also with a new responsibility to come face-to-face with the political nature of all acts of interpretation and with the political consequences of excluding for too long the musics of women [see **feminism**], people of color [see **race**], the disenfranchised, or Others [see **alterity**] we simply do not see and hear.
>
> (Bohlman 1993, 435–6)

Recognition of the political aspect of musicological interpretation and consideration of neglected voices is to be found in Georgina Born and David Hesmondhalgh's multiple-author book *Western Music and its Others* (Born and Hesmondhalgh 2000), while issues of music and **class** have been the concern of Richard Middleton and Derek B. Scott (Middleton 1990; Scott 1989). Much critical musicology questions and examines the ways in which music is used, socially and individually, and this focus on human interaction with music is an important extension of the more subjective (see **subjectivity**) approaches introduced by the new musicology.

Further reading: Radano and Bohlman 2000; Scott 2000, 2003

CRITICAL THEORY

Critical theory is readily invoked but difficult to define. Interestingly, the entry on critical theory in the *Encyclopaedia of Aesthetics* (Kelly 1998) simply tells us to look elsewhere, to 'Adorno; Barthes; Benjamin; Criticism; Derrida; Feminism; Foucault; Habermas; Marcuse; Postcolonialism and Post-structuralism' (ibid., 462). This gesture, in what is an important source of general information on **aesthetics**, reveals critical theory to be a broad, umbrella-like term that to varying extents can form some relationship to many key thinkers, concepts and contexts but itself remains resistant to definition as a concept.

However, critical theory does have its own history and intellectual identity. The first and most direct usage is linked to the work of the so-called Frankfurt school. On the models provided by the Frankfurt school, critical theory was formed as a rigorous critical engagement with philosophical and sociological issues through an interpenetration of these respective disciplines within an essentially Marxist-derived and -oriented framework (see **Marxism**). David Held, in his impressive overview of critical theory, states:

> Critical theory, it should be emphasized, does *not* form a unity; it does not mean the same thing to all its adherents. The tradition of thinking which can be loosely referred to by this label is divided into at least two branches – the first centred around the Institute of Social Research, established in Frankfurt in 1923, and the second around the recent work of Jürgen Habermas.
>
> (Held 1980, 14)

The first of Held's two branches has become synonymous with the work of Theodor Adorno (defined by Held as philosopher, sociologist and musicologist) and Max Horkheimer, although many other thinkers were also active around the Institute of Social Research, including the philosopher Herbert Marcuse, the psychologist Erich Fromm and, from a rather different angle and less clearly defined way, the literary theorist and critic Walter Benjamin.

The fundamentally political nature of critical theory is captured in a brief essay by Horkheimer titled 'Traditional and Critical Theory', which articulates the importance of human agency as a shaping force of history, a reflection of the Marxist orientation of critical theory:

> The critical theory of society... has for its object men as produ-cers of their own historical way of life in its totality.... Objects, the kind of perception, the questions asked, and the meaning of the answers all bear witness to human activity and the degree of man's power.
>
> (Horkheimer 1972, 222)

Max Paddison, the foremost English-language commentator on Adorno and critical theory, provides a neat synopsis of the critical nature of this particular project:

> In brief, Critical Theory has to do with how a theory relates to its object, and how it deals with the contradictions of its object.

At the same time it has to do with the contextualization of the object of inquiry – a process which embraces not only the 'objective' social and historical context, but also the interaction between individual and society (the 'Subject–Object relationship') which is embedded in that context.

(Paddison 1996, 14–15)

On this account, critical theory involves a critical relationship with the object under consideration, a process that can also be situated within another, broader context ('contextualization of the object of inquiry') and that has implications for our understanding of music. Adorno's writings on music, which include surveys of Beethoven, Berg, Mahler and Wagner (Adorno 1998, 1991a, 1992a, 1991b, respectively) and a comparative study of Schoenberg and Stravinsky (Adorno 1973), present a critical understanding of the subject and provide models for further inquiry and critical reaction.

In addition to Paddison's accounts and critiques of Adorno, some aspects of recent musicology have reflected a new-found interest in his work. The most notable attempt to build new interpretations upon an essentially Adornian framework come in American theorist Rose Subotnik's book *Developing Variations: Style and Ideology in Western Music* (Subotnik 1991). In this book, Subotnik presents a series of essays that engage with specific issues that emerge from Adorno, including 'Adorno's Diagnosis of Beethoven's Late Style' (see **periodization**). In this essay, Subotnik confirms the importance of Beethoven, specifically his late **style**, for Adorno, within which the self-contained, self-reflexive nature of the musical language formed a critical relationship to the real world and anticipated **modernism** (see **autonomy**):

According to Adorno . . . Beethoven's third-period style marked the beginning of the modern world, that is, a reversal in the prospects for a fully human species, a reversal that made eloquent and effective social protest imperative in art; and yet, it was with this very style that the social impotence of the artist was established irrevocably.

(*ibid.*, 33)

This statement brilliantly reflects what for Adorno was the paradoxical position of music, and the arts in general, in the modern world: the requirement for a critical art that simultaneously acknowledges the isolation of the artist.

As outlined at the outset of this discussion, it is possible to interpret a wider critical theory beyond the already broad boundaries of the Frankfurt school and its related theorists. Many recent and current trends involve a critical relationship to past theory. Much writing defined as **post-structuralism**, another broad term, can be read as a critique of **structuralism**, likewise **postmodernism** involves a critical relationship to **modernism**. The critical reflex towards already existing theory is most sharply defined in **deconstruction**, in which much of Derrida's writing exists through a critical reaction to already existing texts (by Rousseau, Hegel and Husserl, among others) and concepts.

See also: **critical musicology, new musicology**

Further reading: Jay 1973; Norris 1992; Paddison 1993; Williams 1997

CRITICISM

Criticism can be understood as the regular activity of reviewing concerts and recordings (see **recording**). This version of criticism is located within professional journalism and might not always form part of a general musicology, but it is also possible to conceive a wider criticism in which evaluative and comparative judgements are made. From this perspective, some aspects of musicology can also be understood in terms of criticism.

If it is possible now to perceive a certain distinction between music criticism and musicology, this was not always the case. Critical writing about music forms a significant part of an evolving **tradition**. The rise of publishing during the eighteenth and nineteenth centuries created a context in which a significant increase in commentary about music occurred. The emergence of journals devoted specifically to the study of music was clearly an important development. The *Allgemeine Musikalische Zeitung*, first published in Leipzig in 1798, is often considered to be the first music journal. It included reviews of new works and performances and became a model for the music journals that were soon to emerge throughout Europe. The late eighteenth century also saw the emergence of music criticism in daily newspapers.

The concern with a critical response and evaluation of new and recent music became a recurrent preoccupation through the **Romanticism** of the nineteenth century, with the music of Beethoven being the most clearly defined object of attention. The most interesting and stimulating critic of the period was E.T.A. Hoffmann, a German writer of fantasy novels who also wrote about music. His review of Beethoven's Fifth Symphony (1807–8), which appeared in the *Allgemeine Musikalische Zeitung* in 1810, was the starting point for a tradition of German Beethoven criticism and a central reference point in the **reception** of this music. Hoffmann begins his review with a statement of the composer's and the work's importance, but he clearly outlines the personal nature of his own response (see **subjectivity**):

> The reviewer has before him one of the most important works by the master whose pre-eminence as an instrumental composer it is doubtful that anybody would now dispute; he is utterly permeated by the subject of the present review, and may nobody take it amiss if he exceeds the limits of conventional appraisals and strives to put into words all the profound sensations that this composition has given rise to within him.
>
> (Charlton 1989, 236)

This gives an indication of the subjective nature of Hoffmann's response and also betrays its own time, but it is clear that the review of this work is also an invitation for Hoffmann to reflect on some larger issues, in this instance the description of instrumental music as a truly romantic art form and its elevation towards an **absolute** music, allowing Hoffmann's **interpretation** to be situated in relation to the large-scale aesthetic issues surrounding music and **meaning** (see **aesthetics**).

This review, like others conceived for the *Allgemeine Musikalische Zeitung*, is notable for the degree of musical detail it contains, a factor that distinguishes it from what we have since come to expect from reviews. The descriptive but detailed account of the **work** allows us to view it in relation to later musicological developments such as **analysis**. This overlap with analysis was to be repeated later in the writing of English composer, conductor and critic Donald Francis Tovey, whose descriptive accounts of music, often in the form of the programme note, managed to contain a remarkable degree of musical detail (Tovey 2001).

The nineteenth century also witnessed the emergence of the composer as critic, the most notable being Robert Schumann. In 1834, Schumann founded the *Neue Zeitschrift für Musik*, with the journal originally conceived as a radical alternative to what was now perceived as the conservatism of the *Allgemeine Musikalische Zeitung*. The progressive Romanticism championed by Schumann, in both theory and practice, was soon to be contrasted by the conservatism of the Viennese critic Eduard Hanslick, who believed in the **autonomy** of music. Hanslick reacted critically to the influence of Wagner, favouring the instrumental music of Brahms, which could be interpreted as self-sufficient, in contrast to the extra-musical connotations and significance of the Wagnerian music drama.

In the Austro-German context outlined above, music criticism had now become a focal point for ideological reflections on the nature of music. The connections between criticism and **ideology** were even more clearly marked in nineteenth-century Russia for example, in which the search for a national musical identity found reflection in music criticism (see **nationalism**).

Music criticism during the twentieth century featured an intensification of factors already active during the previous century. If composers no longer cared to review new music in the way that Schumann did, composers still sought justification through the written word, with Schoenberg, for example, producing an abundance of written commentary on music (see **modernism**). However, in some contexts music criticism and the role of the critic were subjected to even greater ideological pressures as music became a source of a more overt political representation.

The further development of a professionalized, academic musicology has intensified the division between musicology and criticism. Criticism has become more widespread through the increase in media such as newspapers, magazines, radio and, more recently, television, all of which can feature reviews of performances, new music and new recordings. However, recent developments in musicology suggest a new-found critical orientation. This does not involve activities of criticism, but it does suggest an evaluative approach to music. American musicologist Joseph Kerman, whose work is mentioned in relation to numerous concepts in this book, suggests a more 'comprehensive "humane" practical criticism of music' (Kerman 1994, 30) as an alternative to the alleged objectivity of music analysis. This proposal opens up the prospect of a study of music that is based on critical and evaluative premises but is carried through with a certain rigour and close scrutiny. It is also possible to look towards a critical response to music that projects a critical relationship to itself as well as to the music under consideration (see **critical theory**).

Popular music and **jazz** also have their own critical discourses (see **discourse**), but they also provide a certain parallel with the classical music **tradition**. The development of specific journals in both jazz (*Downbeat*) and popular music (*Rolling Stone*) helped to shape tastes and provide a framework within which critical responses could be made. Critical discussions in terms of reviews also reflect a certain power, with new groups and recordings subjected to criticism and comparison. In popular music, the division between journalistic criticism and academic study can often be neatly obscured, with important voices such as Simon Frith and Greil Marcus able to move across both dimensions.

See also: **critical musicology, new musicology**

Further reading: McColl 1996

CULTURAL STUDIES

The term cultural studies can be understood as a generalization that embraces all aspects of the study of culture, including music. However, although it is clearly surrounded by multiple meanings and contexts, it has a distinct lineage and is often related to quite specific practices and theories. The point of origin is generally given as the work of Raymond Williams, one of the most important and imaginative writers on **culture**, and Richard Hoggart. The formation of the Birmingham Centre for Contemporary Culture in 1964, directed by Richard Hoggart and then Stuart Hall, represents the beginnings of cultural studies as an academic discipline and the increasingly rigorous theorization of culture. The theoretical work that emerged from Birmingham embraced a multi- (or inter-)disciplinary force and engaged with a diverse range of cultural practices, factors that are now central to most versions of cultural studies.

Cultural studies have often been concerned with popular culture (see **popular music**), the distinction between different formations or levels of culture being a recurrent issue. This focus on the popular has often taken a political dimension through engagement with issues such as **class**. These tendencies are well articulated in Dick Hebdige's *Subculture: The Meaning of Style* (Hebdige 1979), a work that is firmly in the Birmingham cultural studies tradition. Hebdige is concerned with the aspiration of young people for emancipation from the realities of every-day life. This leads to consideration of the **identity** of youth subcultures and the opposition between this aspiration and the commodity status and pressures of the wider cultural and economic contexts. Essentially, Hebdige constructs a dialectical resolution of this opposition, bringing these tensions together through the focus on **style**, which becomes a site of interplay between different conflicting, competing pressures. These issues are situated in the popular music of the period, with references made to styles such as glam, reggae and punk.

Some of the most insightful work on popular music/culture to emerge from an explicitly cultural studies background comes from American cultural theorist Lawrence Grossberg, who views popular music within broad cultural contexts and, often, through political and ideological perspectives (see **ideology**). In the introduction to a collection of essays tilted *Dancing in Spite of Myself* (Grossberg 1997a), Grossberg situates his 'project' 'between an interest in the social effects and logics of popular culture, especially rock music and youth culture, and a commitment to the possibilities of cultural studies as a form of progressive intellectual work' (*ibid.*, 1). This situation leads Grossberg to summarize his work through 'four trajectories': 'a concern with the specific practice of cultural studies; a philosophical interest in cultural and communication theory; an exploration of the popularity and effectivity of rock music; and an investigation into the apparent success of the new conservative hegemony' (*ibid.*, 1). These 'trajectories' outline some important areas and, in many ways, can still be interpreted as an agenda for the future mapping of cultural studies and popular music. The final trajectory, the 'new conservative hegemony', reminds us that music as a cultural practice exists in political contexts and locations, both of which are formed by what Grossberg perceives as the dominant political and cultural climate of America at the time of writing.

Although cultural studies may relate most directly to popular music, many recent trends in musicology, through a new-found inter-disciplinarity, provide some telling parallels (see **new musicology**). Texts such as Gary Tomlinson's *Music in Renaissance Magic* (Tomlinson 1993b), Susan McClary's *Feminine Endings* (McClary 1991) and John Shepherd's *Music as Social Text* (Shepherd 1991), while not always engaged with specific traditions and agendas of cultural studies, remind us, in many different ways, that music is a cultural practice and exists in and through cultural contexts.

Further reading: During 1993; Grossberg 1993, 1997b; Inglis 1993; Mulhern 2000

CULTURAL THEORY *see* **critical theory, cultural studies, culture**

CULTURE

According to the influential cultural theorist Raymond Williams, culture 'is one of the two or three most complicated words in the English language' (Williams 1988, 87). Williams made this statement in a book titled *Keywords*, itself an important cultural text. The complications suggested by Williams emerge from the different contexts in which the word is used and the different meanings that attach to it. While culture has generally been used as an all-embracing term for creative, educational and artistic activities, Terry Eagleton stresses the physicality of the term and its relationship with nature: 'though it is fashionable these days to see nature as a derivative of culture, culture, etymologically speaking, is a concept derived from nature'. Following further consideration of earlier usages, he concludes: 'We derive our word for the finest of human activities from labour and agriculture, crops and cultivation' (Eagleton 2000, 1). This 'cultivation' conveys an image of development and growth, terms descriptive of nature but which relate to human activity, specifically education. This understanding of culture has a clear applicability to both music and musicology, both of which are inextricably linked to educational processes and contexts.

Culture is often thought of as both a context and a set of practices that define that context. The suggestion of context indicates that culture exists as a collective practice. This view was projected by T.S. Eliot in a text titled 'Notes Towards the Definition of Culture', in which Eliot explored the interrelationships of three levels of culture: the individual, groups or classes (see **class**), and the whole of society. Each of these levels depends on the next and results in an understanding of culture as 'the whole way of life' (Eliot 1975, 297). Eliot's perspective, which was driven by his own religious beliefs, raises certain fundamental issues. Clearly, any individual asserts **identity** through his or her cultural associations, and, social and/or economically defined groupings may also form identities through shared interests and issues, but how all this can be subsumed within a cultural totality that is the 'whole of society' remains problematic. It is notable that Eliot uses the singular rather than the plural (*the* rather than *a* definition of culture). From our contemporary multicultural perspective (see **ethnicity**), Eliot's definitions of culture seem somewhat outdated, but even in the context of Eliot's own time there were issues of diversity and difference (see **alterity**) that would form a resistance to his interpretation of culture.

Raymond Williams continually produced insightful discussions of culture and its study (see **cultural studies**), and he also engaged with

Eliot's 'whole way of life', coming to quite different conclusions (Williams 1958). Williams talks of culture as a fluid process and the need to 'recognize not only "stages" and "variations" but the internal dynamic relations of any actual process' (Williams 1977, 121). This relationship between change ('stages' and 'variations') and the internal dynamic leads Williams to state that:

> We have certainly still to speak of the 'dominant' and the 'effective', and in these senses of the hegemonic. But we find that we have also to speak, and indeed with further differentiation of each, of the 'residual' and the 'emergent', which in any real process, and at any moment in the process, are significant both in themselves and in what they reveal of the characteristics of the 'dominant'.
>
> (*ibid.*, 121–2)

These terms (dominant, residual, emergent) are important for Williams, and they purposefully reflect the dynamic nature of culture as process. 'Residual' relates to past cultures: 'By "residual" I mean something very different from the "archaic".... Any culture includes available elements of its past, but their place in the contemporary cultural process is profoundly variable'. Clearly, any culture or cultural context has a past, an inheritance, but how that is reconstructed in the present is open to change (is 'variable'). This residual culture coexists with what Williams terms 'emergent' cultural practices: 'By "emergent" I mean, first, that new meanings and values, new practices, new relationships and kinds of relationship are continually being created' (*ibid.*, 122–3).

In other words, against a recognizable background culture (the 'dominant') we can project reflections of past cultures ('residual') and trace new ('emergent') cultural formations. This theoretical outline is a good reflection of how music operates as culture. Music is an evolving art that always carries some reflection of its past (see **tradition**). However, how we might locate Williams's cultural 'dominant' in a contemporary context is more problematic. Music exists in many different cultural contexts – national, regional, ethnic, among others – and different types of music reflect different cultures. This cultural difference is also reflected in musicology, in which different scholars will focus on different cultural contexts and types of music. This sense of difference is extended through ethnomusicology, in which different ethnomusicologists specialize in different cultures and their respective musical repertoires. This focus on difference questions the possibility of Williams's 'dominant' culture and negates the singular, unifying perspective of Eliot (see **postmodernism**). However, while musicology is a cultural practice, a way of engaging in a culture, it is often retrospective and can be external in terms of time and location to the culture under consideration. It therefore more consistently engages with and reflects Williams's 'residual' rather than 'emergent' culture.

See also: **cultural studies, nationalism, place, popular music**

Further reading: Denning 2004; Kramer 1993b; Mulhern 2000; Tomlinson 1984

CULTURE INDUSTRY

The culture industry is a concept constructed by German critical theorist Theodor Adorno (see **critical theory**) to describe and critique the industrial and commercial nexus that forms around the production, dissemination and **reception** of **culture** (Adorno 1991c). It results in a deliberate paradox, setting culture, with its connotations of both nature and art, against the reality of industrialization, a reality that, in other formulations, would be the antithesis of culture.

One of Adorno's main texts on the culture industry is an extended chapter of the book *Dialectic of Enlightenment*, which he wrote with Max Horkheimer, originally published in 1944 (Adorno and Horkheimer 1979). In this chapter, titled 'The Culture Industry: Enlightenment as Mass Deception', Adorno and Horkheimer characterize the productions of mass culture through processes of industrial standardization, suggesting that the production of film is identical to that of the motor car (*ibid.*, 123). For Adorno and Horkheimer, this standardization is also the defining nature of the **popular music** of the period:

> Not only are the hit songs, stars, and soap operas cyclically recurrent and rigidly invariable types, but the specific content of the entertainment itself is derived from them and only appears to change. The details are interchangeable.
>
> (*ibid.*, 125)

This suggests a highly pessimistic view of the production and reception of popular culture, but there is a degree of accuracy. Much popular music reverts to a certain typology and **genre** classification that is targeted by the industry towards certain markets as defined by age group, **gender** and social background (see **class**). However, it is also a problematic understanding of the human response to culture, which, for Adorno, is blinded by the ideological effects of capitalism (see **ideology**).

It is notable that Adorno's writings on popular culture and the culture industry date from around the 1940s, and that his rather fixed view of these issues were not reconsidered in the light of the trans-formations that popular culture underwent in the period up to his death in 1969. Some writers have sought to focus on exceptions to Adorno's model that can be used as a critical response. For example, Max Paddison proposes a genre of 'radical popular music' that resists Adorno's standardization. This music has a radical potential to assume a critical orientation to which an Adornian perspective might be sympathetic. Paddison mentions the eclectic experimentation of Frank Zappa, and British groups such as Henry Cow and the Art Bears (Paddison 1996, 101), as examples of music that is generally defined as popular but that can be heard as articulating a critical relationship to the culture industry. However, we still buy reissued CDs of Henry Cow recordings through economic structures (CD stores, the Internet) that form part of, or reflect, the commodity fetishism and consumerism of other more neatly defined commercial contexts and therefore they could be argued to reflect the presence and operations of a culture industry. The exceptional nature of such music might have been dismissed by Adorno through his terminology of 'pseudo-individualism' (Adorno 1994), which sees exceptions as merely the appearance of difference (see **alterity**), further reflecting the deceptive nature of mass culture.

The marketing of classical music has come to reflect the operations of a culture industry, which impacts on the reception of the music and, for some cultural and critical theorists (see Strinati 1995, 225–6), has led to the blurring of the boundaries between art and popular culture within the contemporary context of **postmodernism**.

See also: **cultural studies**

Further reading: Gendron 1986; Mulhern 2000; Negus 1999; Paddison 1993

DECONSTRUCTION

Deconstruction is a trend in philosophy and literary theory that has recently been applied to music. The concept is most clearly identified with French theorist Jacques Derrida through his classic texts of the 1960s, such as *Of Grammatology* (Derrida 1976) and *Writing and Difference* (Derrida 1978), and while it remains remarkably resistant to definition, it generally suggests a critical reading of texts and a questioning of the status of **language**.

Derrida insists that deconstruction is not a methodology or a system, but it can be understood as a way of reading and interpreting texts that is subversive. Deconstruction involves a process 'always already' present in a text, and the deconstructive reading is one that involves the identification and explication of this presence as a counter-logic to what may initially appear to be the most logical and natural **interpretation**.

Deconstruction emerges through the preoccupation with language present in both **structuralism** and **post-structuralism**, and it takes issue with de Saussure's construction of language as a series of binary oppositions. For example, apparently simple binary distinctions such as nature/culture and speech/writing can, on closer inspection, be unstable and undecidable in terms of priority and hierarchy. Nature may appear to precede culture, but how we think about and interpret nature is also a reflection of culture and cultural experiences. From this perspective, culture would seem to displace nature in the original hierarchy of the binary opposition. While this subversion, perhaps 'deconstruction', of a binary opposition does not constitute a method, Derrida, in an interview published as *Positions* (Derrida 1981), refers to 'a kind of *general strategy of deconstruction*' that is intended to 'avoid both simply *neutralizing* the binary oppositions . . . and simply *residing* within the closed field of these oppositions, thereby confirming it'. Rather, we need to recognize that 'we are not dealing with the peaceful coexistence of a *vis-à-vis*, but rather with a violent hierarchy. One of the two terms governs the other . . . or has the upper hand' (*ibid.*, 41). This suggests that language, and its use, is imbued with images of power as defined in this instance through the hierarchy situated within the binary opposition. This aspect of Derrida's thought does have a certain parallel with music. We often speak of conflicting keys, or themes, and their state of opposition to each other (tonic–dominant key relationships, for example), but they always, in the context of common-practice tonality and the constraints of **style** and **genre**, achieve a resolution that reflects the realization that 'one of the two terms governs the other'. However, in music that is less clearly defined in terms of the consonance/dissonance relationship, for example that of **Romanticism** and early **modernism**, this situation and its interpretation becomes more open as the relationship between the two terms shifts and, perhaps, begins to deconstruct itself. It is also significant that such music often seems enclosed in its own reflection and thus invites the prizing open of its processes and meanings through a deconstructive interpretation. American musicologist Rose Rosengard Subotnik intriguingly suggests that 'romantic music provides an explicit basis for its own deconstruction' (Subotnik 1996, 45).

Derrida introduces other terms and concepts that, even if they do not help to constitute a method, enjoy a certain consistent use and reference in the literature consistent with a 'general strategy of deconstruction'. Two in particular invite consideration in this immediate context. The first is *'différance'*, which Derrida states is neither a word nor concept (Derrida 1981, 39–40), but it is generally understood as a conflation of difference and deferral. In the words of Gayatri Chakravorty Spivak, '"difference" and "deferment" – both senses present in the French verb "différer" and both properties of the sign under erasure – Derrida calls "différance"' (Spivak 1976, xliii). This conflation of difference and deferral could reflect certain issues in music and musicology. How, for example, do we locate and interpret the **meaning** of music? Each piece is different, but often there is also a feeling that what the music may actually mean is always deferred. However, Derrida's *'différance'* has a larger resonance. It can suggest the construction of a past, a sense of history through distance. We know that the past is different from the present, but the point of separation is endlessly deferred, a suggestion that also maps on to the problematics of defining the distinctions between various musical styles and genres as well as stylistic and historical periods (see **periodization**).

Derrida also makes reference to the 'supplement' as part of a telling binary opposition between essence and supplement. The supplement 'means *both* the missing piece and the extra piece' (Subotnik 1996, 65). A typical strategy of deconstruction may involve consideration of something that may appear incidental or marginal in a text, something that is quickly passed over in pursuit of a main **narrative** or argument. However, this moment can actually be the supplement, that which both completes ('the missing piece') and supplements ('the extra piece') the text. In other words, the supplement is no longer supplementary: it is essential. This can be translated into musical terms. We may initially interpret a certain harmony or thematic idea, for example, as incidental, as a supplement to the structural flow of the music, but it could conceivably be the moment that constructs the doubleness of 'missing piece'/'extra piece'.

It is through this notion of the supplement that Derrida makes one of his few telling references to music. The later sections of *Of*

Grammatology contain his encounter with the thought of Rousseau (see **Enlightenment**) and his specific ideas about music. Rousseau's thought is driven by the construction of binary oppositions, privileging speech over writing and nature over culture. In this sequence, Rousseau also posits the primacy of melody over harmony. For Derrida, however, the logic of supplementarity will suggest that rather than remaining fixed on one side of a binary opposition, harmony will inhabit the actual essence of melody, becoming both the 'missing piece' and the 'extra piece' of musical language.

The various strategies of deconstruction outlined above and their suggested parallels with music are located in the specifics of the text, its language and structure. Derrida's much quoted claim that 'there is nothing outside the text, there is no extra-text' can be interpreted as a preoccupation with the text that is bound by its own **formalism** and **autonomy**. However, rather than limiting textuality, Derrida opens up the text to a new-found **intertextuality** that reaches out from text to the realization that there is no extra-text because everything is text. This vision of textuality coincides with the differing/deferral that is *différance* to explode the narrow confines of text and language.

While deconstruction may appear more relevant to how we write and speak about music, since clearly the texts of musicology can be deconstructed just as readily as any other body of texts, there have been some striking recent attempts to engage directly with actual music through deconstruction. Rose Rosengard Subotnik continues Derrida's avoidance of 'method' when she makes 'no claim to lay out a doctrinally pure deconstruction' (Subotnik 1996, 45). However, in a chapter titled 'How Could Chopin's A-Major Prelude Be Deconstructed?' she sets out to present a 'concrete demonstration of how a musical deconstruction might work' (*ibid.*, 41) through the contrast and comparison of two different analyses of the Chopin prelude (A major, Op. 28, no. 7 (1828–9)). However, it is notable that some of the most interesting writing on deconstruction and music takes the form of critical responses to other writing, most notably Craig Ayrey's virtuoso critique of Subotnik (Ayrey 1998) and also the overviews of music and deconstruction by Adam Krims (Krims 1998b) and Christopher Norris (Norris 1999).

The emergence of a deconstructive approach to music is aligned with wider notions of **postmodernism** and post-structuralism and forms part of a larger challenge to traditional musicology (see **new musicology**). However, while it may be too soon to talk of a 'deconstructive musicology' (*ibid.*), and there is some uncertainty as to what the continued mapping of deconstruction on to music and musicology may produce, the critical close readings of deconstruction do have the potential to unlock alleged certainties and casual assumptions. Alan Street's deconstruction of the notion of musical unity (see **analysis**), which takes its theoretical starting point from Paul DeMan rather than Derrida (Street 1989), and Craig Ayrey's response to Subotnik, suggests that there is still much that could be gained by a project of deconstruction in musicology.

Further reading: Culler 1983; Norris 1982; Sweeney-Turner 1995; Thomas 1995

DIEGETIC/NONDIEGETIC

Diegetic (diegesis) is a concept used in studies of film music to refer to music that is produced and received within the constructed world of the film and therefore forms part of its **narrative**. It could take the form of music heard as a recording by characters in a film, as for example, in *The Big Chill* (1983) or *High Fidelity* (2001), both of which foreground **popular music** and its **discourse** in its narrative and structure.

If diegetic signifies the presence of music in the narrative of a film, then nondiegetic represents the presence of music that is external to that structure or context. Nondiegetic music is thus music composed as an accompaniment or commentary on the visual dimension of the film through the form of a soundtrack. As the characters on screen cannot hear this music, it exists as external to the fictional world represented on screen (see Kalinak 1992). However, there are films in which music does not fit easily into either of these two categories. For example, *American Graffiti* (1973) is a remarkable film that, like *The Big Chill* and *High Fidelity*, bases much of its content around popular music. The film is set in a small Californian town in the early 1960s and involves a series of young characters who are enjoying their last night before departing for college. This context immediately suggests popular music as both a background and foreground dimension. However, although we hear a great deal of popular music, from Bill Haley and the Comets' 'Rock Around the Clock' (1954) to the Beach Boys' 'All Summer Long' (1965), this does not always fit readily into a diegetic/nondiegetic model. David Shumway, in his study of this film, explains:

> Given the ubiquity of the music and the fact that its volume changes without clear narrative explanation (e.g., the music is always loud when we get an establishing shot of Mel's Burger

World, but the volume then decreases to allow conversation to be foregrounded), we cannot classify the music in *American Graffiti* as straightforwardly diegetic even though the movie wants to assume its quasi-diegetic origin. Rather, the line between diegetic and nondiegetic is impossible to establish.

(Shumway 1999, 41)

If *American Graffiti* blurs the distinction between diegetic and non-diegetic, it is also possible to achieve a slippage from one category to the other, as occurs, for example, in the classic western (see **genre**) *High Noon* (1952).

Diegetic and nondiegetic are terms that could also relate to opera and other dramatic contexts, which could reflect distinctions between the internal and external role of music (see Joe and Theresa 2002).

See also: **identity**

Further reading: Davison 2004; Flinn 1992; Kassabian 2001; Wojcik and Knight 2001

DISCOURSE

Discourse has been used since the sixteenth century to describe different forms of speech, but more recently it has been adapted by postmodern (see **postmodernism**) cultural theorists both to expose rigid cultural belief systems and to argue for new fluidities of **identity**, **meaning**, expression, and knowledge in society. For French anthropologist and cultural theorist Michel Foucault, discourse is the system of statements through which the world, society, and the self are known, understood and brought into being in a relational context (Foucault 1972). In this sense, discourse may be understood as the commentaries and aesthetic beliefs (see **aesthetics**) that surround musical practices, shaping and influencing the views of performers, composers, scholars and listeners alike. The nature of the relationship between discourse and musical activities is reflexive and subject to a process of evolution. In the case of composer biographies (see **biography**) or conversation books, however, the discourse may be more confused as the voices of composer and author become irretrievably mixed, for example in the Stravinsky conversation books written by Robert Craft (see Stravinsky 2002). Such books may, in turn, have an effect on a composer's own perception of his or herself. More importantly, through such commentaries, composers are also able to influence discourses about their music. This is especially important in influencing discourse concerning a composer's views on **nationalism** (see Vaughan Williams 1996) or aesthetic positions such as **modernism** (see Schoenberg 1975) and postmodernism.

Although discourse about music is problematized by the fact that discussion of music takes place in a different **language** to music, linguistics has influenced musicological thought. The Russian linguist and literary theorist Mikhail Bakhtin's ideas about an author's discursive distance from his or her characters, which leads to a double-voiced utterance in novels, is reflected in American musicologist Edward Cone's suggestion that a 'composer's voice' in which the idea of a composer's voice gives way to other narrating voices in the orchestra (Cone 1974) exists in a piece of music. This idea has since been developed by Jean-Jacques Nattiez (Nattiez 1990a) and other musicologists such as Carolyn Abbate, who restyled Cone's idea as 'the unsung voice' (Abbate 1991; see also Taruskin 1992). Another development of linguistics is the idea of discursive coding, when, for example, a speaker switches from speaking in a formal situation to an informal one. In the same way that the register of everyday speech will vary depending on context, so we can expect a different form of discourse in different sections of a piece, for example between a scherzo and a finale. However, this kind of analogy is more commonly made in relation to tonal works (see Spitzer 1996).

Certain analytical approaches to music have reflected the influence of linguistics (see **analysis**). One example is semiotic analysis (see **semiotics**), which reflects the influence of structural linguistics (see **post-structuralism**) and **narrative** theory. This is illustrated by the interest that semiotic analysts have in the way music treats certain topics, such as love, war and desire; how these ideas are 'coded' into musical language; and how music may 'switch' between such codes (see Samuels 1995). In considerations of black popular music, a number of writers have realized the potential of linking Bakhtin's ideas about double-voiced discourse to the theories of Henry Louis Gates Jr's book *The Signifying Monkey* (Gates 1988), which explores double play in black fiction between African speech-based traditions and the Western literary **canon**. David Brackett has explored this idea in relation to the foregrounding of shouts and other vocal noises in the music of James Brown (Brackett 2000), while Gary Tomlinson has used this approach to explore Miles Davis's evolving relationship with the jazz canon (Tomlinson 1992).

Discourses on music have constructed musical practice to ensure the continuation of particular genres and styles (see **genre**, **style**), the division of music history into distinct periods (see **periodization**) and the formation of musical canons. The discourse of canon, which promotes the idea of **value** according to standards set by **genius** composers working within a central (Western) practice, inevitably excludes what is perceived as different (see **alterity**) and gives rise to the idea of a periphery of works of a 'lower' standard. In some instances, this interpretation has been placed on **popular music** and **jazz** (see Adorno 1994), although these forms exist and are sustained by a separate set of discourses with their own very different sets of values, traditions (see **tradition**) and critical language. As the popular music scholar Simon Frith has noted, 'Part of the pleasure of popular music is talking about it' (Frith 1996, 4). However, he goes on to point out that in order for meaningful dialogue to take place, there must be a degree of common ground, a framework for 'shared critical discourse' (*ibid.*, 10). Arguably, **popular music** and **jazz** are related more by a set of commonly shared discourses than musical languages or styles, although with the increasing stylistic pluralization in popular music there may be occasions when no shared critical discourse is available.

Musical discourses will directly influence the way in which a musical work is interpreted. For example, in musicology the 1970s and 1980s witnessed a shift to highly formalist (see **formalism**) interpretations and an emphasis on the inner details of a musical **work** (see **analysis**). The roots of formalist thinking can be traced back at least as far as the publications of the nineteenth-century Viennese music critic Eduard Hanslick, who attacked the idea of programme music. This view arose in the context of a contrasting tradition of hermeneutic (see **hermeneutics**) readings, which included the search for **meaning** in **absolute** music. Hanslick's views about the value of absolute music over programme music, in particular his support for Brahms over Wagner, created a discourse that influenced musical thought well into the twentieth century, as reflected, for example, in the music and writing of Arnold Schoenberg (see **modernism**).

Schoenberg, through his claim for the continued supremacy of German music (see Haimo 1990, 1) articulated a nationalist discourse. This example illustrates the ideological function of language (see **ideology**), a feature that has been widely considered in sociology and political science, for example by Giddens and Althusser. Ideological discourses that equate nations, races and ethnicities (see **race**, **ethnicity**) with ideas about cultural value, such as those propagated in Nazi Germany in the 1930s, point to a set of cultural myths that do not maintain historical and geographical realities but pre-construct visions of those realities.

Increasingly, especially since the rise of a **new musicology**, discourses on music have introduced a much wider range of intersecting concerns, embracing aesthetics, race, **gender**, **class** and politics. For example, recent considerations of nineteenth-century music have increasingly drawn on orientalist discourse, which is the subject of the cultural theorist Edward Said's book *Orientalism* (Said 1978) (see **Orientalism**). Said considered a range of texts, including travel correspondence, fiction and autobiography, written by Western authors during the European colonization of other parts of the world. However, as Robert Young observes:

> Said's Orientalism describes a system of apparent knowledge about the Orient but one in which 'the Other' [see **alterity**] from that Orient is never allowed, or invited to speak: the Oriental Other is rather an object of fantasy and construction.
>
> (Young 2001, 398)

A significant number of operas composed since the eighteenth century have been based on oriental subjects, and although the Others in those works are allowed to speak, their words inevitably reflect the views and values of the composers and librettists and their historical context. This fact extends even to recent operas that attempt to give a more authentic voice to the Other, such as John Adams's *The Death of Klinghoffer* (1993). Adams's opera actually brings contrasting discourses into conflict: those of Palestinian hijackers, American hostages and the sound bites of American news media.

Further reading: Gendron 2002; Parker 1997

ENLIGHTENMENT, THE

The Enlightenment is usually interpreted as a general intellectual movement that occurred in the latter part of the eighteenth century. Although often associated initially with France (d'Alembert, Diderot, Voltaire), it also featured significant contributions from Germany (Kant), England (Burke) and Scotland (the 'Scottish Enlightenment' of Hume). The principal concerns and ideas of the Enlightenment were based on the supremacy of reason and the rejection of superstition and thus focused on general education and the cultivation of the arts.

The preoccupation with reason had its origins in Descartes's famous dictum, 'I think, therefore I am', a statement that situated the power of rational thought at the centre of human existence. Enlightenment thought developed this rationalism in a number of ways, one of the most significant being the codification, organization and dissemination of knowledge, resulting in an increase in publications, including the significant development of dictionaries and encyclopedias. This attempt to construct a systematic account of knowledge had implications for music and writing about music. One of the most widely available texts of the later eighteenth century was Jean-Jacques Rousseau's *Dictionnaire de musique*, published in Geneva in 1767 and Paris in 1768 (le Huray and Day 1981, 108–17). This dictionary consists of short definitions of concepts, topics and issues such as **genius** and taste. The attempt to make sense of, to rationalize, such topics is clearly a reflection of the Enlightenment project, yet Rousseau can also be read as an anticipation of **Romanticism**, producing a double perspective that is evident from his discussion of musical genius. But while Rousseau anticipates the **subjectivity** of Romanticism, he also, through the privileging of experience, reflects the presence of empiricism in the origins of the Enlightenment (see **aesthetics**). This sense of departure, or escape, through experience is reflected in the Enlightenment concern with the **sublime**, the moment of transcendence that escapes the grasp of normative, conceptual models. The contrast between the sublime and the beautiful was articulated by Kant in his *Critique of Judgement* of 1790 (Kant 1987; see le Huray and Day 1981, 214–29), but it was English writer Edmund Burke who, in his *Philosophical Enquiry into the Origins of Our Ideas of the Sublime and the Beautiful* (Burke 1998; see le Huray and Day 1981, 69–74) produced the sharpest focus on this comparison. It is the vast greatness of the sublime that forms a bridge between the Enlightenment and Romanticism.

The diffusion of culture and the dissemination of music as reflected in the writing of Rousseau was also active in other areas of music, most notably in the rise of the public concert. For example, the very public nature of Handel's musical activities in London (opera and oratorio) reflect the enlightening role of **culture** and the arts during the eighteenth century. However, it is the Viennese Classicism of Haydn and Mozart that is usually seen as the most apposite musical reflection of the Enlightenment.

The rise of a **historiography** of music can also be seen to emerge through the Enlightenment. English writer and musician Charles Burney was very much a product of the Enlightenment. A musician with professional experience, he was also an admirer of Rousseau and a friend of Burke. Originally published in 1776, Burney's *A General*

History of Music: From the Earliest Ages to the Present Period (Burney 1957) gives a systematic account of what were then conceived as the elements of music within a historical survey, an exercise that reflects the rationalism of the Enlightenment. The attempt to construct a rational account of music is reflected in other specifically musical texts such as those of Sulzer and Koch (see Baker and Christensen 1995).

The Enlightenment has cast a long shadow over later developments, extending through **modernism** to the present. For some, such as German theorist Jürgen Habermas, modernism and the Enlightenment are closely related. Habermas claims that 'The project of modernity... [was] formulated by the philosophers of the Enlightenment' (Habermas 1985, 9) and goes on to pose the question: 'should we try to hold on to the *intentions* of the Enlightenment, feeble as they may be, or should we declare the entire project of modernity a lost cause?' (*ibid.*, 9). For Habermas, the values and intentions of the Enlightenment continue to hold some relevance through their relationships with modernism, which he sees as an 'incomplete project'. This is in contrast to the rejection of Enlightenment ideals in certain theories of **postmodernism**, as reflected in Lyotard's 'incredulity toward metanarratives' (Lyotard 1992, xxiv), with the rational spirit of the Enlightenment acting as a potential metanarrative and therefore no longer sustainable within the critical parameters of postmodernism.

Recent musicological writings have formed a new engagement with the ideas and consequences of the Enlightenment, most notably Rose Rosengard Subotnik's *Deconstructive Variations* (Subotnik 1996), which carries the subtitle *Music and Reason in Western Society*. Subotnik addresses Mozart's *Die Zauberflöte* (1791), a work often seen as an ideal musical representation of the Enlightenment. This work is explored from the perspectives of both the Enlightenment and Romanticism, with the oppositions between the two perspectives and the alternatives they enclose resulting in a contemporary critical relationship to the ideals, values and concerns of the Enlightenment (*ibid.*, 1–38).

Further reading: Heartz 1995; Kramnick 1995

ETHNICITY

The term ethnicity applies to social groups that share a sense of cultural heritage and **identity**, as opposed to biological descent, although part of this sense of shared identity may well reflect discourses of **class** and **race** (see **discourse**). As such, it is a concept that allows for a degree of choice, whereas race more often implies a lack of choice and opportunity. As an indication of the more flexible nature of ethnic identity, Benedict Anderson has argued that it represents 'imagined communities' (Anderson 1983).

The earliest attempts to theorize populations in terms of societal and cultural similarity date from the nineteenth century, especially in the work of German sociologist Ferdinand Tönnies and French sociologist and philosopher Émile Durkheim. The concept of ethnicity grew in importance in the social sciences in the 1960s at the culmination of decolonization in Africa and Asia and in response to the associated migration of post-colonial societies into Northern Europe (see **post-colonial/postcolonialism**). As a result of the emerging anti-racist and anti-colonial views of the time, ethnicity was coined by sociologists in order to represent the positive feelings of belonging to a cultural group. More recently, since the collapse of the Soviet Union and its satellite states, the concept has attracted more negative connotations, arising from the notion of 'ethnic cleansing' in the former Yugoslavia. This points to more recent opposing notions of ethnicity as, on the one hand, a positive sense of shared culture, identity and belonging and, on the other hand, a target of political hostility.

However, there is a boundary problem: where does one ethnicity (or one race) begin and another end? Musicologists have been involved in rewriting ethnic boundaries. Nazi Germany, during the 1930s and 1940s, saw what Potter describes as the cultural annexing of the rest of Europe's music (Potter 1998), resulting in claims that composers such as Chopin and even Berlioz were in fact German. Particular effort went into reclaiming Handel as a German composer in response to his apparent adoption by the English. This led to claims that Handel felt alienated in England, and the Jewish texts of some of his oratorios – such as *Jeptha* (1758) – were rewritten. Handel's predilection for choral music, which developed through his experience of English choral traditions, was claimed as an anticipation of Germany's National Socialist need for utilitarian music, which spoke simply and directly to the people. However, all attempts at defining what German music was – a concern of such important musicologists as Hugo Riemann and Friedrich Blume – proved illusive, not least because Germany had been one of the most cosmopolitan musical centres in Europe.

The anthropologist T.H. Eriksen has argued that:

ethnicity is essentially an aspect of a relationship, not a property of a group...ethnicity is an aspect of social relationships between agents who consider themselves as culturally distinctive from members of other groups with whom they have a minimum of regular interaction.

(Eriksen 1993, 12)

This definition points to the idea that ethnicity operates in a relational context, where a cultural distinction is felt to exist, for example in cities with minority groups (such as Hispanics in New York), countries with culturally heterogeneous populations (such as India and China), or where groups live in diaspora (Celts, Romas). In each case, ethnic identity is most likely to be defined against a (perceived or real) hegemonic norm. However, music associated with certain ethnicities, such as gypsy music and Jewish *klezmer*, is not restricted to one geographical location, and its reception and use throughout history may vary significantly (see Radano and Bohlman 2000, 41–4). Such music will not always be performed by members of the associated ethnic group, and in some cases it will be transformed by composers and other musicians into a **style**, as in Mozart's orientalist use of the *alla Turca* style (see **Orientalism**) and Schubert's use of gypsy style, especially in his later works, for example at the opening of the last movement of the String Quintet in C major, D. 956 (1828) (see Bellman 1998a).

Ethnic identity may evolve or change during the lives of certain individuals, sometimes as a means of accessing opportunities or exercising influence. As *fin-de-siècle* Vienna excluded Jews from many institutions, Mahler converted to Catholicism in order to conduct the Vienna State Opera. Liszt, although now considered Hungarian, spoke German and was considered one of the New German School, along with Wagner. Bartók, on the other hand, stressed the importance of speaking Hungarian (even to his own German-speaking family) and was especially concerned with the formation of a modern music that was linked to the idea of an authentic (see **authenticity**) Hungarian ethnicity – one that he felt resided in Hungarian peasant music, whereas Liszt had believed that the true national compositions of Hungary were those performed by the gypsies (see Brown 2000; Trumpener 2000). As a result of his studies of peasant music in places such as Romania, Croatia and North Africa, Bartók was one the earliest ethnomusicologists.

The term ethnomusicology is attributed to Dutch scholar Jaap Kunst, who used it in the subtitle of a book published in 1950. The practice is interdisciplinary, involving linguistic and anthropological skills, and broadly speaking it applies to music that resides outside the

Western concert music **tradition**. It has been variously described as 'the study of music in culture' (Merriam 1959) and the study of society in music (Seeger 1987). The British ethnomusicologist Martin Stokes states that:

> Music 'is' whatever any social group considers it to be, contrary to the essentialist definitions and quests for musical 'universals' of 1960s ethnomusicology, or text-orientated techniques of musicological analysis.
>
> (Stokes 1994, 5)

As Stokes indicates, ethnomusicologists, and anthropologists, have moved away from the structuralist view that performance simply reflects social and cultural structures (see **structuralism**). Ethnomusicology, like European-centred musicology, originally focused on musical form and musicians, expressing a belief in the possibility of an objective, scientific approach. Ultimately, however, ethnomusicological studies reflect the ideologies (see **ideology**) of their exponents. For example, Radano and Bohlman have pointed out that 'particularly problematic is ethnomusicology's investment in rather fixed concepts of ethnicity, culture, and subjectivity' (Radano and Bohlman 2000, 4). However, as musicology begins to question its exclusive focus on Western concert music, so the boundaries between the two disciplines begin to blur and their shared concerns grow.

Issues of ethnicity are increasingly bound up with **globalization**. The global spread of hip-hop, for example, can be seen to bring racial discourse – ideas of oppression and struggle originally codified by African-Americans in New York – into the hands of ethnic minorities living in parts of Europe, such as France and the Netherlands. In this way, musical styles are shared and adapted by different ethnic groups to convey similar ideas.

Further reading: Krims 2000, 2002

ETHNOMUSICOLOGY *see* ethnicity

FEMINISM

The original stimulus to a movement broadly defined as feminism has been a concern to reverse situations in which women are marginalized by, or subordinated to, men, particularly in political, economic, social and cultural (see **culture**) forms of **discourse**, in order to construct a more equal and inclusive society. As a theory, it can be dated from Mary Wollstonecraft's *A Vindication of the Rights of Women*, published in 1792. Following on from concerns for women's economic and political position in society from the immediate post-Second World War period, feminist theory turned its attention more towards women's cultural experiences. In more recent times, a number of different types of feminism have emerged, including Marxist (see **Marxism**) and liberal feminism.

Feminism became a principal concern of musicology in the 1980s alongside other interdisciplinary approaches broadly categorized under the **new musicology**. Prior to this, in the 1970s musicologists were already beginning to rediscover forgotten women composers and performers and in this light had begun to review existing concepts, such as **genius**, **canon**, **genre** and **periodization**. However, through the 1980s and 1990s, musicologists such as Susan McClary, Marcia Citron and Ruth Solie began to consider the cultural reasons for the marginalizing of women composers from the received canon. Other writers have questioned essentialist views that women were somehow less biologically suited to composing than men, a claim that could never be substantiated (see Halstead 1997). Instead, explanations for the lack of female composers must rest with social and political conditions.

Marcia Citron has explored issues of **gender** and the musical canon, the concept of music as gendered discourse, the idea of professionalism, and the **reception** of women's music (see Citron 1993). Her work also re-examines sites of musical production. She has drawn attention to the fact that in the early nineteenth century, sonatas and other chamber works by composers such as Beethoven, Schubert and Chopin were received in private salons, often established by women, and that these locations were also home to a large number of Jewish women composers. These women were able to pursue music making because of favourable social conditions; they came from liberal-minded families with substantial wealth and learning.

One area that has also received the attention of feminist musicology is **popular music**. In her seminal study of the music of Madonna, McClary examines the accusation that Madonna cannot have meant what we see and hear because she 'isn't smart enough', that she's 'a mindless doll fulfilling male fantasies' (McClary 1991, 149). McClary develops a powerful argument to refute this claim, instead demonstrating the complete control that Madonna exercises over her art, its production and, in particular, her **identity**. McClary also explains that the framework in which Madonna operates is somewhat different to that of the Western art **tradition**, in which feminine subjects associated with desire (Carmen, Isolde, Salome, Lulu) must be destroyed. Instead, Madonna is associated with the physicality of African-American vocalists such as Aretha Franklin and Bessie Smith, for whom, it is argued, there are no male counterparts, women who 'sing powerfully of both the spiritual and the erotic without the punitive, misogynist frame of European culture' (*ibid.*, 153). Similar points are made by Lucy Green in her notion of 'affirming femininity' (Green 1997, 21–51).

Feminist studies have also engaged directly with music, leading to McClary's description of 'horrifying' patriarchal violence in Beethoven (McClary 1991, 128). This kind of approach clearly positions sound itself in relation to gender, which stems from a much older tradition of describing particular themes, for example in sonata form, in terms of masculine and feminine (see Burnham 1996). While such a practice was previously used as an extension of patriarchal ideas of strong masculine and weak feminine, for example the so-called feminine ending, more contemporary writers have turned their attention to the nature of subject positions in music (see **subject position**). For example, in relation to the beheading of Jochanaan (John the Baptist) in Strauss's opera *Salome* (1905), Carolyn Abbate remarks that the composer 'coaxes the listening ear into occupying a female position, by *erasing* any sense of a male authorial voice and replacing it with a deluding chorus of disembodied singers' (Abbate 1993, 247). Such a statement interprets Barthes's idea of the 'death of the author' in the light of feminist thought (see **post-structuralism**).

Through the 1990s, feminist musicology became more closely bound up with notions of gender and difference (see **alterity**), ideas that in turn relate to other increasingly important topics, such as **body**, **ethnicity** and **narrative**.

Further reading: Abbate 2001; Clément 1988; Cusick 1999a, 1999b; Dibben 1999; Fuller 1994; Solie 1993; Williams 2001

FORMALISM

The concept of formalism signifies an aesthetic perspective (see **aesthetics**) that prioritizes formal detail above other factors (such as **identity**, **meaning**, expression and **interpretation**) and is most commonly associated with the study of musical form through the discipline of music **analysis**. The philosophical background of formalism is located in the aesthetics of Immanuel Kant. His critical considerations of judgement and taste as articulated in the *Critique of Judgement*, originally published in 1790 (Kant 1987; le Huray and Day 1981, 214–29), elevates what is being observed (the **work**) above any related or contextual factors. The most clearly defined aspect of Kant's thinking in relation to the work is that of the 'disinterested', in which the outcome of the critical process is separated from predetermined expectations and aspirations (see **ideology**). This results in a critical distance that claims to inject a degree of objectivity into the process and thus shifts the priorities of interpretation towards the internal properties of the work, leading to the claim that the basis of the work's **value** resides in the finality of its form.

In the arts in general and specifically Western art music, formalism, as both an aesthetic ideology and a cultural practice, emerges with the rise of **modernism** during the late nineteenth and early twentieth centuries. In this historical and stylistic context, a preoccupation with the formal elements and requirements of music finds a new, higher focus. Both Schoenberg's development of serialism and Stravinsky's construction of neoclassicism involved a realization of music as a self-reflexive practice. The concern with form that this involved in modernist musical contexts also finds its way into the study of music. The rise of **analysis** as a musicological practice reflects the background of formalism and translates the primary status of formal details from a compositional practice into a mode of inquiry that has its own internal logic. The analytical methodology identified with Austrian music theorist Heinrich Schenker, for example, accentuates the privileging of internal detail as distinct from external factors and exemplifies the Kantian desire for the work's 'formal finality' through the search for a specific structural paradigm and the requirement for the teleological closure of that structure (see Schenker 1979).

See also: **absolute**, **autonomy**

GAY MUSICOLOGY

Gay musicology is a response to, and part of, what is more broadly labelled 'queer theory', that is, studies in humanities subjects that interpret topics from a gay, lesbian or bisexual perspective. Although the term is used here in a general sense, it should be noted that lesbian musicology is gaining currency in its own right. Gay studies have arisen in response to homophobic attitudes, coupled with patriarchal resistance to alternative gender positions. They consist of personal responses by gay or lesbian scholars but may equally be the work of heterosexual scholars, and while they frequently focus on gay or lesbian subjects, this is not exclusively the case. Gay studies have arisen in a number of academic fields, including literary criticism (see Sedgwick 1994, 1997), philosophy (see Butler 1990), and **cultural studies** (see Doty 1993).

One of the key motivations behind gay musicology is a belief in 'diversifying our discipline and rescuing it from the rigid ideology and hidden agendas to which only a few years ago it seemed unduly attached' (Brett *et al*. 1994, vii). As such, it forms part of the broader initiative referred to as the **new musicology**. An important early example is Philip Brett's article 'Britten and Grimes' (Brett 1977), which examined ways in which the central character of Benjamin Britten's opera *Peter Grimes* (1945) had been interpreted, variously, as a flawed characterization, a maladjusted aggressive psychopath, a man who could not fit in and 'an ordinary weak person...classed by society as a criminal and destroyed as such' (Keller and Mitchell 1952, 111). Brett explains Grimes's plight in the opera in terms of the character's reflection of Britten's own homosexuality, claiming that:

It was *Peter Grimes*, representing the ultimate fantasy of persecution and suicide, that played a crucial role in his [Britten's] coming to terms with himself and the society which he both distrusted and yet wished to serve as a musician.

(Brett 1977, 1000)

Brett's work is a paradigm for a historically situated approach, drawing parallels between its musical subject and similar themes in contemporary literature and politics. In this way, Brett draws attention to what he calls 'the dynamics of the closet' (Brett 1994, 21). While Britten's homosexuality was generally common knowledge, he did not make it public and devised various strategies in his music and personal life to avoid direct expression of the fact. This may explain a sense of difference (see **alterity**) that informs the music of gay composers, reflecting Brett's observation that:

To gay children, who often experience a shutdown of all feeling as the result of sensing their parents' and society's disapproval of a basic part of their sentient life, music appears as a veritable lifeline.

(*ibid.*, 17)

It might be argued that Brett's 1977 article, published the year after Britten's death, represented a form of 'outing' of the composer. Such a practice has formed part of the more radical politics of queer theory, following the belief that raising public awareness of the role that gay people have in society will help to tackle prejudice. This drive has informed certain musicologists who have focused on composers who have been classed as different in terms of their musical language, style or reception. Examples of this include Gary C. Thomas on Handel and Susan McClary on Schubert (see Brett *et al.* 1994).

Gay musicology can take any number of forms and can be used to inform almost any kind of analytical or critical approach to music, from the way that we listen to an opera with a lesbian subject, such as Alban Berg's *Lulu* (1929) see Lochhead 1999), to a consideration of the notion of a lesbian compositional process (see Wood 1993; Rycenga 1994). In **popular music**, gay musicology has often turned its attention to the **identity** and performance styles of artists, but some scholars have also considered ways in which gay or queer identity may be encoded in musical **language**. For example, Fred E. Maus has interpreted harmonic evasion and ambivalence in the Pet Shop Boys as an expression of an alternative kind of masculinity (Maus 2001). Future areas that require further reconsideration in the light of queer theory include the **historiography** of music (see also **historical musicology**), music **analysis** and ethnomusicology (see **ethnicity**).

Further reading: Brett 1993; Gill 1995; Kielian-Gilbert 1999

GENDER

In the context of **cultural studies**, gender may be understood as the social constructedness of what maleness and femaleness mean in a given **culture**. In other words, it is an ideological (see **ideology**) concept that is contingent on socio-historical context, rather than the actual biological sense of sex and sexuality.

Traditionally, music has itself been gendered female, and represented as such in paintings, for example as a female muse, as in *The Musical Hall of Fame* (Solie 1993, 32), or referred to in this way in texts and debates. In her consideration of Artusi's attack on Monteverdi and contemporary music in the late **Renaissance**, Suzanne Cusick has drawn attention to the role of gendered metaphors in rhetoric (see **metaphor, language**), in particular Artusi's attempts to discredit contemporary music of the time as 'unnatural, feminine, and feminising of both its practitioners and its listeners' (Cusick 1993, 3). This association between music and gender, which Cusick dates back to Plato's *Republic*, has led to exaggerated attempts by some musicians to negate that image. Notable examples include McClary's claim that Beethoven's Ninth Symphony (1822–4) is 'probably our most compelling articulation in music of the contradictory impulses that have organised patriarchal culture since the **Enlightenment**' (McClary 1991, 129), Charles Ives's feeling that music 'has been, to too large an extent, an emasculated art' (Kirkpatrick 1973, 134), and the gestures, ideologies and posturings of much guitar-based rock music (see Walser 1993).

Musicologist and biographer Maynard Solomon (see **biography**) was one of the first to introduce gender and feminist issues into musicology (Solomon 1977, 1989), as indicated by Susan McClary, who admires the 'seriousness, grace, and courage with which Solomon has introduced questions concerning misogyny in Beethoven, homophobia in Ives, or homoeroticism in Schubert into a discipline that has steadfastly refused to address such issues' (McClary 1994, 208).

In addition to considering the gender of rhetoric and of composers, also of interest is the gender of performers, composers, listeners, even scholars. Particularly insightful in this regard is Cusick's exploration of performance-centred music criticism, following the ideas of gender theorist Judith Butler (Cusick 1999a). The essence of Butler's idea is that gender is something that is performed, that neither the social nor the biological conceptions of gender are stable. This, it is argued, results from a choice that we have between the way we perform social roles and the way we perform, or use, our bodies (see **body**; see also Butler 1990). Cusick develops this idea through an examination of the seventeenth-century singer, composer and teacher Francesca Caccini, and Eddie Vedder, lead singer of rock band Pearl Jam.

Cusick considers what kind of male body audiences would hear in these performers' voices, the former a castrato, the latter using a high tessitura but without falsetto, 'cracking as it strains into the androgynous space eschewed by most males in puberty' (Cusick 1999a, 35). She also considers the Indigo Girls, a paradigmatic girl group on the mid-Atlantic college scene, who 'With their voices ... perform their gender, their sex, and a sexuality (a way bodies might relate intimately to each other) that is culturally intelligible in our time as lesbian' (*ibid.*, 37).

This form of inquiry, Cusick argues, may offer an effective means of considering the ways in which artists and performers remake both their world and ours. Similar ideas to those discussed by Cusick are explored by Mitchell Morris in the context of the gendered rhetoric of the Weather Girls and their 1980s disco hit, 'It's Raining Men' (Morris 1999).

Increasingly, gender is being considered in relation to other factors, such as religion, **class**, **ethnicity**, and national **identity**, and the way in which it is approached will be influenced by the context of study: ethnomusicology, **popular music**, or opera, for example, will each require slightly differing approaches. Studies of gender have also led to the emergence of distinct methodologies, such as queer and lesbian studies (see **gay musicology**).

See also: **alterity**, **biography**, **feminism**

Further reading: Barkin and Hamessley 1999; Bradby 1993; Citron 1993; Cook 1998a; Dame 1994; Dibben 2002a; McClary 1993a

GENIUS

A term that invokes certain musical qualities, with the implication of greatness and a heightened sense of **value** that relates to the wider concept of the **canon**.

Genius was first conceptualized during the **Enlightenment** of the eighteenth century and appears in the dictionaries that were a central feature of that period and project, including that of the Swiss writer on **aesthetics** Johann Georg Sulzer, who, in his *Allgemeine Theorie der schönen Künste*, produced the first wide-ranging survey of the arts in German. He describes the genius as 'those who have greater skill and spiritual insight than others in the tasks and occupations for which they are gifted' (le Huray and Day 1981, 127). The view of the genius as the exception, 'those who have greater skill', would be a standard interpretation, but the suggestion of 'spiritual insight' also connects with the Enlightenment concern with the **sublime** and its suggestion of the journey beyond the grasp of normal concepts and understanding.

Jean-Jacques Rousseau's *Dictionnaire de musique*, one of the most widely known works of its type during the later eighteenth century, contains a fascinating description of genius:

> Seek not, young artist, the meaning of genius. If you possess it you will sense it within you. If not, you will never know it. The

musician of genius encompasses the entire universe within his art. He paints his pictures in sound; he makes the very silence speak; he expresses ideas by feelings and feelings by accents, and the passions that he voices move us to the very depths of our hearts.

(ibid. 1981, 108–9)

Rousseau immediately asserts that genius is something natural, perhaps God-given – a commonly held view – but his passionate description is also notable in that it suggests an anticipation of the **Romanticism** of the nineteenth century and provides a contrast to the rationalism of the Enlightenment. Rousseau continues:

Would you like to know then whether any spark of this devouring flame inspires you? Run, fly to Naples! Listen to the masterpieces of Leo, Durante, Jomelli and Pergolesi. If you are seized with trembling, if in the middle of your rapture oppressive feelings weigh you down, then take Metastasio and set to work. His genius will warm yours.

(ibid., 109)

Rousseau mentions the genius of Metastasio, the librettist whose work was set by many composers of the period, but his list of composers is interesting, with Leo, Durante and Jomelli now most likely to be described as minor figures of the period. This suggests that any description of genius is likely to be highly subjective (see **subjectivity**) and is dependent upon the preferences of the person making the claim. It is also likely to reflect the historical and cultural circumstances of the period in question.

The nineteenth century witnessed a fascination with the concept of genius, usually portrayed through a Romantic image of the composer as hero. This is reflected in the **reception** of Beethoven, in which his biographical circumstances were seen to form a framework for the understanding of the music (see **biography**). During the later nine-teenth century, the cult of the heroic composer was extended by Wagner, who was portrayed as the pathway to the future, an image that Wagner himself conspired to shape.

During the twentieth century, the concept of genius may also be found in the specific notion of an *avant-garde*, which further extended the preoccupation with the future. The isolation of the composer, dramatized by Schoenberg in his music and writings ('How One Becomes Lonely', Schoenberg 1975), was a recurring feature of the century. However, from our contemporary perspective the concept of genius may be less readily acceptable and achievable through our understanding of the social, political and commercial contexts that surround all music (see **culture industry**). In contrast to the Enlightenment view of genius as a consequence of nature, sociologist Tia DeNora, writing from a contemporary critical perspective on Beethoven, suggests that 'Genius and its recognition require social and cultural resources if they are to be cultivated, and these resources are often micropolitically charged' (DeNora 1997, xiii). From this perspective, genius is shaped and conditioned by context, which is often politically and economically determined. DeNora goes on to emphasize the social dimension, proposing that Beethoven provides a case study that enlarges 'the potential for thinking about talent and genius as fundamentally social achievements' (*ibid.*).

GENRE

Genre is a term that reflects a desire, dating back to Greek philosopher Aristotle, to classify and categorize works of art. As a result of this, generic terms often appear in the titles of works (for example, symphony or concerto). Genre necessarily constructs a set of codes and expectations and therefore may be understood as something that is imposed upon music by musical cultures (see **culture**), influencing the way in which music is written. For example, composers and popular musicians will often play with genre conventions, and this is potentially useful to musicologists considering the possibility of **meaning** in music. Understanding genre also suggests ways of listening. According to ethnomusicologist William Hanks, when viewed as an interaction between social constructs and musical content, genre may be seen to offer (1) a framework that a listener may use by which to orient themselves; (2) procedures to interpret the music; and (3) a set of expectations (Hanks 1987; see also **ethnicity**).

One confusion that may at times arise is the overlap between the terms **style** and genre as encountered in musicological writing. Allen Moore has noted that, in general, **popular music** studies employ the term genre, whereas writing on classical music tended, at least until the mid-1980s, to mix genre and style freely (Moore 2001b). Since the mid-1980s, however, musicologists have tended to use genre to describe the external, socially conditioned aspects of a **work**, and style is reserved for consideration of the formal, internal features (see **analysis**).

Prior to the seventeenth century, generic titles in music were defined by a work's function, its text, if there was one, and its textures (see Dahlhaus 1987). In the eighteenth century, scoring and form determined genre, although these and other internal features were increasingly influenced by external social factors. The term gained particular importance in music during the eighteenth and early nineteenth centuries. For example, the Romantic (see **Romanticism**) lied encompasses a range of works by composers such as Franz Schubert and Robert Schumann. These works are related through language (German), scoring (piano and voice) and function (composed for an attentive audience, usually performed in intimate surroundings). The word lied also carries with it a suggestion of the kinds of subject matter to be conveyed through song (nature, love, tragedy) and dictates certain formal and stylistic approaches (a clear link between words and musical devices). The same applies to popular song. For example, musicologist Robert Walser has noted that the genre of heavy metal imparts a particular **ideology**, noting that 'the generic cohesion of heavy metal until the mid-1980s depended upon the desire of young white male performers and fans to hear and believe in certain stories about the nature of masculinity' (Walser 1993, 109; see also **discourse**). This observation points to the importance of genre in the formation of fan cultures. It also indicates that certain genres will be associated with a sense of truth, or **authenticity**. Alternatively, they may, as in the case of glam rock, be concerned with the artificial and the inauthentic.

One view of genre is hierarchical, implying a parent genre, such as symphony, within which other genres, such as *Ländler* or scherzo, may be found. In all these cases, genre defines a context for musical gestures. In general, the concept of genre attempts a limited, finalized account of musical works (see **work**), but this is contrary to the natural diversity of styles and their tendency to evolve. Genre attempts to fix musical practice, pointing to what is consistent and repeated, but this does not take account of the fact that certain features used to determine genre, such as style, technique and form, will change through time.

German critical theorist Theodor Adorno (Adorno 1997; see also **critical theory**) and German musicologist Carl Dahlhaus (Dahlhaus 1987) both believed in the social and historical contingency of genre. They also both noted that, throughout the nineteenth century, society concentrated more on composers and individual works and that musical genres began to lose their importance. In particular, Dahlhaus remarked how the idea of the masterpiece arose directly from the conventions of genre. This shift, which stressed the autonomous status of musical works (see **autonomy**), is reflected in the rise of musical **analysis** during the nineteenth and twentieth centuries, a discipline that places form and gesture over genre. It is also reflected in a change of listening strategy, away from (prior to the late nineteenth century) hearing works as variations of a type towards a consideration of pieces on their own terms. Recently, these ideas have been developed in relation to a range of musical genres, notably by ethnomusicologist Franco Fabbri (Fabbri 1982), musicologist Jeffrey Kallberg in relation to Chopin (Kallberg 1987, 1987–8), and Adam Krims concerning rap (Krims 2000). Krims's work, in particular, indicates that in **popular music** the idea of genre may be central to listening and performing. In the case of club music, for example, DJs are noted less for the specific tracks they play and more for the dance genre they embrace.

A number of disciplines have seen developments in conceptions of genre, most notably Vladimir Propp's work on fairy-tale classification (first published 1928; see Propp 1968), Bakhtin's work on linguistics (Bakhtin 2000), Jameson on literature (Jameson 1981), and film and television studies (see Neale 1980). The latter field has been particularly influential on genre studies in recent musicology, especially through its emphasis on the idea of genre as social convention. One of the central definitions of genre in relation to film is its role in alerting viewers to an established practice and thereby arousing in them a set of expectations based on their memory of similar texts. In relation to music, Kallberg argues that genre guides the listener through a '"kind of generic contract"... the composer agrees to use some of the conventions, patterns, and gestures of a genre, and the listener consents to interpret some aspects of the piece in a way conditioned by this genre' (Kallberg 1987–8, 243). This points to the importance of the interaction between a work's title and its content in forming meaning. For example, Moore has remarked that 'understanding a song like Bowie's "Fashion" means understanding it as ironic, which is dependent upon understanding the genre conventions of uptempo dance music' (Moore 2001b, 441). Furthermore, what makes music interesting are those moments when the social codes or conventions of a genre are challenged or subverted, when the generic contract is broken. Fabbri notes that new genres may be formed from such transgressions. This may be achieved through mixing genres, for example in Vaughan Williams's *Tallis Fantasia* (1910; see Pople 1996). Alternatively, musical genres may cease to operate as controlling factors and instead be used referentially. For example, this can be seen in the way that Mahler's symphonies critique certain genres, such as the waltz and the march, in ways that may reflect social concerns of the time (see Samuels 1995).

Although a shift has taken place in terms of contemporary classical listening and practice, and despite the apparent desire of **modernism** and the *avant-garde* to subvert, overthrow and invent new generic conventions (such as the concerto for orchestra), **postmodernism** has revived interest in older genres. This can be seen, for example, in Heiner Goebbels's *Eislermaterial* (2001), which explores cabaret in the context of post-tonal languages. And genre is still relevant to certain postwar modernists, for example in the symphonies of Maxwell Davies and Lutosławski, and the operas of Tippett and Birtwistle. Genre is increasingly central to the marketing of popular music. This is expressed through the myriad of categories that have arisen, including what Roy Shuker calls meta-genres – loose collections of related genres, such as dance, or world music, within which are any number of sub-genres (such as house and techno), which themselves may be further subdivided (hard house, classic house) (Shuker 1998). Even within these distinctions, there will be references to other genres, leading to hybrids (see **hybridity**). The development of genre in this way can be seen to be constructing ever more sophisticated modes of **reception**, consumption and marketing.

Further reading: Bauman 1992; Fornäs 1995a; Harrison and Wood 2003; Pascall 1989; Samson 1989

GLOBALIZATION

The possibility of a global economy is reflected in the concept of globalization, one of the most sharply contested and deeply politicized terms of the present and recent past. It is suggested that globalization weakens the nation-state, representing the current situation of capitalism as a global economy, and brings with it the implication of a hegemony of cultural practices. A fundamental consequence of globalization is the interdependency of cultural (see **culture**), economic and other structures of life. American literary theorist Michael Hardt and Italian political philosopher Antonio Negri, in their epic work *Empire*, state:

> In the postmodernization [see **postmodernism**] of the global economy, the creation of wealth tends ever more toward what we will call biopolitical production, the production of social life

itself, in which the economic, the political, and the cultural increasingly overlap and invest one another.

(Hardt and Negri 2000, xiii)

In other words, under the impact of globalization it has become impossible to separate the personal from the political and the cultural from the economic.

Many cultural theorists argue that the world is now organized and defined by increasing economic globalization, which reduces the importance of small-scale production and imposes standardized economic practices on a worldwide pattern. The social and critical theorist Douglas Kellner provides an effective summary of globalization and its surrounding **discourse** through the construction of a 'dialectical framework that distinguishes between progressive and emancipatory features and oppressive and negative attributes' (Kellner 2002, 285). From this perspective, globalization becomes a more complex balancing act than simply something purely negative that must be opposed.

One of the most direct ways in which globalization manifests itself is through information and communication technologies. According to American cultural and critical theorist Fredric Jameson, 'globalization is a communicational concept, which alternately masks and transmits cultural or economic meanings' (Jameson 1998, 55). We can relate this view to the way in which certain products and producers (McDonald's and Disney, for example) not only sell a product on a global basis but in doing so transmit certain cultural values (see **value**), which are often simultaneously concealed, a situation that connects globalization with notions of **ideology** and **identity**.

The interpenetration and interdependence of national and economic markets have consequences for music and its **reception**, which is clearly evident in the global spread of MTV and 'mainstream' Anglo-American pop. However, one of the most interesting cultural reflections of globalization is formed through the emergence of 'world music', a term that was concocted by a collection of independent record companies involved in the dissemination of non-Western music. In a penetrating article on the subject, the British popular music scholar Simon Frith (Frith 2000) outlines the origins of the term and highlights its economic and marketing functions. The desire for Other music (see **alterity**), which may include music from all regions of the world, reflects issues of **authenticity** and the recurrent search for the exotic in music by Western audiences (see **Orientalism**). The example of 'world music' could reflect the 'oppressive and negative' features of globalization. The wide dissemination of such music reflects the flattening of the cultural landscape, and the marketing of music from economically disadvantaged regions and locations reflects the exploitation of indigenous cultures. However, it is also possible to interpret 'progressive and emancipatory' features of the spread of localized music on a wider scale. Such music could be heard as a voice of resistance, reflecting Kellner's suggestion that globalization can be 'contested and reconfigured from below' (Kellner 2002, 286). The consequence of this musical contestation is that the diversity of much of the localized music now available can be heard as a mechanism through which the cultural hegemony of globalization is questioned and challenged.

A number of recent publications have sought to grapple with the issue of music and globalization. One of the most immediate and accessible attempts has been Timothy Taylor's *Global Pop: World Music, World Markets* (Taylor 1997). Taylor considers a worldwide range of popular music practices against the background of globalization but also engages with the adoption of world music by Western musicians (including Peter Gabriel and the Kronos Quartet). Other writers look at more specific contexts and cultures through issues of globalization. For example, Koichi Iwabuchi scrutinizes the relationship between popular culture and Japanese transnationalism (Iwabuchi 2002), with the context of Japan providing a highly relevant situation through which the global economy is dramatically visible and, through the influence of Japanese popular culture throughout Asia, defines the recentring of globalization.

See also: **ethnicity, hybridity, nationalism, place**

Further reading: Denning 2004; Harvey 2003; Nercessian 2002; Tomlinson 1999

HERMENEUTICS

The conceptual essence of hermeneutics is the proposal of a theory, or theories, of **interpretation**. While the origins of the term are situated in biblical and legal usages, the philosophical starting point is usually defined through the work of German philosopher Friedrich Schleiermacher. Writing during the early nineteenth century, Schleiermacher defined hermeneutics as 'the art of understanding ... the ... **discourse** of another person correctly' (Schleiermacher 1998, xx). It is significant that Schleiermacher chooses to designate hermeneutics as an 'art', a designation that allows for a **subjectivity** that cannot always be bound or determined by rules. Clearly, the desire to construct a correct understanding is the inevitable aim of a hermeneutic process, but what constitutes the correct understanding can itself be a question of interpretation. If this points to a certain circularity, this becomes dramatized through the so-called hermeneutic circle: 'the attempt to understand the part via the whole and the whole via the parts' (Bowie 1993, 157). In other words, the various parts of a text depend on the whole for their **meaning** to become clear, and that whole is clearly a consequence of the parts. For Schleiermacher, the desire for a correct interpretation and the recognition of meaning through the relationship between part and whole were still located in the intentionality of the author, a view that has been questioned by later philosophers and theorists.

Schleiermacher's hermeneutics are best known through their transmission via Hans-Georg Gadamer, whose monumental *Truth and Method* (Gadamer 2003), first published in 1960, sought to construct a hermeneutic theory grounded in interpretation as an activity. In contrast to Schleiermacher's focus on authorial intent, for Gadamer meaning and its interpretation are more accurately constructed by the context and traditions (see **tradition**) in which specific texts can be located. However, the mobility of hermeneutic interpretation is reflected in Andrew Bowie's claim that 'the account of Schleiermacher given by Gadamer in *Truth and Method* needs radical revision' (Bowie 1993, 146).

If Schleiermacher and Gadamer outlined hermeneutics as an art of interpretation, how we might theorize the act (or art) of interpretation has a deep resonance for music and musicology. Our musicological responses to musical works can reflect a hermeneutic process and experience, as can our reading of musicological and other texts. In both contexts, **theory** can be a prerequisite for understanding, but the quality of that interpretation is required to legitimize theory. As Lawrence Kramer states: 'though interpretive practices benefit enor-mously from hermeneutic theorizing, a hermeneutic theory is only as good as the interpretations that it underwrites' (Kramer 1993b, 2). Much writing on music during the nineteenth century reflected a hermeneutic perspective (see Bent 1994, 1996b), and both the music and writing about it during this period reflects Kramer's retrospective hypothesis of the relationships between theory and practice.

The work of Lawrence Kramer (see **new musicology**) has raised again questions surrounding hermeneutic models and processes.

Kramer has proposed the construction of a 'hermeneutic window' through which we see the potential interpretation of the work:

> Hermeneutic windows tend to be located where the object of interpretation appears – or can be made to appear – explicitly problematical. Interpretation takes flight from breaking points, which usually means from points of under or overdetermination: on the one hand, a gap, a lack, a missing connection; on the other, a surplus of pattern, an extra repetition, an excessive connection.
>
> (Kramer 1993b, 12)

On this account, the musical **work** allows its interpretation to be seen through the cracks in its structure and identity, a proposal that shifts a hermeneutic response towards **deconstruction**, an intellectual context that is formed around interpretations of texts and **language**. Kramer's 'hermeneutic windows' form part of a recent trend in musicology towards interpretation and, by implication, away from 'facts' (see **positivism**). Current preoccupations with issues such as **gender** and sexuality reflect a hermeneutic perspective through interpretation and the embracing of new levels of subjectivity.

See also: **aesthetics, authenticity, biography**

Further reading: Bent 1996a; Dahlhaus 1983a; Hoeckner 2002; Tomlinson 1993b; Whittall 1991

HISTORICAL MUSICOLOGY

The practice of historical musicology can be dated from the publication of German musicologist Guido Adler's 'Umfang, Methode und Ziel der Musikwissenschaft' (The Scope, Method and Aim of Musicology) in 1885 (Adler 1885; Bujić 1988, 348–55). This text, which was much influenced by positivist (see **positivism**) scientific thought, divided the 'science of music' into two disciplines: historical musicology and systematic musicology. The study of historical musicology was intended by Adler to deal exclusively with the history of Western concert music and included musical palaeography (the study of notation), performance practice and the history of instruments. Systematic musicology included ethnomusicology (see **ethnicity**), **aesthetics** and 'elementary' music **theory** (harmony, counterpoint)).

A form of this division was present at the time of Joseph Kerman's seminal study titled *Musicology* (*Contemplating Music* in America), published in 1985 (Kerman 1985), since Kerman clearly separates historical musicology from systematic forms such as **analysis** (although Adler had included 'classification of musical forms' in his definition of historical musicology). Kerman's book represented a desire to reinvigorate historical musicology, which, he suggests, had focused too much attention on text-based projects such as the preparation of manuscripts, dating, cataloguing, editing, biography, transcription and historical performance studies (see Stevens 1980, 1987). Kerman argued that historical musicology had neglected the critical, interpretative side of the subject, a situation that he hoped might be remedied if it were to explore developments in music analysis and literary theory (see **post-structuralism**).

The certainties and assumptions of an historical musicology have been subjected to increasing critical scrutiny through the contemporary impact of new interdisciplinary critical perspectives (see **critical musicology**, **new musicology**).

HISTORICISM

Historicism arose in the nineteenth and twentieth centuries as an alternative to the **Enlightenment** sense of history as human self-development. This idea may be traced back to Immanuel Kant and later G.W.F. Hegel. According to Kant, 'The history of the human race as a whole can be regarded as the realisation of a hidden plan of nature to bring about...[a] perfect political constitution' (see McCarney 2000, 16). Hegel believed in the ability of 'world-historical individuals' to determine world history, and he proposed a dialectical model to illustrate how history is linked to the development of human rationality. Accordingly, history is seen as a continuous and connected process, in which 'products of the past which are active in the present... will shape the future in knowable ways' (Williams 1988, 146). In music history, this viewpoint is captured in Hubert Parry's *The Evolution of the Art of Music* (first published as *The Art of Music*, 1893), which characterized medieval chant as primitive (Parry 1909).

In contrast, historicism rejects the notion of universal historical principles of development, promoting instead the idea of cultural (see **culture**) relativism, interpreting historical subjects as products of social, political and cultural circumstances in a given historical moment. It therefore values (see **value**) the past as much as, if not more than, the present. This has had ramifications for theories that promote the idea that **identity** is influenced by historical conditions (see also **ethnicity, gender**). The origins of historicism reside in eighteenth-century views that promoted a reverence for the past (see **nationalism**). These gave rise, in the nineteenth century, to **historiography**, which resulted in the publication of major composer biographies (see **biography**), the promotion of early composers such as Palestrina (see Garratt 2002), and the development of the research methods for what Guido Adler, in 1885, termed **historical musicology**.

In the 1970s and 1980s, a fresh desire arose to locate and interpret cultural objects in their social and historical contexts while resisting traditional **narrative**-based historical methodologies. The origins of this so-called 'new historicism' are present in the work of French theorist and cultural anthropologist Michel Foucault and cultural theorist Raymond Williams (see **cultural studies**), emerging more fully formed in the work of literary historian Stephen Greenblatt (see Greenblatt 1980, 1982). An example of the influence of this thinking on musicology is Gary Tomlinson's study of magic and **Renaissance** music (Tomlinson 1993b). Tomlinson aims:

> to suggest a hermeneutics more observant of difference [see **alterity**] and less dependent on shared perceptions and understanding than most historical hermeneutic approaches have been ... [an emphasis on dialogue in interpretation] helps us to underscore the situatedness of anthropological and historical knowledge, to keep in full view the negotiation of divergent viewpoints – the intersection of differing interpreters, texts, and contexts – from which such knowledge emerges.
>
> (*ibid.*, 6)

Tomlinson's aim to set up a truly reciprocal dialogue with the 'interpreters, texts, and contexts' of Renaissance music clearly reflects the relativist views of **post-structuralism** and the shift of methodological emphasis encouraged by the **new musicology**, an approach that can be seen reflected in a number of other recent studies (see Born and Hesmondhalgh 2000; Abbate 2001).

Further reading: Frigyesi 1998; Hamilton 1996; Veeser 1994

HISTORIOGRAPHY

Historiography is the discipline of writing history, so the historiography of music (music historiography) is the writing of music history. The development of a music historiography, like other forms of history, is influenced by changing historical and cultural conditions, and it therefore has its own history, which reflects different attitudes and approaches to music during different historical moments (see **reception**).

Although the act of writing music history can be identified through the importance of a mythologized past in the medieval and **Renaissance** periods, evident through documents such as theoretical treatises, a historiography of music has its origins in the eighteenth century and reflected the wider context of the **Enlightenment**. The Enlightenment concern with progress provided a model for the writing of music's history, with several histories published in the late eighteenth century, including Burney's *A General History of Music* (Burney 1957), reflecting recurrent issues of historiography such as continuity between past and present, **periodization** and the classification of **style**. National **identity**, and the role of music in its formation, also became a significant factor in music historiography, particularly during the nineteenth century (see **nationalism**).

The periodization of history, the division and subdivision of the past into manageable categories such as Baroque, Classical and Romantic (see **Romanticism**), or distinct periods usually formed through the use of centuries as models, was intensified throughout the twentieth century, which witnessed the expansion of attempts to construct comprehensive and systematic histories of music. Many generations of past students, as well as the current generation, will have had contact with such historical accounts of music. Many of the issues, and problems, of music historiography are evident in the *New Oxford History of Music*. First published in 1957 and reprinted in 1960 and 1966, this project, which replaced an earlier *Oxford History of Music* published between 1901 and 1905, is now a historical document that reflects its own time. Consisting of several volumes and contributions for a wide range of writers, it is presented 'as an entirely new survey of music from the earliest times down to comparatively recent years' (Westrup *et al.* 1957, vi). This survey approach was by then a well-established historiographical **genre**. Shorter, but still comprehensive, surveys also became prevalent. One of the best known and widely used has been Grout's *A History of Western Music* (Grout and Palisca 2001). Since it first appeared in 1960, this book has been a central reference for generations of students and was clearly intended as a pedagogical work. It constructs a history from ancient Greece and Rome to contemporary music of the post-Second World War period within a linear chronology, which implies connection and progression. But there are problems with this approach. To continue to privilege historical continuity removes the possibility of rupture, elevating similarity over difference. From our contemporary perspective, the exclusive focus on the Western **tradition** seems exclusive, and inevitably the compact yet comprehensive structure implies a history of great composers and great works, but one that excludes music that may suggest other, perhaps alternative, historical perspectives (see **canon**).

The survey of a complete period, or century, is a well-established strategy and has remained a popular and useful part of the historiography of music. For example, German musicologist Carl Dahlhaus's *Nineteenth Century Music* (Dahlhaus 1989c) gives an overview of the century, providing commentary on many different types of music and related issues. However, any such history is selective, and that process of selection may reflect wider issues of **ideology**. Although Dahlhaus makes reference to Italian opera and Russian music, there is a feeling that this is primarily a history of German music and that these other musical examples are exceptions to what, from a German perspective, may be perceived as the mainstream of music history. American musicologist and theorist James Hepokoski writes of 'the vexing reality of his [Dahlhaus] apparent unwillingness to consider non-Germanic music on its own terms' (Hepokoski 1991, 221).

The presentation of music history through century-long surveys continues with the current series of Cambridge Histories. However, they reflect a late twentieth-century perspective on their respective periods. This is evident in the history of the twentieth-century volume (Cook and Pople 2004), which reflects the problems of writing the history of more recent times. Its inclusion of **popular music**, alongside that of the art music contexts of the century, suggests a contemporary, and perhaps comparative, understanding of that more recent history. This late twentieth-century concern with diversity and inclusion is reflected in the current edition of the *New Grove Dictionary of Music* (Sadie 2001), which, through the structure and genre of the dictionary, the history of which stretches back to the Enlightenment, constitutes the most ambitious attempt to construct a comprehensive body of knowledge about music and its history. Each version of this dictionary has reflected its own time, and the current edition is no exception, with its inclusion of **jazz**, popular and non-Western music reflecting the concerns and ideologies of the present.

See also: **historicism**

Further reading: Dahlhaus 1983a

HISTORY *see* **historical musicology, historicism, historiography**

HYBRIDITY

A concept that has been much developed by cultural criticism and **post-colonial** studies, hybridity is concerned with degrees of cultural exchange between **race**, **ethnicity**, **gender** and **class**. Although often considered to have contemporary origins, the term was first used in seventeenth-century botany and zoology, where it referred to the crossing of two separate species of animal or plant; it was expanded to include humans during the eighteenth century. Imperialism and Western colonialism in the nineteenth century saw both segregation and assimilation policies; the latter were seen as a way of ridding a race of the characteristics that marked it as degenerate.

Theories of hybridity may also be developed to account for new cultural forms that have arisen as a result of borrowings, intersections and exchanges across ethnic boundaries, some of which are con-troversial or contradictory. An example of this is the appropriation of Aboriginal art by white Australians as a means of promoting Australian culture in a manner that glosses over the poor state of Aboriginal civil rights and the country's history of persecution (see Brah and Coombes 2000). However, colonial subjects seeking emancipation have them-selves sought to appropriate the colonizer's language in order to develop an effective anti-colonial critique (see **post-colonial/post-colonialism**). This has led to the creative hybridization of languages. In Africa, English is reappropriated as a common language, while in Britain, musicians and writers have developed localized ethnic varia-tions of English, as expressed in the poetry of Lynton Kwesi Johnson (commonly cited as the first major dub poet) or the rap of Roots Manuva.

Hybridity, as the cultural theorist Homi Bhabha has pointed out, is contained in the act of mimicry that occurs when a colonized subject copies the occupying culture, since 'each replication...necessarily involves a slippage or gap wherein the colonial subject produces a hybridized version of the "original"' (*ibid.*, 11). The result, in Bhabha's terms, is a third space that contains 'something different, something new and unrecognisable, a new area of negotiation of meaning and representation' (Rutherford 1990, 211; see also Bhabha 1994). However, a contrasting view was presented by the Russian theorist Mikhail Bakhtin. In his work on literature, he noted a form of intentional hybridity. Intentional hybrids, in Bakhtin's formulation, consist of an ironic double-voicedness, a collision between differing points of view on the world that 'push to the limit the mutual non-understanding represented by people *who speak in different languages*' (Bakhtin 2000, 356).

A number of types of cross-cultural exchange have been noted since Bakhtin, leading to mutual, subversive or transgressive hybrids. Another commonly discussed form is strategic essentialism, which may sometimes be seen to benefit a certain ethnic group (see Spivak 1993). American cultural theorist George Lipsitz has considered various musical examples of this in his book *Dangerous Crossroads* (Lipsitz 1997). One example concerns a group of gay Hispanic dancers in New Orleans who parade on Mardi Gras dressed as Native Americans. This strategy reflects the fact that black people were for several years banned from wearing masks in the carnival, so using warpaint was a way around that prohibition. According to Lipsitz:

> These forms of 'play' are deadly serious; they enable members of aggrieved communities to express indirectly aspects of their identity that might be dangerous to present by more direct means.
>
> (*ibid.*, 71)

A more controversial example concerns Paul Simon's album *Graceland* (1986). In this project, Simon performed with South African musicians, including Ladysmith Black Mambazo. Although the African musicians received fair pay and recognition for their work, they nonetheless appear as support acts to Simon's conception. Consequently, Lipsitz argues, Simon appears to have used the other musicians as a means of strategically redefining the ethnicity of his album in order to present his own music in a new, alternative – and commercially attractive – light. This argument appears to be supported by the subsequent wave of white performers who produced collaborative albums with non-white musicians under the commercial banner of world music (see **globalization**).

Cultural theorist John Hutnyk has presented further critical arguments against so-called world music, in particular regarding festivals such as WOMAD. Hutnyk argues that such festivals sanitize difference 'into so many varied examples of a World Music culture that is everywhere the same' (Hutnyk 1997, 133). Hutnyk is concerned with:

> The appropriations, and questions of appropriate behaviour, in . . . a scene where authenticity operates through incomprehension and fracture of context. . . . CNN's reports on Womad 1994 stressed little of the grass-roots politics and made much of the most 'exotic' of the musicians.
>
> (*ibid.*, 110–12)

While the comments about detaching music from its context – the society in which it was created – and the role that technology has in this are important, the problem with Hutnyk's concern is his conflation of non-Western and ethnic minority music, as well as his belief that both are always an expression of politics and resistance. He also notes that multiculturalism is often promoted in the West but in such a way that blurs, or overlooks, the differences contained within ethnic groups. Hybridization, therefore, runs the risk of hiding internal difference (see **alterity**). Essentially, Hutnyk does not feel that hybridity is radical enough, and his preferred hybrid bands are the ones that emphasize politics and difference the most, such as the British-based Asian Dub Foundation. However, absent from Hutnyk's discussion is a consideration of different types of hybrid experience, for example those offered by Cornershop or Nitin Sawhney. Cornershop's music expresses the kind of double-voiced, intentional hybridity that Bakhtin described, whereas Nitin Sawhney presents political ideas in an ambient, 'easy listening' context.

Brah and Coombes stress 'the necessity of historicizing the concept of hybridity and of acknowledging the geopolitical contexts in which the terms of debate circulate' (Brah and Coombes 2000, 2). A historical perspective on the subject in music should consider that cross-cultural exchange was the life-blood of **Renaissance**, Baroque and classical music as a result of musicians and composers crossing national boundaries. In the Baroque period, for example, although dance forms were associated with particular countries, such as the allemande, gigue, gavotte and courante, their treatment by composers from other nations (such as Bach's French Suite and Italian Concerto) represented a crucial focus for the hybridization and proliferation of Baroque and classical styles (see **style**). The twentieth century has seen further boundary crossing between genres and styles and across the art music/ **popular music** divide. Paris in the 1920s and 1930s saw several attempts at hybridizing African music, jazz and the *avant-garde*, as in Milhaud's *Le Creation du Monde* (1923; see Gendron 2002); more recently, around the late 1960s, various attempts have been made to hybridize jazz and rock, most notably by British band the Soft Machine and by Miles Davis on *Bitches Brew* (1970), which includes performers from classical, rock and jazz backgrounds.

Further reading: Hutnyk 2000; Sharma *et al.* 1996; Werbner and Modood 1997; Young 1995

IDENTITY

A concept closely linked to **subjectivity**, identity has its origins in philosophy, **psychology** and **cultural studies**, all of which have defined identity as a response to something beyond an individual, something Other (see **alterity**). The early nineteenth-century German philosopher G.W.F. Hegel was possibly the first to reverse ideas dating back to Descartes when he suggested that a fully developed self required recognition of its status from others (see Alcoff and Mendieta 2003, 11–16). French sociologist Émile Durkheim developed this idea by proposing that the individual was the product of society, with society determining an individual's attitudes and values (see **value**). Following Karl Marx, Durkheim noted that in industrial societies there is greater likelihood of a variety of attitudes and values, therefore individual identity is not primary but is a product of economic organization. Subsequently, social psychologist George Herbert Mead explored the idea that an individual is constructed through his or her interaction with others. He distinguished between consciousness and self-consciousness, the latter consisting of the internalization of another's point of view. Other social psychologists who have explored the concept of identity include Erik Erikson (see Erikson 1968) and Jacques Lacan. Erikson realized that if an individual breaks with community it can lead to an 'identity crisis'. The cultural anthropologist Michel Foucault also developed important theories concerning the way in which an individual is constructed through his or her positioning in relation to a set of social discourses (see **discourse**) or narratives (see **narrative**). One example of this, revealed through **post-colonial** studies, is orientalist discourse (see **Orientalism**), in which the identities of colonial subjects are determined by Western powers.

From the 1960s onwards, awareness of the range of established identity structures increased, leading to the construction of, and attempts to dismantle, negotiate and defend, identities associated with **class**, **culture**, nationality (see **nationalism**), **ethnicity**, **gender** (see also **feminism**, **gay musicology**), religion, age and disability. Such processes represent forms of identity politics. In the words of Linda Martín Alcoff: 'For some, the emphasis on identity is a threat to democracy and an incitement of ceaseless conflict; for others, it is a struggle long overdue (Alcoff and Mendieta 2003, 1).

These comments point not only to differing views about specific identities but also to the fact that identities can be agents of oppression as well as of liberation. For example, there are good reasons to move beyond caste and class divisions, but the variation of humanity in terms of gender, ethnicity and nationality might be argued to be valuable, ensuring, at least, a rich array of cultural traditions (see **tradition**). However, identities are not stable concepts. For example, race identities such as 'black' signify differently in Britain, America and Jamaica (see Lipsitz 1997; Gilroy 1999), and new conceptions of cyborgs (human–techno hybrids; see **hybridity**) have emerged in postmodern theory (see **postmodernism**), breaking down the binary of self/other, challenging notions of **authenticity** and redefining identities as plural and fluid (see Auner 2003; Haraway 2003).

Identity, therefore, is expressed through a set of attitudes that relate to, or are shared with, a group; identity inheres in the relationship between personal experience and public **meaning**. Cultural 'texts', such as music, enable identities to be expressed, formed and sustained, for example through what psychologists call priming, where 'a network of associations that are linked by shared mood connections is activated by music' (Crozier 1998, 79), a fact that will lead to narratives of **subjectivity**, accounts of how these experiences, or readings, came about for individuals in a certain place at a particular time (see also **psychology**). Implicit in the question 'how is music used to regulate and constitute the self?' is a recognition that music may represent an Other to the self and thereby set up the reflexive relationship described in earlier accounts by philosophers and psychologists (see Kramer 2001). Identity theories also examine the way in which the subjective activities of listening and performing are influenced by objective social, economic and political conditions.

Music was first considered in relation to identities in cultural studies, for example through the work of the Birmingham Centre for Cultural Studies, established in 1964 (see Hebdige 1979). However, this work tended to focus on the sociological aspects of identity formation as resistance rather than passive consumption, and on the role of the media in fixing meaning and **value**; it also prioritized the identities of fans and critics over those of performers (see Thornton 1995; for further work on identities of resistance in music, see Sakolsky and Ho 1995). One important issue that remained unexamined was identification, the mechanism by which a listener finds or locates his or herself in music. More recent sociological work on these questions has been carried out by Tia DeNora in her book *Music in Everyday Life* (DeNora 2000), and the communications theorist Anahid Kassabian has explored identification in relation to contemporary Hollywood film music. One topic that Kassabian considers is the ways in which 'music facilitates perceivers in assimilating into one of the available subject positions of [a] film' (Kassabian 2001, 113). **Subject position**, a term developed in film studies, describes the concerns or viewpoints that a film tries to convey. By constructing music that is closely linked to a particular character in a film, a perceiver is more likely to engage with the subject position associated with that character, whereas a score that is less narrowly committed to a single position will encourage more mobile processes of identification (*ibid.*, 114). Kassabian also considers strategies for appealing to a range of different identities, including those of gay, heterosexual, black, male and female perceivers.

Attempts have been made to develop this concept in relation to **popular music** by examining the music's construction (see **analysis**), or by analyzing performance details such as vocal or instrumental styles, production techniques, music videos, promotional materials and other visual aspects, for example in the music of Madonna (see Hawkins 2002; Whiteley 2000; Clarke 1999). Where individual performers, such as Bob Dylan or Madonna, may invent or take on new identities, there are whole styles, or genres (see **style**, **genre**), that may be said to represent single identities, such as the aggressively male perspective associated with heavy metal (see Walser 1993). In the case of hip-hop, as a result of the processes of **globalization**, the idea of ethnic struggle, conceived in the Bronx in the 1970s, is recast in a wide variety of very localized identities (see Krims 2000, 2002), some of which are hostile towards gay, lesbian and female identities, while recent African immigrants to America may construct a sense of their own 'blackness' – a form of identity that was not necessary in Africa – through exposure to American hip-hop (see Forman 2002).

Further reading: Barkin and Hamessley 1999; MacDonald *et al.* 2002; Williams 2001

IDEOLOGY

Ideology is often taken to refer to any set or system of beliefs through which we view and interpret the world or an engagement with any set of specific issues and circumstances. Our responses to **culture**, including music, also reflect these beliefs, as does alignment with specific approaches and attitudes in musicology. For example, the pursuit of a formalist (see **formalism**) understanding of music through strategies of **analysis** could be understood as reflecting a specific ideology. In musicology, Joseph Kerman's critique of analysis provides a useful reference to the operations of ideology through the conflation of ideology with **organicism**, analysis and **value**: 'From the standpoint of the ruling ideology, analysis exists for the purpose of demonstrating organicism, and organicism exists for the purpose of validating a certain body of works of art' (Kerman 1994, 15). In this construction, the perceived orthodoxy projected by analysis becomes, in Kerman's terms, a ruling ideology, a normative framework through which musical works (see **work**) are interpreted and evaluated (see **interpretation**). Other possible ideological processes in musicology would include that which leads to the formation of a Marxist (see **Marxism**) understanding of music in its social and political contexts.

However, this somewhat casual understanding of ideology is in sharp contrast to the more specific Marxist conception of the term. In this construction, ideology is understood as 'false consciousness', a condition that occurs when a **class** is blind to the forces that shape its existence and unaware of the actions that are in its best interests. In other words, ideology as false consciousness is the obscuring of truth for political purposes and is bound up with notions of power. The musical implications of this version of ideology are most clearly defined in German critical theorist Theodor Adorno's highly negative view of **popular music**. Adorno (see **critical theory**) views popular music as reflecting the constraints of the industrialized standards of capitalism (see **culture industry**), with the musical characteristics of 'standardization' and 'pseudo-individualism' satisfying the false needs of the masses: 'Standardization of song hits keeps the customers in line by doing their listening for them, as it were. Pseudo-individualization, for its part, keeps them in line by making them forget that what they listen to is already listened to for them, "pre-digested"' (Adorno 1994, 208).

Louis Althusser, a French structuralist Marxist (see **structuralism**), coined the term 'ideological state apparatus' (Althusser 1994). For Althusser, this was the processes through which the ruling class not only projected a dominant ideology but also reproduced the conditions of production necessary for its own continuing survival and domination. This model could be used to understand the use of culture in totalitarian societies, with music and other art forms used to sustain the ruling ideology. Musicology could also form part of this process through the selection of 'great' composers and 'great' works that are appropriated by the state as part of the construction of a 'national' (see **nationalism**) cultural **identity** (see Potter 1998; Levi 1994). As well as promoting certain composers and works, these ideological apparatuses also work to suppress music, and ideas about music, that do not correspond to the ruling ideology (see Sitsky 1994), but it could also be extended into the consideration of the dissemination of music and related ideas in so-called democratic societies, in which there may be apparatuses such as broadcasting and other media that project a political orthodoxy that is fundamentally ideological.

See also: **canon**, **cultural studies**, **culture**

Further reading: Eagleton 1991; Middleton 1990; Paddison 1993; Žižek 1994

INFLUENCE

The term influence might not be readily identified as a concept in musicology, but it is a recurrent theme in many different musicological contexts. In the writing of music history (see **historiography**), for example, influence is often claimed to be present in the relationships between different composers, works or periods. It also appears frequently in biographical studies of composers (see **biography**), often through reference to readily identifiable influences on the young composer. But what does it mean to describe or identify influence? In many contexts, influence is interpreted as a consequence of similarity or resemblance, but this may not always relate to what might, in some contexts, be an almost subliminal process of influence.

During the early 1990s, there were several notable attempts to provide a more theoretically focused understanding of influence. The starting point for this was the work of American literary theorist Harold Bloom, who developed his theories of influence through a series of important books, most notably *The Anxiety of Influence: A Theory of Poetry* (Bloom 1973). In this book, Bloom outlines a series of 'revisionary ratios' that seek to account for the identification of influence through certain strategies in relation to the precursor, such as 'misreading or misprision' and 'completion and antithesis' (*ibid.*, 14–16).

Two large-scale efforts by American music theorists to utilize Bloom appeared almost simultaneously: Kevin Korsyn's 'Towards a New Poetics of Musical Influence' (Korsyn 1991) and Joseph Straus's *Remaking the Past: Musical Modernism and the Influence of the Tonal Tradition* (Straus 1990). Korsyn begins by outlining his project: 'These pages unfold a theory of **intertextuality** in music, proposing a model for mapping influence, which, by usurping conceptual space from the literary criticism of Harold Bloom, also swerves towards a new rhetorical poetics of music' (Korsyn 1991, 3). The introduction of intertextuality into the debate is significant as it immediately reminds us that to talk about influence is to talk about the relationships between musical works (see **work**). Korsyn gives a musical representation of these issues through the initial consideration of scherzos by Brahms (Op. 4, 1851) and Chopin (Op. 31, 1837). Korsyn's starting point is the discussion by American musicologist and pianist Charles Rosen of the relationship between these two works: 'having steeped himself in Chopin's style in order to absorb a now canonic [see **canon**] conception of the virtuoso piano scherzo, Brahms displays the thematic reference at the opening in order to signal the presence of imitation' (Rosen 1980, 94). But does imitation signify influence? Rosen demonstrates some striking similarities between the two works, but, according to Korsyn, 'it is not enough merely to accumulate data by observing similarities among pieces; we need models to explain which similarities are significant, while also accounting for differences among works' (Korsyn 1991, 5). It is this search for models of explanation and **interpretation** that leads Korsyn to the work of Bloom.

Straus's engagement with Bloom is distinct from that of Korsyn. While Korsyn focuses in great detail on specific relationships, Straus considers a wider musical perspective and context, that of **modernism**. Straus's concern is with the central composers of modernism – Bartók, Berg, Schoenberg, Stravinsky, Webern – and the relationship of their music to the tonal traditions of the past (see **tradition**). This is clearly an ambitious engagement, but Straus also focuses his attention on specific details and the tracing of precise relationships. This is evident from his discussion of Alban Berg's violin concerto (1935), a work that forms a significant representation of modernism and its relationship to the past. This work, like much of Berg's music of the period, uses serialism but also articulates strong echoes of the tonal past. Following detailed analytical discussion of triadic shapes, Straus concludes: 'Their presence simultaneously establishes a link to the past and proclaims the subsumption and domination of that past' (Straus 1990, 81–82). This conclusion, through its reference to the domination of the past, echoes Bloom's suggestions of strong misreadings of poetic precursors. However, it is possible to suggest that Berg's conscious use of triadic references in his serial music is a deliberate compositional strategy and need not automatically be defined as reflecting the influence of the past. In other words, why assume that using the past is the same as being influenced by the past? While Straus produces some fascinating insights into these relationships, how he has transferred Bloom's theories into a musical context requires greater theoretical reflection. What is the revisionary relationship between the two contexts? Does Straus 'misread' Bloom, and if so in what way?

It is notable that since this period of engagement with Bloom's theories, little further work has been produced in this area, which suggests that musicology may have to begin to look elsewhere for models of understanding and interpretation that can illuminate the difficult question of what we mean when we say that one composer is influenced by another.

Further reading: Gloag 1999b; Street 1994; Taruskin 1993; Whitesell 1994

INTERPRETATION

Interpretation suggests a level of understanding and the communication of that understanding. All music making and all musicological activity constitutes a form of interpretation. Playing a musical composition, or improvising, on any musical instrument can be understood as an experience that involves a degree of interpretation. Clearly, the act of performance, and the musicological study of performance through contexts such as period performance practice, is the context that is most directly relatable to the concept of interpretation. The study of performance practice involves the interpretation of performance instructions, notational and editorial problems, and the interpretation of treatises and other historical documents (see **historical musicology**) that relate to the performance of music. The absorption and interpretation of such information can lead to a historically informed realization of a musical **work** (see **authenticity**). However, the communication of such a realization is a reflection of the context in which the music is heard, not in which it was composed. According to the pioneering English musicologist Thurston Dart: 'First of all we need to know the exact symbols [musical notation] the composer used; then we must find out what these signified at the time they were written; and lastly we must express our conclusions in terms of our own age, for we live in the twentieth century and not in the eighteenth or fifteenth' (Dart 1967, 14). However, deciding what the 'symbols' 'signified' in their own time remains an act of interpretation.

Popular music also involves acts of interpretation through concepts such as the **cover version**, while the reinvention of past material is an interpretative dimension of **jazz**. The nature and status of interpretation is different in these musical contexts in comparison with classical music due to the absence of a musical score, an absence that focuses attention on the processive, spontaneous act of interpretation.

However, other aspects of musicology also require interpretation. Biographical documents (see **biography**), historical evidence and source material (see **sketch**) are all musicological contexts that present information that requires interpretation. The activity of **analysis** is another area that is closely bound up with acts of interpretation. The determination of a work's structure or thematic content, for example, could be conceived as an interpretation. British musicologist Arnold Whittall extends this proposed relationship between analysis and interpretation to suggest that analysis is a performative act, so when we analyze music we execute a certain performance of it: 'We need, as analysts, to "perform" the music in different ways in order to achieve an interpretation alive to all nuances of the "text"' (Whittall 1991, 657). This proposal of an intellectual performance suggests that interpretation is a process, not a fixed entity or outcome, and as such it enjoys a certain fluidity. However, this poses problems around the degree of correctness that can be attached to any interpretation. Different performers will interpret the same music in different ways while also providing valid interpretations. This is also the case in musicology. Different interpretations of a musical work's structure, for example, can result from different strategies and theoretical starting points (see **theory**). However, while different interpretations may be equally valid, there remains the problem of how we respond to that which we sense to be inaccurate, misleading or misinformed. For example, Stravinsky's *The Rite of Spring* (1913) is a work that has provoked very different responses, with these differences dramatized by the polemical exchanges between Allan Forte (Forte 1986) and Richard Taruskin (Taruskin 1986). It remains a work that is difficult to situate in terms of even basic categories such as tonal or atonal (see Whittall 1982).

The intellectual context of **post-structuralism** has tended to privilege interpretation and, according to the literary theorist Roland

Barthes, has elevated the reader (the interpreter) over the author (the interpreted) (see Barthes 1977, 142–8). However, the free play of interpretation unleashed by some aspects of post-structuralist thought remains problematic. If the meaning of texts and, by implication, musical works is always in a state of flux, do they lose **value** and identity, and do we have to accept as valid readings that may be wilfully inaccurate? The literary theorist and novelist Umberto Eco has reflected upon the problems of interpretation and what he defines as 'overinterpretation' (Eco 1992, 1994). Following his earlier study of the 'open work' (Eco 1989), Eco now wants to raise issues of the limits, or perhaps boundaries, of interpretation, suggesting that authorial intent can still have some relevance in terms of how we interpret texts and that the content of any text goes some way towards influencing potential interpretations. However, in comparison with intellectual concepts and contexts such as post-structuralism, much musicological writing has remained fixed within recognizable boundaries of interpretation, with these boundaries being expanded through the emergence of a **new musicology** that has refocused attention on issues of **meaning** and interpretation (see Kramer 2002).

See also: **autonomy**, **criticism**, **discourse**, **hermeneutics**, **subject position**

Further reading: Grey 1995; Krausz 1993; Lawson and Stowell 1999; Rink 1995

INTERTEXUALITY

Intertextuality is a concept that has developed through **post-structuralism** to signify the sense in which any text is defined through its relation to other texts. The term was coined by Julia Kristeva in her seminal essay 'Word, Dialogue and Novel', originally published in 1967 (Kristeva 1986) and implies that the focus of **interpretation** shifts from creator to receiver, a process that is also active in Barthes's claim of the 'death of the author' (Barthes 1977, 142–8). The act of reading or, in the context of music, listening, involves tracing echoes and reflections of other texts. Therefore, all music can in some sense be seen and heard as intertextual. We are always inclined to make comparisons, highlight similarities and recognize familiar traces of past music. Borrowing, and more recently sampling (see **popular music**), is a recurrent feature of music, but intertextuality as a concept goes beyond the musically familiar to suggest that there is no such thing as a unified original musical **work**, that all music exists in relation to other music (see **alterity**), thus interrogating and displacing the assumptions of **organicism**, a central notion of much traditional musical thought.

In the context of twentieth-century music, the inherent inter-textuality of music has been enlarged upon as a compositional practice. For example, Luciano Berio's *Sinfonia* (1968) presents a timely cele-bration of the intertextual. Its central third movement is based upon the scherzo of Mahler's Second Symphony (1888–94), while a collage-like surface envelops the Mahlerian material. Other composers, such as Schnittke, exploit a deliberate intertextuality, often as part of a post-modern parody (see **postmodernism**).

The concept of intertextuality has emerged as a prominent feature in recent writing on music as part of a new-found understanding of the fluidity of the musical work. Tippett's oratorio *A Child of our Time* (1939–44), for example, has been interpreted through its relation to Handel's *Messiah* (1741), while Tippett's text for the work is defined via the **influence** of and references to T.S. Eliot and Jung (see Gloag 1999a). Other writing seeks to uncover less obvious relationships and shared meanings, a process that is evident in Korsyn's studies of the rela-tionships between the music of Brahms and Chopin (Korsyn 1991, 1996).

Further reading: Barthes 1990b; Gloag 1999b; Worton and Still 1991

JAZZ

Jazz may be best understood as a context rather than a concept, but it is a context that reflects the operations of a number of related concepts, some of which are specific to jazz, others absorbed from other contexts. Like **popular music**, jazz is a broad term that envelops a wide range of musical practices. However, it is commonly associated with musical styles (see **style**) that emerged from New Orleans in the early twen-tieth century and were defined through a certain rhythmic vitality, often referred to as 'swing', in collaboration with a degree of spon-taneous improvisation.

Jazz historian Alyn Shipton, in a recent overview of the historical development of jazz, identifies the first use of the term in print as occurring in San Francisco in 1913, when it was used to 'describe a dance music full of vigor and "pep"' (Shipton 2001, 1). This asso-ciation with dance was to remain with jazz for some time, suggesting that the music formed part of a social and recreational culture. It was also a music that emerged from distinct ethnic origins (see **ethnicity**): 'Because the music had African-American origins, the question of race also was bound up in it from the start, and to a white public it symbolised something "Other" [see **alterity**], something daring and exotic, while simultaneously, to a black public it was a unifying force, an aspiration' (*ibid.*, 1). That jazz provided a form of cultural expression for an African-American community and an object of exotic curiosity for a white public is clear, but at many points in jazz history the music became a highly self-reflexive project, one that often further problematized the process of defining the term. According to Krin Gabbard, 'Jazz is a construct. Nothing can be called jazz simply because of its "nature"' (Gabbard 2002, 1). In other words, there is no natural essence that is jazz. Rather, it becomes a set of discourses (see **discourse**) that mutate around a series of often very different musical practices. Gabbard continues, stating that 'the term jazz is routinely applied to musics that have as little in common as an improvisation by Marilyn Crispell and a 1923 recording by King Oliver and his Creole Jazz Band' (*ibid.*). Crispell and Oliver are situated in very different worlds and musical contexts. Cornettist Oliver emerged in New Orleans during the early years of the twentieth century and, like a number of musicians, migrated north to Chicago, where, during the 1920s, he led his own band, employing a number of developing talents, including a young Louis Armstrong, who had followed him from New Orleans. The music that Oliver made was unquestionably an essential jazz – fast, rhythmic and, to a certain extent, spontaneous. In contrast, Marilyn Crispell is a contemporary pianist who was educated in a classical music environment and whose music reflects a diverse and broad perspective. It is also an often improvised music, but it is far removed from the rhythmic regularity or harmonic vocabulary of early jazz.

Much writing on jazz has focused on individual performers, accentuating the image of the instrumental soloist as **genius**. The writing of American theorist, historian and composer Gunther Schuller often reflects this while also providing what, in its own time, was some of the most informed literature on the music:

When on June 28, 1928, Louis Armstrong unleashed the spectacular cascading phrases of the introduction to *West End Blues*, he established the general stylistic direction of jazz for several decades to come. Beyond that, this performance also made quite clear that jazz could never again revert to being solely an entertainment or folk music. The clarion call of *West End Blues* served notice that jazz had the potential capacity to compete with the highest order of previously known musical expression.

(Schuller 1968, 89)

There are several notable aspects to this statement by Schuller. The first is that it positions Armstrong in a pivotal moment in jazz history, a position that he certainly deserved, but we can also read it as a reflection of the construction of a jazz **canon** in which a series of individual performers and recordings are elevated above their surrounding context. This strategy runs parallel with the claim that this recording marks the emergence of jazz as an art form, as distinct from entertainment. While jazz demands to be understood as an art form, it is unclear why it must be seen to compete with other art forms, presumably the classical **tradition**, on the basis of 'previously known musical expression'. It is also significant that what Schuller is actually referring to is a recording, Armstrong's 'West End Blues'. It is one of the defining paradoxes of jazz and its study that our understanding and **interpretation** of the music is largely based upon the recording process and its dissemination, creating a perspective that may at times be distinct from that of a live performance, with the potential repeated hearings further distancing the spontaneity of the musical experience (see **recording**).

The tension between conceptions of jazz as art or entertainment were further accentuated with the emergence of bebop in the 1940s. This period was dominated by the 'swing' style of the big bands, and bebop is often interpreted as a reaction to this. This was the moment at which jazz became modern (see **modernism**). The innovations implemented by musicians such as Charlie Parker, Dizzy Gillespie, Thelonious Monk and others reflected a search for artistic status. According to Bernard Gendron, 'Though the idea that jazz is a modernist art form appeared in full force in the revivalist–swing debate, it is bebop that gets credit in the jazz canon for being the first modernist jazz, the first jazz avant-garde, the first form in which art transcends entertainment' (Gendron 2002, 143).

While jazz reached for artistic status, or in terms of critical strategy had this status conferred upon it, the music remained enclosed within issues of **race** and ethnicity. The trumpeter Miles Davis, who played a pivotal role in jazz after the high point of bebop, stated, with reference to Dizzy Gillespie: 'I love Dizzy, but I hated that clowning shit he did for them white folks . . . I decided . . . when people come to hear me, they were going to be coming to hear my music only' (Kahn 2000, 29). This statement reflects the musician's desire for control, power and status.

The current position of jazz is that of an increasingly diverse range of musical practices and interpretative strategies. This diversity presents formidable challenges for musicological study of and response to the music. Earlier writers such as Schuller could be seen to be involved in the construction of a jazz canon, while Gendron, writing from a contemporary critical perspective, questions the relevance of such a construction.

Recent writing on jazz reflects an interdisciplinary perspective, reflecting the essentially hybrid nature of the music (see **hybridity**). Several musicologists have embraced ideas derived from the black literary theory of Henry Louis Gates Jr, including Gary Tomlinson (Tomlinson 1992) and Robert Walser (Walser 1997), specifically his seminal text *The Signifying Monkey* (Gates 1988). In this book, Gates states:

> Free of the white person's gaze, black people created their own unique vernacular structures and relished in the double play that these forms bore to white forms. Repetition and revision are fundamental to black artistic forms, from painting and sculpture to music and language use. I decided to analyze the nature and function of Signifyin(g) precisely because it *is* repetition and revision, or repetition with a signal difference.
>
> (*ibid.*, xxiv)

This has a clear relevance for jazz. Gates's suggestion of 'Signifyin(g)', a specifically black form of signification (see **semiotics**), reflects the African-American origins of the music, but it also captures the performative nature of the musical experience, articulating it as a dynamic process and experience. As part of this construction, Gates draws attention to the relationships between repetition and revision in black cultural practices. Jazz is evidently a musical discourse that is bound up with patterns of repetition and difference. For example, standard song material is repeated by many different musicians in different contexts, but each individual will infuse this repetition with a degree of difference. This is evident, for example, in the music of John Coltrane, and specifically from his various reconstructions of Rodgers and Hammerstein's 'My Favorite Things', which featured in the Broadway musical, and later film, *The Sound of Music* (1965). Gates has commented directly on this specific example: 'Repeating a form and then inverting it through a process of variation is central to jazz – a stellar example is John Coltrane's rendition of "My Favorite Things", compared to Julie Andrews's vapid version. Resemblance thus can be evoked cleverly by dissemblance' (Gates 1984, 291). American ethnomusicologist Ingrid Monson provides a detailed discussion of Coltrane's 1960 recording of this song in which she details the 'transformations and reversals' of the original, a process that she defines as an 'ironic reversal, or transformation of a "corny" tune into a vehicle for serious jazz improvisation' (Monson 1996, 107). Monson concludes her discussion of 'My Favorite Things' with reference to Gates: 'In the case of "My Favorite Things", the transformation of the tune simultaneously communicates the resemblance between the two versions and the vast differences between them – Gates's signifying "repetition with a signal difference"' (*ibid.*, 127).

This statement forms part of an overview of what Monson defines as 'Intermusicality', a musical form of **intertextuality**, a context that invokes the Russian literary theorist Bakhtin's concept of 'dialogism', ideas of ironic parody derived from the postmodern literary theory of Linda Hutcheon (see **postmodernism**) and reference to the black cultural history of W.E.B. Du Bois. Given the diverse range of music generally defined as jazz and the different contexts that have shaped the music, such broad yet specific theoretical reflections highlight the impact of conceptual thought on jazz studies, providing an appropriate framework for further interpretations of the music and the development of a musicology of jazz.

Further reading: Ake 2002; Berliner 1994; DeVeaux 1997; Gebhardt 2001; Helbe 2000; Monson 1994; Wilmer 1992

LANDSCAPE

Through the work of social geographers (see Matless 1998), landscape has been developed in conjunction with ideas about preservation, **identity** and nation (see **nationalism**) to indicate the extent to which a particular **place** or location may shape or be shaped by cultural as well as economic considerations. From this perspective, the reflexive link between music and landscape may be understood in terms of the role it has played, at various points in history, in the construction of a nation's identity. This aspect of Vaughan Williams's music, for example, has been explored by Alain Frogley, who has argued that the early **reception** of Vaughan Williams was founded on an association of his music with the pastoral (images of a rural idyll, of a past that was irretrievably lost, and of a need to preserve a disappearing folk music), and that this stemmed from specific historical and political conditions in Britain in the 1920s and 1930s (Frogley 1996). Similar investigations may explain the role that the reflexive relationship between music and landscape has had, for example, in the music of Sibelius and Copland.

Conversely, a later generation of composers emerged that related some of its aesthetic concerns to observations about specific landscapes. In such instances, the more complex relation between the threat of imposed urban intrusion into a natural, organic (see **organicism**) landscape may be called upon. In Harrison Birtwistle's *Silbury Air* (1976), this idea is given a deeper modernist (see **modernism**) significance as the prehistoric site of Silbury Hill, near Avebury in the south of England, is evoked by the composer as an example of an 'organic intruder' into the landscape. There is also an implied sense here of landscape as a **metaphor** for musical technique. In the same way, Peter Maxwell Davies has likened the effects of storms on the Orkney Isles to the tonal ambiguity and reconfigurations of symphonic form in his music (see **analysis**).

Musicologist Annette Richards has explored how eighteenth-century aesthetic ideas (see **aesthetics**) of the picturesque and landscape had a metaphorical counterpart in certain genres (see **genre**), such as the keyboard fantasias of C.P.E. Bach (Richards 2001; see also Barrell 1980). Central to Romantic (see **Romanticism**) conceptions of landscape is travel. Schubert's *Winterreise* (1828) portrays aspects of landscape to convey this, just as American rock has drawn on the topic of travelling on highways through open and wild expanses. Urban landscapes also inform and are informed by music. Citing street names and describing other geographical features of urban landscapes, such as street corners, parks and bridges, is a component in claiming identity and **authenticity** in music, including the Beatles ('Penny Lane' (1967)) and Otis Redding ('Sitting on the Dock of the Bay' (1968)). This is, in part, because references to specific landmarks reinforce claims to location and authorship.

The conception that music can in some way reflect the landscape in which it is conceived appears to be strong in the minds of artists and composers. However, the work of social geographers points to the need for musicologists to begin to investigate how and why such associations are constructed.

Further reading: Brace 2002; Leyshon *et al.* 1998; Skelton and Valentine 1998

LANGUAGE

Music is often referred to in terms of language, and musicology is presented through the written word. Descriptive references are often made to factors such as a composer's stylistic (see **style**) or harmonic language, but it is difficult to specify in what sense music may be a language, or what is the nature of the relationship, or resemblance, between music and language.

The suggested parallel between music and language has a long history. Music, for a great deal of its history, has been inextricably linked to the voice and word, with the articulation of text in dramatic and liturgical contexts creating a framework for the development of music. The relationship between music and language was given some theoretical basis through the art of rhetoric, formed upon the ancient Greek and Roman literature on oratory, particularly Quintillian's *Institutio Oratorio*, which was rediscovered in the early fifteenth century and had a significant impact on musical thought. Rhetoric essentially outlined a verbal discourse through five distinct stages, from the invention of an argument (*inventio*) through its articulation (*elecutio*). The transfer of rhetorical theory to music forms an early musicology, with many treatises based on this relationship or making reference to it.

During the Baroque period, the parallels between music and language through the framework of rhetoric was most clearly defined and was given a theoretical basis in Mattheson's *Der Vollkommene Cappellmeister*, published in 1739, which is one of the most important treatises of the period. It presents a rational basis and structural plan for composition (see Harriss 1981). Mattheson refers to the 'oratorical' terms disposition, elaboration and ornamentation as the basis of the structuring of melody (*ibid.*, 469). The Baroque era also saw attempts to categorize musical figures into something approaching a musical vocabulary, with numerous treatises taking an often extensive, taxonomic approach. In contrast, the **Romanticism** of the nineteenth century saw quite different appropriations of language. The setting of text remained prominent, as evident in the lieder of Schubert and Schumann, among others. Opera, too, through the use of *leitmotifs* by Wagner, again recognized the linguistic potential of music. The rise of music **criticism** and the ongoing development of **aesthetics** also emphasized the problems involved in trying to describe and articulate music through language.

However, describing similarities between music and language or defining music in terms of language does not necessarily result in an understanding of music as language. The most extended attempt to create this understanding comes in Deryck Cooke's *The Language of Music* (Cooke 1959), which attempts to outline a common vocabulary through recurring musical characteristics of tonality, but the assumption that music is in some sense a language has also been questioned.

According to German critical theorist (see **critical theory**) Theodor Adorno, 'Music resembles a language. Expressions such as musical idiom, musical intonation, are not simply metaphors. But music is not identical with language. The resemblance points to something essential, but vague. Anyone who takes it literally will be seriously misled' (Adorno 1992b, 1). Perhaps the similarities between music and language have led to the misinterpretation of resemblance as relationship: music resembles language without actually becoming language.

See also: **metaphor, post-structuralism, semiotics, structuralism**

Further reading: Bonds 1991; Bowie 1993; Clarke 1996; Paddison 1991; Ratner 1980; Street 1987; Thomas 1995

LITERARY THEORY *see* **deconstruction, influence, intertextuality, post–structuralism, structuralism**

MARXISM

Marxism refers initially to the writings of Karl Marx and his associate Friedrich Engels and to later attempts to interpret and build on these writings. The main areas of concern and influence are economic and political, but there are also social and philosophical dimensions to Marxism.

Marx attempted to highlight the economic basis of society through reference to capitalism and the conflicting, competing interests of distinct socially and economically defined classes (see **class**). For Marx, society was defined by an economic base. This determined social and political relationships, which were predicated upon the suppression and exploitation of a subordinate class, the proletariat. However, Marx viewed this class as having a latent power, which could be unleashed in a revolutionary political context.

The revolutionary upheavals throughout Europe in 1848 provide a dramatic context for Marx's writings of the period. His *The Communist Manifesto* of that year presents a view of history as a series of striking polarities:

> The history of all hitherto existing society is the history of class struggles. Freeman and slave, patrician and plebeian, lord and serf, guild-master and journeyman, in a word, oppressor and

oppressed, stood in constant opposition to one another, carried on an uninterrupted, now hidden, now open fight, a fight that each time ended either in revolutionary reconstitution of society at large or in the common ruin of the contending classes.

(Marx and Engels 1998, 34–35)

This view of history determined Marx's interpretation of the present. It also reflects an awareness of the philosophy of Hegel and the presence of dialectical thought. Marx saw these conflicts and oppositions as moments of thesis and antithesis, opposite poles brought into collision, and out of this a new, revolutionary moment would emerge. However, much debate has surrounded the question of the inevitability of such actions and events.

Although Marx's writings have great relevance for an understanding of **culture** in relation to society, he did not provide any fully developed theory or even much specific commentary on the position of the arts and culture. For Marx, however, cultural activities clearly belong to the superstructure of society and are therefore dependent on the economic base. This dependency indicates the material nature of culture and its role as a reflection of society. It therefore subverts the art work's claim of **autonomy**. It is also possible to see cultural contexts as ideological operations, helping to produce the 'false consciousness' that blinds a class to its true historical and political destiny (see **ideology**).

While the attempted realization of Marxism through the Russian Revolution of 1917 led to unprecedented experimentation in the arts, the onset of Stalinism in the USSR reduced Marxism to a crude, rigid dogma. The attempt to translate Marxism into a realizable view of culture led to a policy of socialist realism as the ideological norm, with the accusation of **formalism** directed at artists, composers and writers who did not conform and whose work was seen not to engage positively with the representation of a social reality and the real-life concerns of the proletariat, a situation that had real consequences for composers, most famously Shostakovich. But musicology was also implicated in this, with music criticism and education distorted to serve the interests of the Stalinist state (see Schwarz 1972).

In contrast to the official rigidity of Marxism in the USSR a number of influential thinkers have engaged positively with Marxism throughout the twentieth century and addressed relationships between culture and society in a more productive manner. The term 'Western Marxism' evolved to define currents of Marxist thought that were independent of official Soviet policy and ideology. The first and most noted thinker from this perspective was György Lukács, a Hungarian Marxist who had real political experience, including the impact of Stalinism. Lukács developed a literary theory of socialist realism through his study of the nineteenth-century novel and its representations of reality. However, while it is difficult to trace a musical parallel with this literary trend, it can be viewed as a powerful precursor of **modernism**. Lukács's most important theoretical work is *History and Class Consciousness*, first published in 1923 (Lukács 1971). This book presents a humanized Marxism, one that situates issues such as alienation within a materialist conception of history. While Lukács's work has implications for an understanding of culture, the work of the Frankfurt school in general and Theodor Adorno in particular bring the relationships between culture and society into clear focus (see **critical theory**). It is rather simplistic to describe Adorno as a Marxist, but Marxism does form a significant part of the intellectual context from which he emerges. However, Adorno would not accept a view of culture as merely part of a superstructure dependent upon an economic base. Rather, for Adorno, there is a process of mediation between the real world and the art work, a mediation that, in the context of music, occurs within the musical materials. Significantly, Adorno did not subscribe to the Hegelian view of a dialectic process that aspired to some ultimate truth or transcendent moment. Instead, he resisted the totalizing impulse of such claims and saw dialectic thought as suspended in a negative relationship: thesis and antithesis may be brought into collision but need not be seen to result in a new synthesis. This negative dialectic rejects simplistic views of historical progress and artistic renewal. It also captures the tension and intensity of certain artistic issues and contexts of the twentieth century, particularly the atonal music of Schoenberg and its relationship to early modernism.

Recent theories of **postmodernism** have signalled a significant shift from the concerns of Marxism, with its central tenets refashioned as the 'meta-narratives' of modernism that we could no longer invest in. However, some recent writing on music and Marxism suggests new possibilities both for Marxism and for an understanding of music (see Krims 2001; Klumpenhouwer 2001). The increased commodification of music demands greater scrutiny, while the hegemonic nature of global capitalism (see **globalization**) raises issues that continue to be susceptible to a Marxist critique.

Further reading: Bottomore 1991; Eagleton and Milne 1996; McClellan 2000; Nelson and Grossberg 1988; Paddison 1993

MEANING

Music has often been described in terms of its expressive potential and character, which leads to the issue of its meaning, or, the posing of the question: what, if anything, does music mean?

This question has been restated throughout the history of both music and musicology and is one of the defining questions of musical **aesthetics**. Although this question has a long history, it comes fully into focus in the nineteenth century, during which the increased **subjectivity** and expressive potential of music as defined through **Romanticism** found a parallel in writing about music.

Debates about the nature of music and its meaning developed from the publication of the Viennese music critic Eduard Hanslick's *Vom Musikalisch Schönen* (On the Musically Beautiful) in 1854 (Hanslick 1986; Bujić 1988, 11–39). This book called into question many of the assumptions that had surrounded the issues of music and meaning and put in place the groundwork for the claim of music's **autonomy** and a formalist (see **formalism**) understanding of the musical **work** (see also **absolute**). For Hanslick, music consisted of 'Tonally moving forms' (Hanslick 1986, 29). In other words, the internal mechanisms of music were the key to understanding its nature and identity.

Hanslick's criticism was directed against the music of Wagner and its influence on other composers and related issues. Wagner's response was to represent Hanslick through the pedantic figure of Beckmesser in his opera *Die Meistersinger* (1867). It is through the context of the Wagnerian music drama that the music of the nineteenth century looks outwards to encapsulate so much that could be defined as 'non-' or 'extra'-musical perspectives. However, although Wagner may have dominated both the musical landscape of the period and its legacy, there is still a powerful lineage that flows from Hanslick's original conception of music as a formal, autonomous force.

In a recent study of musical meaning, the British musicologist Nicholas Cook considers the legacy of Hanslick and suggests that discussions of meaning are still grounded in formalism:

> The problematic Hanslickian inheritance is most evident in the work of those philosophers and, more recently, music theorists who have readmitted issues of meaning within academic debate, but on terms which maintain the underlying values of formalism. . . . The basic premise . . . is that, in Hatten's words, 'musical meaning is inherently musical', so that in speaking of the expressive qualities of music, of its qualities of acquiescence, resignation, or abnegation,

we are as much talking about the music as when we speak of themes, harmonic progressions, or formal prototypes.

(Cook 2001, 174)

On this account, rather than an opposition between formalism and meaning, there is a perceived relationship between the two, but the foundation of that relationship is constructed through and around the musical materials. This perspective is defined by American musicologist Edward Cone: 'formal and expressive concepts are not separable but represent two ways of understanding the same problem' (Cone 1974, 112).

Recent writing on music, much of which has been defined as **new musicology**, has again confronted the problem of defining the meaning of music, or at least considering music's representational qualities. The most wide-ranging attempt has been that made by Lawrence Kramer in his book *Musical Meaning: Toward a Critical History* (Kramer 2002). In his introduction, Kramer considers the relationship between musical meaning and modern experience and sees meaning as a central factor in music: 'The book celebrates meaning as a basic force in music history and an indispensable factor in how, where, and when music is heard' (*ibid.*, 1).

For Kramer, the illusiveness of the issue becomes not the barrier to understanding but its key: 'The underlying point of this book is that the apparent dilemma of musical meaning is actually its own solution', and he claims that to ask the question of music's meaning is part of the meaning of music: 'the question of whether music has meaning becomes, precisely, the meaning of music' (*ibid.*, 2). In other words, we surround music with various discourses (see **discourse**), which begin to attach meaning to music or reflect what music may be perceived to mean. However, the pursuit of musical meaning remains a fundamentally subjective process, and it is one that will continue to invite differing responses and interpretations (see **interpretation**), all of which can add to the diversity of what music might mean.

See also: **hermeneutics**, **language**, **post-structuralism**

Further reading: Head 2002; Robinson 1997

METAPHOR

Metaphor is a concept that defines our relationship to music. For example, music cannot be said to be sad; rather, sadness is a quality that we may ascribe to it (Neubauer 1986, 151). Metaphor arises in all forms of **discourse** about music, even when, as in **theory** and **analysis**, it attempts to treat music as an autonomous object (see **autonomy**). Naomi Cumming has summarized metaphors about music as 'a projection onto sound of aspects of our own mentality' (Cumming 1994, 28). In a critical appraisal of Roger Scruton's discussion of ways in which metaphor has informed musical descriptions, Cumming comments:

> If explanations of music commonly make it an 'intentional object' by treating it as the object of understanding, not as a thing which can be described 'in itself'... then references to qualities which derive from our own cognitive mechanisms rather than from any acoustic property of the music are bound to appear.
>
> (*ibid.*, 28)

Such metaphors, therefore, often reflect a cognitive link between music and the **body**. Austrian music theorist Heinrich Schenker, for example, spoke of *der Tonwille* ('the will of the tones') and of sensing a 'life-impulse' in the motion of his analytical reductions. Roland Barthes also sensed the presence of the composer's body in his description of the musical motion of Schumann's *Kreisleriana*, Op. 16, No. 2 (1838) (Barthes 1985, 299). These examples point to the habitual tendency of musical metaphors to reflect types of motion. This has been extensively examined by Robert Adlington, who explores metaphor theory (see Lackoff 1993) that proposes that the 'spatialization of change – and particularly the conceptualization of change as motion – is a necessary and unavoidable aspect of human cognition' (Adlington 2003, 300). However, Adlington discusses a range of post-tonal works that suggest that non-motional metaphors, such as those describing states of weightlessness or accumulation, are often more appropriate. He argues that music:

> has the potential to provide a counterbalance to... prevailing ideas about the form of existence... a fact sometimes obscured by the words we use to describe music, which may seem to align it with favoured concepts of time, rather than highlight its points of difference [see **alterity**].
>
> (*ibid.*, 297)

An indication of a way in which this may be applied in analysis is provided by a semiotic (see **semiotics**) analysis by Craig Ayrey of

Debussy's *Syrinx* (1913). Ayrey adopts French psychologist Jacques Lacan's definition of metaphor as paradigmatic ('one word for another') and metonymy as syntagmatic ('word-to-word connection') (Ayrey 1994, 136). He therefore likens musical units that reveal a sense of process and transformation to metonymy, and units that are more static and repetitive to metaphor. He then compares this with the rhetorical structure in Marcel Proust's novel *A la recherche du temps perdu* (1913–27), in which 'the trigger of memory is metaphor, but the expansion and exploration of a particular memory is metonymic' (*ibid.*, 151). In other words, the musical discourse of Debussy's piece consists of a creative tension between ideas that slide, metonymically, and metaphorical attempts to reassert paradigmatic structures.

The role that metaphor has played in musicology has recently been the subject of more historically informed musicological approaches (see Zon 2000; Spitzer 2004). Throughout history, cultural values (see **value**) have informed and constructed metaphors used to describe music, and these have changed through time, reflecting shifting discourses and metaphors in other areas, such as religion, politics and science.

See also: **language**, **narrative**

Further reading: Lackoff and Johnson 1980

MODERNISM

Modernism means different things in different contexts. It implies a historical epoch while simultaneously referring to specific composers and works, but it is generally used as a comprehensive term that embraces major developments in the arts during the late nineteenth and early twentieth centuries. The emergence of musicology as a distinct discipline can also be seen to be aligned with certain aspects of modernism.

Modernism has had a long history, and there is continuing debate around when it ended, or indeed if it has ended (see **postmodernism**). Clearly, any historical epoch thinks of itself as 'modern', as the new in contrast to the old (see **historicism**, **periodization**), but modernism reveals a higher self-conscious preoccupation with the new, projecting a desire for progress that borders on the utopian.

The origins of modernism are intertwined with the **Enlightenment**, the seventeenth- and eighteenth-century project that defined itself through a new spirit of rationalism and enlightened progress. Modernism is no longer that which is most current but becomes that which is most progressive. This association of modernism with progress is given explicit meaning in the political dimension, with modernism as we now understand it being seen to emerge in the aftermath of the revolutionary upheavals of 1848. This moment and its sense of modernity are given theoretical reflections in the writings of Karl Marx and Friedrich Engels, most specifically in *The Communist Manifesto* of 1848 (Marx and Engels 1998). The project of **Marxism** will be seen to provide an apt reflection of modernism. Its preoccupation with the future, the inevitability of history and the power of the dialectic all find echoes in more aesthetic formations of modernism (see **aesthetics**). The attempted political realization of Marxism in the form of the Bolshevik Revolution also finds a certain parallel with modernism through the actions of a political *avant-garde*.

The year 1848 is also a moment of significance in the history of music, and it is possible to see these political and philosophical statements of modernism as precursors to the emergence of a full-blown aesthetic modernism in the late nineteenth and early twentieth centuries. The mid-nineteenth century (*c.* 1848) witnessed distinct changes in **Romanticism**, the prevailing aesthetic and stylistic context of the period. For Carl Dahlhaus, one of the most significant and persuasive writers on the music of this period, this moment in the mid-nineteenth century marks a symbolic division in Romanticism and the period in general:

> Early nineteenth-century music could be said to be romantic in an age of Romanticism . . . whereas the neo-Romanticism of the later part of the century was romantic in an unromantic age, dominated by positivism and realism. Music, *the* romantic art, had become 'untimely' in general terms, though by no means unimportant; on the contrary, its very dissociation from the prevailing spirit of the age enabled it to fulfil a spiritual, cultural, and ideological function of a magnitude which can hardly be exaggerated: it stood for an alternative world.
>
> (Dahlhaus 1989b, 5)

For Dahlhaus, then, the later nineteenth century had become dominated by **positivism** and realism. Positivism, which constitutes a view of knowledge as validated through observation and evidence, has a clear relationship to the emergence of musicology. The classification of knowledge and the identification of material became essential features of musicology, as evident from Adler's division and classification of the discipline (see **historical musicology**). Dahlhaus's proposal of a dominant realism is best reflected in the art and literature of the period and provides anticipatory traces of the heightened expressiveness of modernism as manifested in the expressionism of the paintings of Munch and the early atonal music of Schoenberg (see **subjectivity**). However, of greater significance is Dahlhaus's claim that music had become untimely. In other words, it no longer fitted easily into its surrounding context, yet it is through this separation from the real world, its positioning of itself as an 'alternative world', that music becomes modernism. This process was initiated by Wagner, whose music dramas constitute an alternative reality, but one that is pregnant with commentaries on and reflections of the real world.

This other-worldly quality (see **alterity**) is often extended in modernist music of the late nineteenth and early twentieth centuries. Often alienated from mainstream audiences, a composer such as Schoenberg faced hostility and rejection. This, along with the increasing radicalism of the music, helped to shape increasingly alienated, self-reflexive contexts. However, this disengagement, or alienation, need not imply that the music is completely decontextualized. For German critical theorist Theodor Adorno, it is precisely this drive towards **autonomy** that allows the art work to become critical, constructing a distance that allows for reflection (see **critical theory**). Of course, this process is never complete or fully formed and, according to Adorno, there is a process of mediation between work and world through which 'art not only reflects society but also opposes it, not only converges with society but also diverges from it' (Paddison 1993, 128). In contrast to Schoenberg, Stravinsky, after the scandal of the first performance of *The Rite of Spring* (1913), did find a wider audience for his music. Stravinsky, through the reinvention of a Russian mythology, could also be seen to be involved in the construction of an 'alternative world'. But, for Adorno, this lacked the critical force of Schoenberg's early music and was fundamentally regressive (see Adorno 1973).

By the early 1920s, modernism had shifted from its early radical spirit to a new-found sense of order, a so-called return to order. This was manifested through the rationalization of musical materials that became Schoenberg's serialism (the systematic ordering of all twelve notes of the chromatic scale) and neoclassicism. Serialism could be seen in some ways as a continuation of the rationalization that modernism had inherited from the Enlightenment but also, for Schoenberg, that which would again extend musical **language** into a new future condition, a belief that was evident in his nationalistic claim (see **nationalism**) that serialism would guarantee the supremacy of German music for the next hundred years (Haimo 1990, 1).

Serialism also had an impact on thinking about music and, by extension, musicology. Schoenberg had always written about music and was an influential teacher of composition (Berg and Webern were his two best-known students), and his theoretical writings on harmony (Schoenberg 1978) and composition (Schoenberg 1970) look towards a systematic understanding of the subject. But Schoenberg was also interested in larger aesthetic ideas, and his attempts to formulate an understanding of the musical 'idea' reflect an understanding of the philosophy of Hegel (Schoenberg 1995). Schoenberg was also self-consciously concerned with his own status and position as a composer, as evident in essays such as 'How One Becomes Lonely' (1937), 'New Music, Outmoded Music, Style and Idea' (1946) and 'Brahms the Progressive' (1947) (in Schoenberg 1975), and this self-consciousness reflected that of modernism as it sought to situate itself as both the cultural dominant and a historical condition. However, this process now involved a search for precedent, the reinvention of the past in order to legitimize the present. This is evident from 'Brahms the Progressive', in which Schoenberg resituates Brahms, often thought of as conservative in relation to Wagner, as a progressive composer and therefore forming an anticipation of Schoenberg's own modernism. This search for precedent and the reconstruction of the past signifies a shift within modernism, a shift that now relates past and present with the future (see Straus 1990).

Serialism continued to have an impact on thinking about music. The complexity of the compositional process, but also how that process could be revealed, influenced composers and theorists, and much writing on contemporary music from the 1950s onwards reflects this influence (see **structuralism**). Neoclassicism also had a wider impact on thinking about music, but it was to manifest itself in different ways to serialism. While serialism was to influence contemporary composition and writing about it, neoclassicism helped to shape attitudes towards performance of early music (see **authenticity**).

Neoclassicism can be understood as a phase and a set of stylistic issues within modernism (see **style**), but it is one in which the originating nature and spirit of modernism is reduced at times to a residual trace. In 1920, Stravinsky took what at the time was conceived as a surprising turn towards the past. The ballet *Pulcinella* heralded the beginning of a sequence of works, all of which had a new-found relationship to past musical styles. This sense of a new **historicism** also came with suggestions of new levels of objectivity. In the German context, this became the *Neue Sachlichkeit* (new objectivity) identified with Hindemith. For Stravinsky, this 'objectivity' involved a denial of the subjective role of performer and interpretation and the implied suppression of the expressive nature of music, issues that were reflected in Stravinsky's much quoted claim that 'music is, by its very nature powerless to *express* anything at all' (Stravinsky 1936, 53). The emergence of this attitude points towards the rise of a more clearly defined historical consciousness and objectivity in the performance of music, as reflected in the work of conductors such as Toscanini and Szell, for example. This relationship between modernism and the performance of music has increasingly been explored by American musicologist Richard Taruskin (Taruskin 1995).

Modernism continues to exert a powerful influence in music and musicology. Many contemporary composers continue to produce music that can still be defined as modernist (Harrison Birtwistle, Pierre Boulez and Elliott Carter, for example), while musicology continues to reflect aspects of modernism and attempts to interpret it. In an important article titled 'Modernity The Incomplete Project', the influential German cultural and critical theorist Jürgen Habermas claims that 'the project of modernity has not yet been fulfilled', with the implication that before we can think of postmodernism the project of modernism must be completed, its tensions resolved (Habermas 1985). However, if modernism continues in some shape or form, its alleged certainties have been subject to wide-ranging critical responses. The assumption of the inevitability of historical progress, the art work's aspiration towards autonomy and the overarching sense of scale and ambition have all been extensively undermined by various theories and strategies of postmodernism. The reflections of this critical situation in musicology involve new formations and alignments around issues such as the shift from consideration of the **work** in isolation towards context, from positivism towards **interpretation**, and from an aura of objectivity towards subjectivity (see **new musicology**).

Further reading: Bradbury and MacFarlane 1976; Butler 1994; Habermas 1990; Nicholls 1995; Samson 1991; Whittall 1999

NARRATIVE

Narrative describes events that have unfolded in time; narrativizing is the attempt to give meaning to such events by accounting for them in terms of a plot, containing such devices as dialogue, action, character, reversal or climax; and narratology is a discipline that has appeared in literary criticism since the early 1980s, specifically concerned with issues of narrative in literature and culture (see Mitchell 1981). According to Hayden White, narrative concerns the problem of 'how to translate *knowing* into *telling*' (White 1980, 1), or in the words of French philosopher Paul Ricoeur, how to 'draw a configuration out of a simple succession' (Ricoeur 1984, 65). Narrating, which is necessary if a story is to be told, requires an act: a plot must be enacted. In this sense, narrative is not only a plot or a story but also an act. Definitions of narrative are highly varied, as are the attempts to discuss narrative in music.

According to Jean-Jacques Nattiez, 'a narrative emerges...only when a temporal series of objects and events is taken over by a metalinguistic discourse' (Nattiez 1990a, 243). As this quotation indicates, narrative is sometimes related to **discourse**, and discourse has a number of meanings. It may refer to the mode in which a narrative is conveyed: the quality of speech, or the musical **style**, for example. It may refer to the distinction, in a narrative, between the story and a narrating voice. Many scholars doubt that music is capable of presenting this distinction, or that music can present different discursive 'points of view', as would be common in a work of literary fiction. In this instance, however, Nattiez is using discourse as a metonym for talking about music. Cultural theorists, such as Italian Marxist Antonio Gramsci and French cultural theorist Michel Foucault, have outlined the presence of grand narratives in such cultural discourses – ideologically determined ways of perceiving and structuring societies and cultures. For example, a modernist (see **modernism**) master narrative, which dates from the time of the **Enlightenment**, can be seen to have determined a Western European belief in the need for progress in knowledge, in the arts, in technology and in human freedom. By the second half of the twentieth century, this had begun to give way to a condition that French cultural theorist and philosopher François Lyotard has described as an 'incredulity towards metanarratives' (Lyotard 1992). Consequently, an alternative set of postmodern narratives, what Lyotard calls 'little narratives', arises. In the words of Wayne D. Bowman:

> Since to postmodern sentiments, [modernist] discourses about truth, knowledge, justice, and beauty are really about political power and control, the conviction that reason provides the neutral, objective machinery enabling human access to foundational or

absolute truths is no longer tenable.... [Postmodernism] often assumes a strenuously defiant...skepticism toward modernist narratives...sensitivity to the ways such stories covertly served the interests of power, control, and oppression.

(Bowman 1998, 395–6)

The basis of an alternative use of the term narrative in relation to music derives from the apparent narrative quality of music. Music's linearity, the fact that objects follow one another in succession, is an invitation to compare music to narrative, what Nattiez describes as the listener's 'narrative impulse'. In relation to this, American musicologist Edward Cone has noted the presence of narrative terms in analytical language about music. He cites the use of the terms subject, answer, exposition, discussion and summary to describe the constituents of a fugue, terms that associate fugue with the model of a conversation (see Cone 1974). However, German critical theorist (see **critical theory**) Theodor Adorno, in his consideration of what he saw as the novel-like quality of Mahler's music, suggested that 'music recites itself, is its own context, narrates without narrative' (Adorno 1992a, 76). Similarly, American musicologist Carolyn Abbate has suggested that 'certain gestures experienced in music constitute a narrating *voice*' (Abbate 1991, 18), but we do not know exactly what the voice is striving to articulate about. However, others have argued that narrative is a semiotic enterprise (see **semiotics**) that can enrich music **analysis** by providing a metaphorical (see **metaphor**), hermeneutic (see **hermeneutics**) layer of **meaning** (see Hatten 1994; Samuels 1995). Despite existing reservations, there persists in accounts of music a commonly shared sense that, in the words of French anthropologist Claude Lévi-Strauss:

The musical work ... is a myth coded in sounds instead of words [which] offers an interpretive grid, a matrix of relationships which filters and organises lived experience, acts as a substitute for it and provides the comforting illusion that contradictions can be overcome and difficulties resolved.

(Lévi-Strauss 1981, 659–60)

The paradigm of conflict and resolution that this quotation outlines represents a narrative archetype that is central to most discussions of music, particularly tonal music. For example, Anthony Newcomb has discussed the presence of plot archetypes in Beethoven's Fifth and Ninth Symphonies (1807–8 and 1822–4), suggesting that they might be seen to correspond to two affective states: 'suffering, followed by healing or redemption'. In his consideration of Schumann's instrumental music, Newcomb remarks that: 'Listening to a work, we recognise the evocation of actions, tensions and dynamisms analogous to those for which the literary work is a vehicle' (Newcomb 1983–4, 248).

However, Nattiez contends that, 'the narrative, strictly speaking, is not *in the music*, but *in the plot imagined and constructed by the listeners* from functional objects ... for the listener, any "narrative" instrumental work is not *in itself* a narrative, but *the structural analysis in music of an absent narrative*' (Nattiez 1990a, 249; italics in original). The key point here is a distinction between a plot 'imagined and constructed by the listeners', which may be implied by a work's title or other programmatic information provided by the composer, and the music's interpretation of an 'absent narrative' in formal, structuralist terms (see **structuralism**). This is a crucial distinction between two types of logic: dramatic and formalist (see **formalism**). According to Nattiez, any description of music's formal structures in terms of narrativity is 'nothing but superfluous metaphor' (*ibid.*, 257). The influence of narrative modes may contribute to the transformation of musical forms, he argues, but musical syntax cannot relate dramatic events in the way that language can. For example, there is no exact musical equivalent for the linguistic association of 'the duchess' and 'left at five o'clock'. Furthermore, as Abbate has argued, music has no past tense; nor is there any way to differentiate between first and third person accounts. Nattiez builds on this by stating that music 'can evoke the past by means of quotations or various stylistic borrowings. But it cannot relate *what* action took place in time' (*ibid.*, 244).

However, by limiting music's ability to narrate to rare 'moments that can be identified by their bizarre and disruptive effect', Carolyn Abbate has revealed numerous examples in music, especially in opera, of musical devices that function as narrative voices (Abbate 1991, 29). This view of narrative appearing in disruptive rather than normative moments in music is also shared by Lawrence Kramer, who is particularly concerned with nineteenth-century instrumental music that has a rhetorical character (Kramer 1993b). Philip Rupprecht has also applied these ideas, as well as those of theorists such as Gérard Genette, C.S. Peirce, Mikhail Bakhtin, J.L. Austin and Eve Sedgwick to the operas and songs of Benjamin Britten (Rupprecht 2001). He points to the importance, when exploring narrative meaning in Britten's operas, of considering the manner in which vocal utterance is presented, both vocally and in terms of orchestral support, as well as the wordless utterances of the orchestra, in terms of *leitmotifs*, timbre and the relationship to the vocalist. Rupprecht is also very much concerned with various kinds of gesture in Britten's operas as indicators of levels of discourse, as well as the different narrative meanings that Britten's music presents in contrast to the meanings of the fictional narratives that his operas are based upon, which include novels by Henry James, Herman Melville and Thomas Mann.

Studies related to this subject continue to be produced, as different interpretations of narrative are applied to music in a search for meaning in wider, cultural contexts, especially in the fields of semiotics and opera studies. Instrumental music that contains heterogeneous musical materials, music with known biographical or programmatic associations, such as works by Schumann, Berg and Shostakovich, is especially attractive to such inquiries, although all music can be discussed in such terms. While the central issues have yet to be resolved, and such studies may risk falling into literal exercises in anthropomorphism, there is still much potential in the subject of narrative and music to offer further insight into analytical and critical debate.

Further reading: Karl 1997; Micznik 2001; Paley 2000

NATIONALISM

Nationalism can be defined as an attitude not just of artists but, often more crucially, of historians, critics and audiences, while nationality is a condition, with the emergence of nation-states pre-dating the concept of nationalism (see Armstrong 1982; Taruskin 2001). A nation is not necessarily defined according to boundaries but results from a mediation of political status and a community's terms of self-definition, according to religion, **ethnicity** (see Smith 1986), **race**, language or **culture**, in which any act of inclusion is, necessarily, an act of exclusion. However, nationalism will depend primarily on a sense of a common, shared history, a concept that tends to cut across local and individual differences (see **alterity**). Of importance in the spread of nationalism, it has been argued, was the development of printed media in the sixteenth century and their role in shaping what historian Benedict Anderson has called 'imagined communities' (Anderson 1983).

A precedent for the concept of nationalism in music stems from an awareness of different musical styles (see **style**). These sometimes arose as a consequence of institutional support, as in the case of Gregorian chant under the auspices of the Carolingian Empire in the eighth to ninth centuries. Although such distinctions at times led to a sense of rivalry, for instance between Italian and French opera in the eighteenth century, there have also been examples of fruitful exchange, for example the export of a *contenance Anglaise* to France in the fourteenth century (see Caldwell 1991). However, the idea of musical styles representing the cultural and political values of a nation-state has a relatively recent history and follows from historical moments such as the beheading of the English monarch in 1649, an event that signalled a new kind of direct political link between music and national **identity**.

One of the primary concerns of musicologists working on nationalism has been to find ways of deciding what constitutes a national style and developing 'models of individual national traditions' (Beckerman 1986, 62; Dahlhaus 1989b; see also **tradition**). What is interesting about such attempts is that they mirror similar studies by German theorists in the 1920s and 1930s, which, for political reasons, attempted to define German-ness in music. Michael Beckerman, in his study 'In Search of Czechness in Music' (Beckerman 1986) concludes that Czechness is a 'subtextual program' that exists in the minds of composers and audiences that '*animates* the musical style, allowing us to make connections between the narrow confines of a given piece and a larger, dynamic context' (*ibid.*, 73). As such, he argues, Czechness, and any other nation-ness, must be considered an 'aesthetic fact' (see **aesthetics**), as real as a national landmark. In other words, nationalism in music depends on a network of cultural ideas that must exist outside a **work**, and the work must engage with these ideas if it is to be interpreted as nationalistic.

Dahlhaus also stressed the importance of reassessing claims that nationalism represented a form of artistic **authenticity**, and a need to consider the different ways that nationalism appeared – for example, through unification, deposing a monarchy, or a struggle for independence – as well as the historical overlaps that occurred between the establishment of various nation-states. The rise of nationalism in art and music, in its modern political sense, has generally been associated with the French Revolution, after which 'nationalism came to dominate Europe as a mode of thought and a structure of feeling' (Dahlhaus 1989b, 85). It dominated the nineteenth century, largely as a result of the Napoleonic Wars and the subsequent nationalist causes that arose as a consequence of the rise of military and political empire building, notably the French, Prussian,

Austro-Hungarian and Ottoman empires. Early expressions of nationalism in this form were Italian *risorgimento* operas, from 1820 to 1850, especially the works of Rossini and Verdi (see Gossett 1990; Parker 1997), and English romantic opera in the 1830s. However, German composers and critics were among the first to question what nationalism might mean in music and, alongside Russia, Germany presented a model that others used to define their own sense of difference (Applegate 1992).

Central to German and subsequently Russian and other European nations' ideas of musical nationality has been the concept of *der Volksgeist*: 'the belief in the spirit of a people as an active creative force' (Dahlhaus 1989b, 85). Collections of songs (*Volkslieder*) and poems gathered in small towns and villages, such as J.G. Herder's *Stimmen der Völker* ('Voices of the Peoples', 1778–9) and *Des Knaben Wunderhorn* ('The Youth's Magic Horn', 1805–8), point to the emergence of German nationalism out of early German Romantic conceptions, such as the superiority of unspoilt nature (see **landscape**) and truth over corrupted, decadent culture (see **Romanticism**). They also provided a repository of material for a composer such as Schubert. German writers, including E.T.A. Hoffmann and A.B. Marx, in particular through their discourses (see **discourse**) on Beethoven, universalized German musical values, leading to the eventual identification of all instrumental music with German music (see **absolute**), a process that, in the main, arose covertly (Applegate 1992). By association, recent scholarship has considered the influence of nationalism on music **theory** (see McClatchie 1998) and **historicism**. For example, the New German School – a term coined by German music historian Franz Brendel in 1859 – included Wagner, Liszt and Berlioz, all of whom were linked, it was argued, by the notion of a German spirit.

The revolutions throughout Europe in 1848–9 were clearly of great significance in encouraging nationalist sentiments, but they also gave rise to a contradiction between the Romantic demands of artistic **subjectivity** and a desire to represent the real world (Dahlhaus 1989b). The awareness of composers of the more positivist (see **positivism**), scientifically and technologically advanced late nineteenth-century context, upon which German nationalism was contingent, marked a break from the Romanticism of the early nineteenth century and was integral in what has subsequently been interpreted as the birth of **modernism** (see Banks 1991; Butler 1994). Likewise, the neo-nationalism of Stravinsky's so-called Russian ballets was a springboard to international modernism. A darker side of the changes after 1848–9 was the emergence of less tolerant forms of nationalism. In music, this amounted to expressions of anti-semitic views, which were rapidly gaining currency in late nineteenth-century Germany (see Weiner 1995; Hallman 2002), and the brash militarism, anti-semitism and decadence of Richard Strauss's tone poems and early operas (Gilman 1988).

One aspect of nationalism in music is emulation – the attempt to out-do a dominant nation. For example, French composers, after 1871, following France's defeat by the Prussian army, wrote absolute music to rival that of Germany. In the case of Russia, emulation was an important step in establishing musical prestige, although in this instance European tradition clashed with an interest in indigenous techniques (see Taruskin 1996, 1997). In other cases, nationalism manifested itself in a conscious rejection of another nation's music. This can be seen in the discourse in *fin-de-siècle* France, which stressed the need for clarity and economy in opposition to German excess.

Of consideration must also be the **reception** of works and their retrospective interpretations by subsequent generations of musicologists. John Deathridge has noted that although Wagner's 'Plan for the Organization of a German National Theatre for the Kingdom of Saxony' was initially received with derision when it was written in 1848, it was highly topical when published in 1871, the year of the founding of the German Reich (Deathridge 1991, 53). Nazi Germany's appropriation of non-German composers is well documented (see Potter 1998), and Alain Frogely has presented fascinating accounts of the appropriation of Vaughan Williams's music according to Britain's desire to construct a nationalist identity between the two world wars to rival that of Germany, examining the importance of critical and composer reception of his music and its influence on audiences (Frogley 1996, 1997). Frogley also considers the extent to which Vaughan Williams modified his views about nationalism and music, a change that can also be seen in the writings of Bartók (see Frigyesi 1998; Brown 2000).

Recent studies have also highlighted the extent to which nationalism has been selectively constructed. Some examples contain deliberate forms of cultural amnesia, as illustrated by the Nazis' exclusion of Mendelssohn and Schoenberg from historical accounts, despite their prominent roles in constructing German nationalism and their own capacity for cultural chauvinism (Potter 1998). Hybrid processes (see **hybridity**) of assimilation and co-option are also based on selection. For example, notions of Hungarian national musical styles have hinged on shifting interpretations of gypsy music (Bellman 1998a), and Parisian neoclassicism was a product of the assimilation of Stravinsky's music to French nationalism (Messing 1996); subsequently, it became a prescription for attempts to form a national musical language in America (Tischler 1986). **Jazz**, too, was variously co-opted by French and American composers to nationalist ends (Fry 2003). Recent studies have also considered nationalism in the music of Sibelius (Franklin 1997b), Elgar's links to British imperialism (Grimley and Rushton, 2005), interpreting nationalism in terms of musical techniques and traditions (Bellman 1998a), the role of language in nationalist music (Beckerman 1986) and the nationalist contribution of musicians living abroad, such as Chopin (Milewski 1999), Bartók and Schoenberg.

Since the Cold War, during which a broad polarity can be sketched between the non-nationalist institutionalization of high modernism in the West (see Born 1995; Carroll 2003) and folk-influenced socialist realism in Soviet bloc countries in the East, the rise of **globalization** has led to a focus on local resistance and diversity, which often side-steps issues of nationality (see **postmodernism**). Often this is achieved by shifting the emphasis more on to **ethnicity** rather than nation, as is the case in the music of Ligeti, although Birtwistle can be seen to draw on symbols of national association, for example in his opera *Gawain* (1991, revised 1994). However, the concept of nationalism does arise directly in some contemporary contexts. For example, black civil rights activism led to the idea of a black nation-state, promoted by jazz musicians such as John Coltrane and Charlie Mingus (Kofsky 1970), while funk and hip-hop have similarly been associated with black nationalism, as illustrated by James Brown's *Revolution of the Mind* (1971) and Public Enemy's *It Takes a Nation of Millions to Hold Us Back* (1988). From a non-black perspective, attempts have been made to co-opt certain American musicians in support of the values and spirit of the American nation, for example Hank Williams and Bruce Springsteen. However, Springsteen's 'Born in the USA' (1984) belongs to a songwriting tradition that is critical of the concept of nationalism; other notable examples include Jimi Hendrix's deconstructive **interpretation** of 'The Star Spangled Banner' at Woodstock in 1969 and Madonna's 'American Life' (2003). The Eurovision Song Contest resists the hegemony of American popular music, although voting often reflects the politics of national and regional affiliations, as well as age-old grudges, while in France regulations are in place to protect French-language popular music. In Britain, resistance to American dominance dates from the success of the Beatles and the Rolling Stones in the 1960s and can also be detected in progressive, folk and punk rock in England in the 1970s, all of which can be seen to examine, in different ways, notions of English nationalism (see Macan 1997; Savage 1991). And Eric Zolov, in an example that illustrates the presence of emulation of national styles in popular music, has explored the co-option of Elvis Presley in the development of a counter-cultural movement in Mexico in the 1960s and the manipulation of its consumption by state agencies (Zolov 1999).

Further reading: Bohlman 2004; Dennis 1996; Hobsbawm 1992; Mäkelä 1997; Ridenour 1981; White and Murphy 2001

NEOCLASSICISM *see* **authenticity, modernism**

NEW MUSICOLOGY

There can be no sense in which the new musicology ever existed as an integrated movement. It would be more accurate to describe it as a loose amalgam of individuals and ideas, dating from the mid-1980s, nearly exclusively based in America, whose work has now largely been absorbed into the common practice. Reference to the new musicology is therefore largely retrospective. However, these individuals bring to their own particular fields of expertise a number of shared concerns and focus on recurring issues and problems that reflect a wider post-modern (see **postmodernism**) move to displace **positivism** and the concept of the autonomous (see **autonomy**) musical **work** (see **modernism**). This is manifested in a will to engage with disciplines outside musicology, in particular those in the humanities and social sciences, and a desire to alter the framework of musicological discussion. Their work reflects the fundamental questioning of accepted forms of knowledge that has affected a range of subjects, including anthropology, sociology and history, and that is influenced by cultural anthropologist Michel Foucault's structural account of the history of knowledge (Foucault 1972).

However, these common concerns should not obscure a number of differences of emphasis between new musicologists. One noted debate is that between Lawrence Kramer and Gary Tomlinson, which stems from Kramer's article 'The Musicology of the Future' (Kramer 1992), itself a response to an earlier article by Joseph Kerman (Kerman 1994). Kramer's interest centres on nineteenth-century music and literature and reflects developments in **post-structuralism**, in particular the idea that **meaning** is to be found in individual, subjective (see **subjectivity**) interpretations of the context of an art work, and that equally valid, multiple interpretations may result (see **interpretation**). The related perspectives of **deconstruction** and narratology (see **narrative**) are also present in Kramer's work. He investigates various literary themes, or tropes, from which he generates a network of discourses in order to construct a literary and historical context for his discussion (see **discourse**). He then attempts to read this context in the content of the music by locating similar discursive practices in the **language** and syntax of music, for example in a composer's use and manipulation of **style**, form and **genre**.

To Tomlinson, however, Kramer's work seems suspiciously reactionary in some respects, for example his falling back on to conventional methods of **analysis** and the careful selection of detail to support his argument.

> Instead of postmodern doubt, play, and a problematizing of the communicative relation, Kramer offers a too-familiar modernist mastery... a postmodern musicology will be characterized most distinctively by its insistent questioning of its own methods and practices.
>
> (Tomlinson 1993a, 21)

In particular, Tomlinson does not find Kramer's approach historical enough. This is demonstrated by Kramer's concern to relate his cultural and linguistically based discussion to conventional analyses of the musical score, leading Tomlinson to note that 'it is the act of close reading itself that carries with it the ideological charge of modernism' (*ibid.*, 22). Tomlinson has advocated locating meaning almost exclusively in what he terms a 'web of culture', a series of interrelated historical narratives that surround the musical subject (Tomlinson 1984).

New developments in musicology can, in part, be linked to the rise of **feminism** and **gender** studies within the discipline. These were first integrated into musicology by Susan McClary, Marcia Citron and Philip Brett (McClary 1991; Citron 1993; Brett 1994; see also **gay musicology**). McClary in particular has been successful in addressing subjects in **popular music**, notably constructions of **identity** in the music of Madonna, as well as reconsidering figures from the Western classical **tradition**. For example, she has used gender discourse to interpret the historical **reception** of Schubert, in particular the sense of difference (see **alterity**) between the music of Beethoven and Schubert (McClary 1994).

Other ways in which the new musicology has attempted to explore contemporary methodologies include Rose Rosengard Subotnik's use of philosophical and linguistic criticism, developing, for example, an insightful interpretation of Beethoven's late style, a post-**Enlightenment** reading of Mozart's *Die Zauberflöte* (1791) and a musical deconstruction of Chopin's prelude in A major, Op. 98, no. 7 (1828–9; Subotnik 1991, 1996). Nineteenth-century opera and instrumental music has been a particular focus of revisionary interest, particularly in the work of Carolyn Abbate, for example her book *Unsung Voices* (Abbate 1991), which, among others, considers the music of Wagner and Mahler. Abbate's work is significant for its interdisciplinarity and imaginative rereadings of standard repertoire (see **narrative**). The new musicology has also initiated debate concerning the nature of **authenticity** in music (see Taruskin 1995), relating this issue to the dichotomy between modern and postmodern perspectives.

The first significant call for a change in musicology was Joseph Kerman's article, 'How We Got into Analysis, and How to Get Out', originally published in 1980, in which he pleaded for a 'new breadth and flexibility in academic music criticism [musicology]' (Kerman 1994, 30). This article was followed by Kerman's book *Musicology* (*Contemplating Music* in America; Kerman 1985), which presents a more detailed account of the context for the developments that were to lead to the new musicology. Interpretations of Kerman's work, and of developments in musicology since the mid-1980s, have largely been presented by academics whose own interests originated in music theory, analysis or **aesthetics** (see Agawu 1997; Cook 1998a; van den Toorn 1995; Williams 2001). Van den Toorn is especially resistant to the new musicology's call to abandon close readings of musical works. Agawu, while presenting grounds on which to question the new musicology's claims, stresses the place of music theory within the broader notion of music criticism and therefore seeks not only a justification of close reading but also a more self-critical theoretical approach. Further responses to the new musicology are also to be found in the attempted formation of a **critical musicology**, and critical assessments of the work of new musicologists are already beginning to appear (Cook and Everist 1999; Head 2002; Krims 1998b).

Further reading: Abbate 2001; Kramer 1993b, 1995; McClary 2000

ORGANICISM

Organicism reflects the idea that the musical work is an organism in which parts combine together as a functioning whole, appropriating the **body** as a **metaphor** for the musical **work**. It therefore restates the concept of musical unity as defined through music **analysis**, but it does so through the specific notions of growth, expansion and transformation, all of which play with organicist images of both nature (see Solie 1980) and body.

The ideas that underlie a musical organicism were common currency in the eighteenth and nineteenth centuries and were most clearly articulated in the philosophy of Hegel. According to Hegel, 'if the work is a genuine work of art, the more exact the detail the greater the unity of the whole' (le Huray and Day 1981, 341). This is a statement about the unity of the art work, and it is significant that Hegel relates the condition of unity to **value** ('a genuine work of art'), a move that will be restated throughout the history of musicology (see **analysis**). This condition of unity is founded upon the assumptions of organicism through the claimed relationships between part and whole, a process that Hegel relates directly to music: 'Now of course inner organisation and overall coherence are equally essential in music, because each part depends on the existence of the others' (*ibid.*, 341). This dependency leads to the musical elements coalescing into a functioning, organic whole. For Hegel, a unified organicism was a representation of the 'Absolute Idea'. This complex philosophical construct is well summarized by musicologist Wayne D. Bowman:

> Absolute idea is neither abstract nor subjective. Rather, it is that ultimate concrete reality toward which understanding and experience constantly strain. All of human history – indeed, the evolution of the entire universe – consists in absolute idea coming increasingly to fruition by infusing the 'material' with Spirit. Eventually, through a succession of stages of ever-increasing self-awareness, mind is destined to achieve full comprehension of the absolute unity of all that is. In absolute idea, conception and reality (thought and its objects) coalesce into a state of complete unity.
>
> (Bowman 1998, 95)

In other words, an evolutionary process, that of growth, leads to the recognition of a prevailing unity formed around concept and reality.

Such organicist ideas find a ready reflection in music and musicological activity. Composers have often described their music in terms of metaphors of growth and relationships between part and whole. Music analysis provides the most immediate context in which such ideas are enacted. The writings of music theorist Heinrich Schenker are enclosed within and defined by organicist assumptions. In the introduction to his major work, translated as *Free Composition*, Schenker states: 'I here present a new concept, one inherent in the works of the great masters; indeed, it is the very secret and source of their being: the concept of organic coherence' (Schenker 1979, xxi).

For Schenker, the musical materials become a life force that rises to the ideal form of a predesignated musical structure, with concept and its realization coalescing into a unity. Through this process, the musical materials act in a manner that is parallel to the human organism: 'Even the octave, fifth, and third of the harmonic series are a product of the organic activity of the tone as subject, just as the urges of the human being are organic' (*ibid.*, 9).

Other music theorists and analysts have invoked organicism as both a guiding principle and desired outcome for their project. Rudolph Réti, although very different in many respects to Schenker, confronted the same music, that of the tonal tradition from Bach to Brahms, and again raised the issue of an organic unity. While Schenker was preoccupied with the unity of harmony and counterpoint, Réti focused more exclusively on the thematic dimension of music, one of his major books being titled *The Thematic Process in Music* (Réti 1961). His study of Beethoven's piano sonatas (Réti 1992) begins with an extended analysis of the Piano Sonata in C minor, Op. 13 (the *Pathétique*, 1797–8). This analysis begins with the two so-called 'prime cells' of the work, the first of which consists merely of a rising minor third from C to E♭, while the second falls from A♭ to D and then rises to E♭. For Réti, these two cells form the essence of the work: 'The basic thematic idea of the *Pathétique*, the core of its structural life, will be found to be a combination of *these two cells*. It will be seen that all the shapes throughout the whole sonata – the themes, groups and sections – are formed from, and are variants of, these two elements' (*ibid.*, 17). Réti's analysis is based upon an **interpretation** that effectively grows outwards from these two cells; using an organicist metaphor, they become the seeds from which the work grows. Such ideas and their representation were already evident in the theoretical writings of composer Arnold Schoenberg (see **modernism**), who wrote of a musical *Grundgestalt* (basic shape) that shaped and influenced the musical materials and their structure. Schoenberg again enacted a metaphor of organic growth and development through the interplay of similarity and difference as reflected in his terminology of 'developing variation' (Schoenberg 1975; see also Frisch 1984).

Questions as to whether the concept of the musical work as an organic unity, a living organism, lives only in the musicological imagination have been raised. In a statement that has been revisited throughout this book, American musicologist Joseph Kerman states: 'From the standpoint of the ruling ideology, analysis exists for the purpose of demonstrating organicism, and organicism exists for the purpose of validating a certain body of works of art' (Kerman 1994, 15). This statement highlights again the presence and function of organicist thought in analysis and draws attention to the essentially ideological nature of an organicist view of music (see **ideology**). It also highlights the evaluative pressures of the concept. Following Kerman, there have been concerted attempts to displace organicism, but in the immediate context of analysis the preoccupations of unity and the desire to realize the organicist metaphor have proved difficult to supplant.

Further reading: Samson 1999; Street 1989

ORIENTALISM

Orientalism is a concept developed by Edward Said in his book *Orientalism: Western Conceptions of the Orient* (Said 1978). Said identifies an antithesis between the Orient (the Middle East, the Far East, Africa and the Indian subcontinent) and the Occident (Western Europe). According to Said, Orientalism constitutes:

> [A] *distribution* of geopolitical awareness into aesthetic, scholarly, economic, sociological, historical, and philological texts; . . . an *elaboration* not only of basic geographical distinction . . . but also a whole series of 'interests' which, by such means as scholarly discovery, philological analysis, landscape and sociological description, it not only creates but also maintains; it *is*, rather than expresses, a certain *will* or *intention* to understand, in some cases to control, manipulate, even to incorporate, what is a manifestly different (or alternative and novel) world.
>
> (*ibid.*, 12)

This definition points to the possibility that Orientalism may result from a genuine desire to understand a foreign culture, but it appears to conclude that the result is effectively to control and maintain a sense of difference and political imbalance. Said makes a direct link between Orientalism and the imperial projects of nineteenth- and early twentieth-century Europe, stating that it has 'less to do with the Orient than it does with "our" world' (*ibid.*).

In the early nineteenth century, the two most important colonizers, and therefore the two main exponents of Orientalism, were Britain and France, particularly following their battles for control of the Indian subcontinent, which took place in the mid-eighteenth century, and France's subsequent interest in Egypt and the Middle East. Musicologist Mark Everist points out that Orientalism in France changed almost by the decade and that 'Individual operatic works therefore need to be set alongside precise and well-defined phases of Orientalism, and not alongside some essentialised view...that takes no account of the diversities of text and culture' (Everist 1996, 225). This remark reflects a danger, which Said himself notes, of positing 'a unified, historically transcendent Western discourse on the Orient' (*ibid.*, 223). Said suggests that future studies could explore Italian, Dutch, German, and Swiss Orientalism (Said 1978, 24), and in his discussion of Meyerbeer's *Il crociato in Egitto* (1824), Everist considers two types of Orientalism: French, *c.* 1813, and Venetian, *c.* 1824.

Said has claimed that Verdi's *Aida* (1871) presents 'an Orientalised Egypt' (Said 1994, 92). However, this view has been challenged by Paul Robinson, who has remarked that:

> *Aida* is an orientalist opera only if the drama Verdi actually constructed...embodies the ideological project Said ascribes to it. Above all, it is an orientalist opera only if its ideological agenda is significantly embodied in its music.... Things that exist in the text [libretto] and that do not find expression in the music for all practical purposes cease to exist.... If *Aida* is an orientalist opera...it will have to be because of its music.
>
> (Robinson 1993, 135)

The suggestion that an opera is orientalist only in terms of evidence in the music overlooks the role of the librettist, not to mention the visual aspects of production. However, Robinson points to the fact that the opera depicts a militaristic Egypt that is tyrannizing Ethiopia, and as such it would appear to represent an anti-imperialist work – a view supported by Verdi's own lack of sympathy for the Egyptian empire. He further remarks that Egypt is represented by 'European'-sounding music ('regular, diatonic and brassy'; *ibid.*, 136), whereas the Ethiopians are represented by Aida and Amonasro, who draw on more 'exotic' styles (see **style**) when singing of their native land. He also notes that all the opera's exotic music is associated with women, so that 'the antithesis between exotic and non-exotic music in *Aida* comes to seem a code as much for gender difference as for ethnic difference' (see

ethnicity, **alterity**). He therefore concludes that it is Egypt's imperial victims (the Moors, Ethiopians and Egyptian women) who are orientalized by Verdi's music, and that it is best viewed as a political Italian opera – a metaphorical expression of Austria's suppression of Italy – relating back to the *risorgimento* operas of the 1840s.

Orientalism has been applied to a wide range of styles and musical periods (see **periodization**), including the *alla Turca* style adopted by composers such as Haydn, Mozart and Beethoven, and the *style Hongrois* used by Liszt. In this sense, Orientalism can be seen to overlap with ethnicity, gender, and **race** issues. Crucial to the discussion of Orientalism is an awareness of the historical context of a given example. In his consideration of Mozart's *Die Entführung aus dem Serail* (1781), Matthew Head points out that 'the historical-cultural distance that separates modern listeners from later eighteenth-century Vienna ensures that Orientalism says different things today than it may have been intended, perceived or even permitted to say "back then"' (Head 2000, 11). He also suggests that Orientalism can be understood as having been a mask through which composers were able to critique the customs of their own time. An example of this is the contrast between the sense of danger that erupts as, in one instance, oriental material in Mozart's opera 'exceeds in length and intensity the formal, stylistic and generic boundaries signalled by the courtly-minuet refrain' (*ibid.*, 12; see **genre**). Compared with the oriental music, the courtly minuet that seeks to contain it sounds 'dainty', echoing Jean-Jacques Rousseau's **Enlightenment** critique of a 'feeble bodied, ornately attired aristocracy'. Head's study is responsible for extending the application of Said's ideas back in time, embracing a period that pre-dates significant empire building by Britain and France, and it therefore calls for slightly different interpretative strategies. Similarly, applications of Orientalism to twentieth-century music, including **popular music** and **jazz**, would necessarily stretch the original intentions of the theory. However, music that draws on exoticism will always contain a trace of orientalist **ideology**, whether it is the *japanisme* of Debussy's piano music or the use of the sitar in recordings by the Beatles.

Further reading: Bellman 1998b; Clifford 1988; Macfie 2002; Scott 1998; Turner 1994; Yegenoglu 1998

PERFORMANCE *see* **authenticity, canon, historical musicology, interpretation, recording**

PERIODIZATION

Musicology has consistently periodized music history, musical **style** and composers' careers (see **biography**). Distinct historical periods have been seen to provide a manageable framework through which specific musical stylistic groupings or periods – Baroque, Classical, Romantic – can be interpreted (see **interpretation**). Representative of this approach is Grout's monumental history of music (Grout and Palisca 2001), which, through many editions over a period of time, has provided one of the standard narratives (see **narrative**) of music history (see **historiography**).

Within certain chronological parameters, specific styles or style periods are widely represented in the musicological literature. Charles Rosen, in his influential study of the Classical style, which he situates in relation to the late eighteenth century, produces a study that is concerned with detailed aspects of musical **language** and style (Rosen 1971, 19). In contrast, American musicologist James Webster has produced a focused and detailed study of Viennese 'Classicism' that expands upon the processes and problems of periodization from a contemporary perspective: 'At the beginning of the twenty-first century, the traditional periodization of European music between 1700 and 1975 – late Baroque; Classical; Romantic; modern – seems increasingly problematic' (Webster 2001–2, 108). The process becomes problematic because much contemporary critical thought (see **postmodernism**) has cast doubt on the validity of the narratives and strategies that underpin the notion of a historical period, a construct that carries an image of a totality. Webster subverts this possibility through his suggestion of a 'first Viennese Modernism' (see **modernism**) and the 'delayed nineteenth century'. The proposal of a first Viennese modernism implies new continuities but also departs from the standard linear succession as outlined above (*ibid.*, 115).

Webster's 'delayed nineteenth century' has a certain parallel with interpretations that seek to displace or disrupt historical models based upon century-long periods, such as the common reference to a 'long eighteenth century'. The history of the twentieth century has been described as 'the long twentieth century' by Giovanni Arrighi (Arrighi 1994), a description that is based on the relationships between the historical development of capitalism and the twentieth century. In contrast, Marxist historian Eric Hobsbawm proposes a 'short twentieth century', bounded by the First World War and the collapse of communism (Hobsbawm 1995). The construction of a historical period on the basis of seminal events is a highly logical strategy, particularly as those selected by Hobsbawm had such a profound effect on **culture**, reflecting the shift from **modernism** to **postmodernism** (see Gloag 2001).

The life and work of individual composers are also subject to periodization, often using issues such as **place** as a reference point. The positioning of a composer's 'early' or 'late' period often produces interesting debates. Beethoven is a powerful example of a composer who has been subjected to this process, with a wide **discourse** formed around his late period and style (see Solomon 2003). The life and work of Michael Tippett is more resistant to periodization than some composers, including Beethoven, but he does provide an interesting scenario, with a shift into a late period occurring, according to British musicologist David Clarke, at a specific point in a specific work – the beginning of the slow movement of the Triple Concerto for violin, viola and cello and orchestra (1978–9) – a claim that is remarkable for its degree of specificity (Clarke 2001, 211).

Because of its compressed nature, the history of **popular music** is often constructed in relation to decades rather than centuries. A distinct moment, such as 'the sixties' (see Marwick 1998; Gloag 2001), is often described in historical terms, but it also presents a number of problems. Much of what is both remembered and written about as history did not come into focus until 1963 and the emergence of the Beatles, while many definitive issues of the popular culture of the 1960s continued to resonate into the early 1970s. In other words, what is now historically conceptualized as 'the sixties' did not begin in 1960 or end in 1969/70. This example, like Hobsbawm's 'short twentieth century' or Webster's 'delayed nineteenth century', suggests that the fluidity of the past is not easily contained within large-scale constructs, but it also indicates that the concept of periodization continues to provide useful reference points for our understanding of history.

See also: **historicism**, **Renaissance**, **Romanticism**, **tradition**

Further reading: Dahlhaus 1983a, 1989b, 1989c; Webster 2004

PLACE

A concept that has received increasing attention in the social sciences since the mid-1980s, place has been considered in relation to a wide range of topics, including Aristotle's concept of place (Morison 2002) and Christian theology (Inge 2003). Spatial concepts such as place and

landscape have gained in importance as a result of the relativism of postmodern theories (see **postmodernism**; see also Soja 1989; Harvey 1990; Jameson 1991) and **globalization**, a concept that draws attention to the role of the local in relation to the global (Verstraete and Cresswell 2002). Place is also highly relevant to considerations of **identity**, **gender**, **ethnicity**, **race** and **subjectivity**, all of which have a discursive, reflexive relationship with place.

Consideration of place in relation to music has informed historical and cultural studies, such as Carl E. Schorske's book on *fin-de-siècle* Vienna (Schorske 1981) and Tia DeNora's study of the construction of the idea of Beethoven's **genius** in Vienna (DeNora 1997), as well as work on **Renaissance** music that draws on urban historical methodology (see Kisby 2001). These examples illustrate the importance that places may have in fostering specific genres (see **genre**) and styles (see **style**), and they indicate the potential that consideration of place has for reappraising historical periods (see **periodization**) and our understanding of musical **reception**. The role of sound **recording** has also been discussed in relation to place; for example, Adam Krims has explored how recording may be used to construct living and consumer spaces (Krims 2001).

Place has always been a central concern of ethnomusicology, and more recently this can be seen to have influenced work on **popular music**, a feature that can be traced back to Charles Keil's study of blues music in Chicago (Keil 1966). Other important contributions in this area include Sara Cohen's study of rock culture in Liverpool (Cohen 1991) and Barry Shank's book on the popular music scene in Austin, Texas (Shank 1994). Cohen was concerned to explore what she called the 'ethnographic and microsociological detail' of the Liverpool music scene, 'the grass roots of the industry – the countless, as yet unknown bands struggling for success at a local level' (Cohen 1991, 6). In contrast, Shank, drawing on the psychoanalytical theories of Jacques Lacan, is concerned with the divergence and dissonance between different musical identities. At the centre of his study is the idea that the cultural function of musical 'scenes' is to enable people to perform 'new, sometimes temporary but nevertheless significant, identities' (Shank 1994, x). Similar ideas are discussed with great skill by George Lipsitz in his wide-ranging consideration of immigrant and diasporic music, including Puerto Rican music in New York and black reggae in London (Lipsitz 1997). Hip-hop has also received much attention in terms of analyses of its relationship with space and place. As studies such as those by Murray Forman (Forman 2002) and Adam Krims (Krims 2000) illustrate, central to hip-hop are **narrative** themes, expressed in the music's textures and lyrics, concerning real and imagined ideas about contested space. As a result of globalization, these themes 'can be heard in other languages around the world, expressed with a shared emphasis on spatial location and identity formation but informed by radically varied contexts and environments' (Forman 2002, 18).

Further reading: Bennett 2000; Leyshon *et al.* 1998

POLITICS *see* **class, culture industry, ethnicity, identity, ideology, Marxism, race**

POPULAR MUSIC

Popular music is a term that describes music that achieves a sense of popularity or strives to be popular. It is often used interchangeably with its abbreviation 'pop' and the associated term 'rock'. Popular music has evolved as a generalization that encompasses multifarious musical styles (see **style**) and practices, much of which can be seen to be situated within a commercially driven entertainment-based industry (see **culture industry**). Each specific **culture** (nation, region) can be seen to generate its own popular music in some shape or form, but the term has become synonymous with American and Anglo-American music (see **globalization**). Given the diversity of what popular music has come to incorporate, the term is inevitably resistant to definition and classification. Popular music in itself may not be a concept as such, but it is a musical context that is replete with concepts, and its **interpretation** requires the application of conceptual thought. While popular music has effectively evolved its own musicology in the form of popular music studies (see Shuker 1998), recent developments, such as **critical musicology**, have helped to form new insights into popular music that positively subvert the separation of music into categories of 'high' and 'low', art and popular.

One common interpretation of popular music has viewed it as inherently inferior to the 'high' culture of classical music. This alleged inferiority of popular music is most clearly marked in the writings of German critical theorist Theodor Adorno (see **critical theory**). In an article first published in 1941, Adorno saw popular music as 'characterized by its difference from serious music'. In this characterization, the music is defined through a common 'standardization', and any sense of individuality or difference is explained as 'pseudo-individualization' that is manipulated by the **culture industry**, clearly a highly negative interpretation that focuses exclusively on recurrent features (standardization) and negates the exceptional nature and individual identity of much popular music (Adorno 1994). Other recurrent definitions of popular music focus on social/sociological frameworks, seeing it as products of certain social groupings (see **class**). However, while it is certainly relevant to view some aspects of popular music as the expression of or response to specific socio-economic circumstances at a specific historical moment, this does not take account of generational change and social mobility: changing social and/or economic circumstances may come to have as great an impact on an individual's subjective response to the music as did the contexts from which the music originally emerged (see **subjectivity**). Nevertheless, the sociology of popular music remains important, and the social, collective dimension plays a significant part in both the production and consumption of the music. However, rather than pursuing an essentially singular and restricted definition of popular music, it is perhaps best to positively embrace its ambiguities and differences (see **alterity**), and view popular music as a fluid, changing musical landscape that has certain recurring characteristics and concerns but also powerful potential to change as part of a drive towards diversification within an ongoing interaction of musical, social and economic discourses (see **discourse**).

In contrast to a sociological understanding of popular music, a specifically music-oriented approach has evolved that provides an analytical focus (see **analysis**) on the music as the 'primary text' (Moore 2001a) and wider discussions of what actually constitutes the text in a popular music context (Middleton 2000c).

A type of popular music can be seen to have existed in many different historical epochs and contexts, including the continuing existence of folk music traditions and the self-conscious search for popularity by some musicians and composers, but a specific sense of a popular music **tradition** and context is most clearly active in the twentieth century. With the rise of **modernism**, and an ongoing process of technological innovation – film, sound recording, television, video – generating the contexts in which popular music is both constructed and disseminated, the music found its place in a wider notion of a popular culture (see **recording**). Clearly, the pre-Second World War era was less marked by this process, and the musical categories that existed, all of which could in some sense be defined as 'popular' – blues, **jazz**, swing, among others – although disseminated through recordings, were essentially defined through the spontaneity of live performance. In the case of the blues, the transformation from an oral folk tradition to an electric urban sound (for example through Chess Records in Chicago) would become a formative **influence** on later popular music styles (see **place**). The pre-war period also witnessed, in conjunction with cinema, the emergence of the personality cult of the performer as star, with Frank Sinatra providing a powerful example of this phenomenon.

Most historical narratives of popular music (see **historiography**, **narrative**) focus on its development from the 1950s (see Gillett 1983) to the present, with a succession of styles contained within a historical chronology (see **periodization**). In this history, the 1950s and the emergence of rock 'n' roll assumes a seminal status, with the early recordings of Elvis Presley, for example, positioned as an almost mythical point of origin. Great attention is also given to the music of the 1960s, as defined through the Beatles, and rock-based narratives of the 1970s (see **canon**), but it is clear that this period also witnessed a separation of the popular music audience, often along generational lines, and a new diversification of style.

The processes of fragmentation and diversification that emerged from the later 1960s continued and indeed intensified in the subsequent development of popular music (see **postmodernism**). This is evident through the multiplicity of styles and terms that coexist at the present moment (indie, r&b, rap, hip-hop, trip-hop and many others). Each of these styles appears to have the potential to attract its own, often exclusive, audience, a fact that further undermines any notion of a singular culture. The pluralization of popular music can now be seen to be a reflection of a wider social and historical process. It suggests that popular music, rather than being just a reflection of this process, is an active agent in its construction and a definitive statement of a contemporary postmodern condition.

See also: **authenticity**, **cover versions**, **criticism**, **ethnicity**, **gender**, **subject position**

Further reading: Frith 1996; Longhurst 1995; Middleton 1990; Palmer 1996; Strinati 1995

POSITIVISM

Positivism reflects a view of the world and conception of knowledge which believes that knowledge and, by implication, **interpretation**, can only be validated through an evident proof. It therefore reflects a scientific determination by which evidence is tested, and a hypothesis is either rejected or accepted on the basis of a proven truth. While positivism has a long history in philosophy and has regularly been subject to critique, the rise of positivist thought coincided with the emergence of industrialization in the nineteenth century, with its processes of rationalization reflecting science while also placing new demands on it. There are several writers and texts from the nineteenth century that reflect the scientific aura of positivism. Hermann von Helmholtz, who was a physicist and psychologist and was interested in the philosophical and aesthetic issues of the period, considered 'the sensations of tone' and commented upon Hanslick's *Vom Musikalisch Schönen* (On the Musically Beautiful) (see **aesthetics**, **autonomy**, **meaning**), embracing what Bojan Bujić describes as 'Hanslick's anti-emotionalist stance' (Bujić 1988, 276; see also Helmholtz 1954). Hanslick's own view of music as 'tonally moving forms' (Hanslick 1986, 29) again reflects the positivistic **ideology** of the period. Other theorists and writers who reflected this scientific engagement with music include Edmund Gurney, whose *The Power of Sound* was published in 1880 and considered the distinction that could be made between 'the two ways of hearing sound' based on the 'definite or indefinite character of music'. These 'two modes of effect' connect with 'perception and non-perception of form' and therefore lead to the 'definite character of music involving the perception of individual melodic and harmonic combinations, the indefinite character involving merely the perception of successions of agreeably-toned and harmonious sound' (Bujić 1988, 292–3). This view, with its concern with the act of listening and related issues of perception, reflects a positivist perspective that seeks to establish a degree of scientific certainty enclosed within a quasi-scientific language. These issues of listening and perception will be revisited in later musicology (see **psychology**).

Many recurrent aspects of musicology can readily be seen as a reflection of positivism. The study of historical documents through issues such as the attribution of a manuscript (see **historical musicology**), and the attempt to determine what constitutes a formal structure for an individual **work** (see **analysis**), are reflections of positivistic thought that, in the case of analysis, can often assume a scientific aura (see Forte 1973). This reflection is questioned by Joseph Kerman in his overview of musicology published in 1985. According to Kerman, 'Musicology is perceived as dealing essentially with the factual, the documentary, the verifiable, the analysable, the positivistic.

Musicologists are respected for the facts they know about music. They are not admired for their insight into music as aesthetic experience' (Kerman 1985, 12). For Kerman, musicology needed to move towards a broader, more humane condition: 'What I uphold and try to practise is a kind of musicology orientated towards criticism, a kind of criticism orientated towards history' (ibid., 19). This opening up of musicology and the proposed shift from a fact-based perspective is one of the paths that, in retrospect, could be seen to lead to the emergence of contemporary developments of new and critical musicologies (see **critical musicology**, **new musicology**) that seek to replace the ideology of positivism, along with concepts such as **formalism** and autonomy, with a wider sense of **interpretation** (see **hermeneutics**).

POST-COLONIAL/POSTCOLONIALISM

The term post-colonial entered political theory in the 1970s to describe the predicament of nations that, following the Second World War, ceased to be part of European empires. By the 1980s, the term was also being used in literary criticism, the history of law, anthropology, political economy, philosophy, **historiography**, art history, and psychoanalysis (see Ashcroft et al. 2002). In the 1990s, the unhyphenated form of the word appeared following the establishment of the term in general and the rise of postcolonial **discourse** theory, which was heavily influenced by **post-structuralism**.

Key contributors to postcolonial discourse theory include cultural theorists Gayatri Spivak, Edward Said and Homi Bhabha, all of whom were born and brought up in regions of the world that had experienced colonialism (Said from Palestine, Spivak and Bhabha from India) but became established at American universities. Edward Said was one of the first to draw attention to the need to investigate the system of discourse by which the world is ordered, administered and divided into self (the 'human' colonizers) and Other (the 'inhuman' colonized peoples) (Said 1978, 1994). This gave rise to a consideration of material previously overlooked, such as travel writing, letters and autobiographies, as well as literature, art and music. Said's work on **Orientalism** has been directly absorbed into musicology, in particular in relation to nineteenth-century opera (see Robinson 1993; Everist 1996).

Where Said apparently views the relationship between colonizer and colonized as fixed and homogeneous, Bhabha describes it as a nervous condition of fantasy and desire, emphasizing instead the ambivalence and heterogeneity of colonial discourse. Bhabha has argued that one result of colonialism is **hybridity**, as the distinction between the colonizer and the colonized is apparently broken down. In reality, the condition is often one in which the colonized mimic or parody the colonizers, either to fit in or to subvert the ruling power (Bhabha 1994). Spivak's work has centred on subaltern groups, those that do not belong to the ruling classes and whose indigenous position often means that they have had no voice in the construction of history. More specifically, she is concerned to point out that while postcolonial discourse theory may speak for subaltern groups, there is no such thing as a single subaltern **identity**. She has illustrated this point by stressing the need to situate discussion of the colonial or post-colonial individual in his or her specific gendered, social, geographical and historical context in order to better understand varying colonial and post-colonial experiences (Spivak 1994).

The musicologists most closely associated with the issues raised by these theorists are ethnomusicologists. American ethnomusicologist Philip V. Bohlman has noted the moral imperative of ethnologists working on indigenous music to reflect as closely as possible the particulars of the music and its forms of practice, to insist on its difference (see **alterity**) from Western practice (Bohlman 1992, 132). Although detailed transcriptions and associated commentaries of non-Western music may reveal the inadequacies of Western notation, they may also narrow, rather than enforce, the gap imposed by colonialism.

According to Vijay Mishra and Bob Hodge, the term postcolonial:

> foregrounds a politics of opposition and struggle, and problematizes the key relationship between centre and periphery. It has helped to destabilize the barriers around 'English literature' that protected the primacy of the **canon** and the self-evidence of its standards.
>
> (Mishra and Hodge 1994, 276)

This description points to the degree of overlap that exists between considerations of postcolonialism and other inquiries for which the notions of periphery and centre are crucial, such as **canon**, **gender** (see also **gay musicology**) and **alterity**. From the specific viewpoint of resisting empire and colonialism, a good example in music is that of Bartók and other Eastern European composers of the early twentieth century, who attempted to resist and critique the prevailing Austro-Hungarian Empire. In Bartók's case, this was expressed through his assertion of the Hungarian language and the revitalization of indigenous folk material in a modernist context (see **modernism**; see also Brown 2000).

Further links between music and empire can be traced back at least as far as the seventeenth and eighteenth centuries, when attempts were made by the French, German and British to account for music from outside Europe – mainly that of China and America. These accounts reflect a growing desire for non-Western difference (see Young 1995), and they usually focused on musical accomplishments. Although this approach reflects the eighteenth-century **Enlightenment** belief in the equality of men, the eventual growth of colonies and empires contradicted this view. Such ambiguities are reflected in some of Mozart's music, for example his varied treatment of the Turkish character Osmin in *Die Entführung aus dem Serail* (1781). Given the history of Turkish rule in Eastern Europe under the Ottoman Empire, it is interesting to hear Mozart's musical characterization of Osmin ranging from admiration to revulsion (Head 2000). Mozart's views were in sympathy with those of French philosopher Jean-Jacques Rousseau, a key contributor to the French Enlightenment who, despite reservations about certain aspects of non-Western civilizations, believed that indigenous peoples had an instinctive 'natural ability', especially for activities such as music. In fact, Rousseau believed that the origins of Western music and language could be found in the primitive 'speech-songs' of 'native peoples'. As colonial interests shifted towards Africa in the nineteenth century, so did the work of ethnomusicologists, although, according to Radano and Bohlman, 'these later studies commonly positioned foreign musics in a decidedly inferior status in ways consistent with the growing orthodoxy of racialist opinion, laden as it was with the pernicious claims of Social Darwinism' (Radano and Bohlman 2000, 17).

In the early twentieth century, the practice of ethnomusicology was encouraged by some institutions, such as the Schola Cantorum in Paris. At this time, such work was closely linked to modernist compositional **aesthetics**, and this has been explored in some detail by musicologist Jann Pasler in an essay on French composer/ethnomusicologists Albert Roussel and Maurice Delage (Pasler 2000). Interest in non-Western music and the cultures of Africa and Asia were of central concern in the establishment of modernist aesthetics, a fact demonstrated by the collections of African masks assembled by Picasso around 1907 and reflected in his painting *Les Demoiselles d'Avignon* from the same year. The French had been responsive to African art for some time before this, as illustrated by the Universal Expositions of 1878, 1889 and 1900, and during the 1920s and 1930s this interest prevailed in the music of Milhaud, Antheil and Ravel. Milhaud's ballet *La Création du Monde* (1923) constitutes a very typical early modernist attempt to fuse contemporary experience (Milhaud's experience of listening to black jazz musicians in Harlem) with an ideological belief in a primitive Other (his belief in the 'negro soul'), together with an orientalist conception of African music (see Gendron 2002).

Later twentieth-century examples of modernism's continued fascination with orientalist conceptions can be found in the experimental works of composers such as John Cage (his *Sonatas and Interludes* (1948) for prepared piano evokes the bell and gong sounds of Balinese gamelan), Harry Partch and Lou Harrison. John Corbett has considered these composers, as well as the responses of the American experimental jazz musician and composer John Zorn to the music of Japan (Corbett 2000). Corbett even notes that in the case of the Chinese composer Tan Dun the usual paradigm of orientalist appropriation is turned on its head, as Cage-like nature sounds are sent 'back' to China, where they are greeted as exotic items. The music of later twentieth-century Americans, in particular, embrace **globalization** through their tendency to mix a range of non-Western sounds from unspecified origins, in some cases in order to develop a form of 'world music'. However, working from the opposite end of the spectrum, minority ethnic groups in Western countries may appropriate popular genres in order to convey culture-specific knowledge that, inevitably and deliberately, privileges the position of certain listeners. An example of this is the music of Cornershop, especially their songs using Hindi or hybrid English/Punjabi lyrics, as well as drones and sitars. In this way, Cornershop's music can be compared to post-colonial texts such as Salman Rushdie's *The Satanic Verses* (1988), which 'can draw on an indigenous precursor tradition that has some of the features of **postmodernism**' (Mishra and Hodge 1994, 283).

Further reading: Hyder 2004; Moore-Gilbert 1997; Spivak 1999; Young 2001

POSTMODERNISM

The concept of postmodernism, and the ideas that it both envelops and reflects, has enjoyed wide usage in most cultural contexts and has increasingly been used in relation to musicological thought and contemporary musical practices. However, it remains a term that is highly resistant to definition. According to Hans Bertens, 'Postmodernism is an exasperating term, and so are postmodern, postmodernist, post-modernity, and whatever else one might come across in the way of derivation' (Bertens 1995, 3). This exasperation echoes Linda Hutcheon's claim that:

> Few words are more used and abused in discussions of con-temporary **culture** than the word 'postmodernism'. As a result, any attempt to define the word will necessarily and simulta-neously have both positive and negative dimensions. It will aim to say what postmodernism is but at the same time it will have to say what postmodernism is not.
>
> (Hutcheon 1989, 1)

These positive and negative dimensions look towards the problematic relationship between postmodernism and **modernism**. Does it imply a rejection of modernism ('what postmodernism is not')? Alternatively, might the implication that modernism is left intact after the prefix 'post' open up a more positive dimension that can suggest some degree of continuity between the two concepts?

The understanding of postmodernism as a rejection of modernism is most clearly articulated in the philosophy of Jean-Francois Lyotard. His *The Postmodern Condition* (Lyotard 1992), originally published in France in 1979, had a great impact on contemporary thought and continues to have a remarkable legacy. Lyotard begins with a seemingly straightforward definition of modernism: 'I will use the term *modern* to designate any science that legitimates itself with reference to a meta-discourse [see **discourse**] ... making an explicit appeal to some grand narrative' (*ibid.*, xxiii). This statement is usually interpreted as defining modernism through all-embracing, totalizing narratives (see **narrative**). In contrast, Lyotard describes postmodernism as 'incredulity toward metanarratives' (*ibid.*, xxiv), and later he states that 'the little narrative remains the quintessential form of imaginative invention' (*ibid.*, 60). In other words, we can no longer believe in the grand meta-narratives of modernism and therefore the focus shifts to the micro-narratives ('the little narratives') of postmodernism: from the large to the small, from the singular to the plural. There is a great deal of evidence to support this claim. Many would accept that we live in a more plural, fragmented cultural context than in the past. This is certainly the case with music. Many different musical styles coexist without there being any culturally dominant set of values (see **value**) or definitive **style**. This is most clearly evident in **popular music**, which in its contemporary manifestations articulates a myriad of changing styles and genres (see **genre**).

However, it is equally possible to challenge the claims made for postmodernism. Musical modernism, for example, although driven by utopian and progressive aesthetic imperatives (see **aesthetics**), did contain its own plurality, as reflected by the very different musical practices of Schoenberg and Stravinsky, and was often also a culture of fragmentation, even if that dimension was ultimately resisted in much modernist thought. Although our contemporary culture may be increasingly fragmented into plural micro-narratives, the apparent homogeneity of the political and economic contexts, as reflected in current debates on **globalization**, suggests a more complex picture than some aspects of postmodern thought might allow.

The problematics of defining the relationship between modernism and postmodernism and, by implication, the relationship between past and present, introduces the possibility of thinking of postmodernism as history in conjunction with the adjacent issue of **periodization**. The evocation of history is most clearly made in the writings of Fredric Jameson, who, through his use of a late Marxist agenda (see **Marxism**), creates a unique perspective on the concept. Jameson seeks to situate postmodernism within a recognizable historical framework while being alive to the paradoxes involved in this exercise: 'It is safest to grasp the concept of the postmodern as an attempt to think the present historically in an age that has forgotten how to think historically in the first place' (Jameson 1991, ix). This process of thinking the history of the present manifests itself in specific musical practices. The increased self-conscious quotation of the past, as reflected in the music of Wolfgang Rihm and Heiner Goebbels, for example, produces an intertextual postmodern music (see **intertextuality**). These musical representations provide a reflection of Umberto Eco's 'postmodern attitude', which involves accepting 'the challenge of the past, of the already said, which cannot be eliminated' (Eco 1985, 67).

Jameson also seeks to project postmodernism into a specific historical location. He draws attention to the juncture between the late 1950s and early 1960s, suggesting that any notion of a postmodernism 'depends on the hypothesis of some radical break ... generally traced back to the end of the 1950s or early 1960s' (Jameson 1991, 1). This proposal has clear musical resonance, with the radical changes of musical styles and languages (see **language**) throughout the 1960s now seen as a reflection of postmodernism (see also Harvey 1990; Jameson 1988; Gloag 2001).

Although Jameson seeks to configure postmodernism as history, he, like Lyotard, embraces fragmentation and difference as the cultural norm, but this now becomes part of a distinction between style and history:

> The conception of postmodernism . . . is a historical rather than a merely stylistic one. I cannot stress too greatly the radical distinction between a view for which the postmodern is one (optional) style among many others available and one which seeks to grasp it as the cultural dominant of the logic of late capitalism.
>
> (Jameson 1991, 45–6)

This statement is an accurate reflection of the contemporary situation of music. The already mentioned pluralism of the present creates a range of possible stylistic options, none of which dominates. But this becomes postmodernism as a cultural dominant rather than any specific style being defined as postmodern. Clearly, one of the endless stylistic options in postmodernism is a continuing, ongoing modernism. This possibility allows us to understand the different modernist music of Harrison Birtwistle and Elliot Carter, for example, as stylistic options within the cultural dominant of postmodernism, but from this perspective they cannot in themselves achieve the status of the meta-narrative, which would allow them to be seen as the stylistic norm that is required for the formation of the cultural dominant.

Jameson's reference to late capitalism introduces an interesting political dimension into the concept, one that is explicitly critical of capitalism. Many aspects of postmodern theory, including the work of Lyotard and Baudrillard, have been criticized for being non-political and, by implication, divorced from reality (Norris 1990, 1992). Some music that has become associated with postmodernism (Górecki, Tavener, for example) can also be seen, through its easy accommodation with past traditions, to be stripped of any critical force. From this angle, the plural coexistence of postmodernism leads to a cultural relativism in which anything goes and culture consequently loses its critical value and voice. This alleged flattening of the cultural field leads to the blurring of the distinctions between 'high' art and popular culture, a move that, for some, is seen as a significant manifestation of postmodernism. In the words of Dominic Strinati: 'There are no longer any agreed and inviolable criteria which can serve to differentiate art from popular culture' (Strinati 1995, 225). There is a great deal of truth in this claim. The marketing of classical music, for example, reflects the manipulations of the **culture industry** and its translation of popular media into the world of 'high' art. There are also notable crossovers and collaborations, which add to the blurring of the distinction between the two contexts, with the minimalism of Philip Glass, for example, producing a music that is situated in its own postmodern relationship to both. However, this interpretation is also open to criticism. As Andrew Goodwin points out, the resemblance of Glass's music to popular music is largely superficial, with the structures of performance and **reception** still distinct from popular music (Goodwin 1994).

Many aspects of contemporary musicology have become associated with postmodernism, with the range of topics and issues enclosed by musicology ever widening and fragmenting and therefore reflecting the wider cultural context. The impact of other concepts and contexts, such as **feminism**, **gender** studies, **critical theory** and **cultural studies**, and the resulting interdisciplinarity, can also be interpreted as a further reflection of postmodernism and thus indicative of the possibility of a postmodern musicology.

The **new musicology** is often portrayed as a reflection of a wider postmodernism, with this interaction most vividly present in the work of Lawrence Kramer. According to Kramer: 'The emergence of postmodernist musicologies will depend on our willingness and ability to read as inscribed within the immediacy-effects of music itself the kind of mediating structures usually positioned outside music under the rubric of context' (Kramer 1995, 18). In other words, the construction of a postmodernist musicology will deconstruct the boundaries between the internal and external natures of music (see **deconstruction**), a move that displaces the claims of a formalist musicology (see **formalism**) and the related concept of the autonomous (see **autonomy**) musical **work** while retaining a focus on the music itself. Gary Tomlinson, writing in response to an earlier article by Kramer, goes further, suggesting that:

> we need to move away from the whole constraining notion that close readings of music, of whatever sort, is the sine qua non of musicological practice. This notion has repeatedly pulled us back toward the aestheticism and transcendentalism of earlier ideologies. (I have felt the pull in much of the nascent postmodern musicology I have read and written.) It is not enough to cast our close readings in the light of new methods – narratological, feminist, phenomenological, anthropological, whatever. For it is the close reading itself that carries with it the ideological charge

of modernism. These new methods, instead, need to be linked to new approaches to music that have distanced themselves from such analytically oriented reading. They need, indeed, to be allowed to engender such new approaches.

(Tomlinson 1993a, 21–2)

For Tomlinson, then, it is not enough to read context in the content of music; we need to escape the ideological grasp (see **ideology**) exerted by a modernist fetishization of the work and its related 'close readings' (see **analysis**). There are significant differences between the views of Kramer and Tomlinson (see Kramer 1993a), and as current patterns of contemporary musicology develop there are further reflections of both positions, but these differences also provide an apt reflection of a musicology that is increasingly shaped by the pluralities and differences of the wider cultural and intellectual landscape of postmodernism.

Further reading: Cahoone 1996; Lochhead and Auner 2002; Miller 1993; Vattimo 1988; Williams 2000

POST-STRUCTURALISM

This is a general movement of thought and ideas in various fields that grew out of **structuralism** but also reacted against the dominance of its precursor. This movement was most clearly defined in the work of a number of French theorists and writers during the 1960s.

Post-structuralism shares structuralism's focus on **language** and its network of meanings (see **meaning**), but it ultimately rejects the possibility that its study can be that of an objective science. From this perspective, post-structuralism can be seen to embrace new levels of **subjectivity** and difference (see **alterity**). It becomes in effect a conceptual space in which possible theoretical paths occur rather than a theoretical paradigm. The reconsideration of language is most clearly defined in the seminal work of French philosopher Jacques Derrida, in which the seemingly stable binaries of de Saussure's model of language are deconstructed and new multiplicities of meaning are explored (see **deconstruction**).

The shift from a structuralist to a post-structuralist mode of thought was most clearly outlined in the work of French literary theorist Roland Barthes. His *Mythologies*, originally published in 1957 (Barthes 1973) analyzed a wide range of social and cultural phenomena in terms of their underlying structures, and this book played a significant part in the wider dissemination of structuralism. However, Barthes also looked to new possibilities and was alive to intellectual change. His essay 'The Death of the Author', for example, argued for interpretation ('the birth of the reader') as the site of meaning in the literary context, a move that shifted the focus from the construction of language as structure towards the plural possibilities of **interpretation** (Barthes 1977, 142–8). Barthes's later work of the 1970s, such as *S/Z* (Barthes 1990b) and *The Pleasure of the Text* (Barthes 1990a), still often concerns itself with language, but by this stage any theoretical precision and analytical rigour is replaced by what may be understood as an idiosyncratic subjectivity that refers to and draws from any number of sources and objects.

Roland Barthes also wrote about music. The essays collected in *The Responsibility of Forms* (Barthes 1985) contain some fleeting but fascinating insights into music. The essay 'The Romantic Song' begins with a reference to Schubert:

> Once again, tonight, I am listening to the opening phrase of the andante of Schubert's first trio – a perfect phrase, at once unitary and divided, an *amorous* phrase, if ever there was one – and once again I realise how difficult it is to talk about what one loves. What is there to say about what one loves except: I *love it*, and to keep on saying it?
>
> (*ibid.*, 286)

Of course, there is more to say, and Barthes will say it, but it is significant that he is writing about music in what may be described as a romantic manner (see **Romanticism**), with the reference to 'love' reflecting the eroticism that he explored in *The Pleasure of the Text* (Barthes 1990a) and *A Lover's Discourse: Fragments* (Barthes 1990c). The subjectivity of his response reflects what he perceives in the music, but it clearly says more about Barthes (as 'reader'/'listener') rather than about Schubert (as 'author'/'composer'). From this perspective, it reflects a wider post-structuralism. It is still in some sense concerned with language (that of both Barthes and Schubert), but it does not concern itself with issues of 'deep' structure in terms of the music; nor does it engage directly with how language is used to describe and interpret the music. And, most significantly, there is clearly no possible claim to objectivity.

Barthes, like other examples of post-structuralism, does not provide a direct model for music, but clearly musicology has experienced its own shift, which parallels that of structuralism and post-structuralism, and the issues of subjectivity and interpretation raised in Barthes's work will reappear in certain musicological contexts. Music **analysis** functions as the disciplinary context that most clearly reflects a structuralist perspective in that it has generally been concerned with the structures of music and the methods used to identify and explicate structure. However, other forms of musicology have also clearly echoed structuralism's claim of objectivity and its scientific aura, enacting a certain **positivism**: the proving of something, the establishment of fact. This can be seen through the standard accounts of the life and **work** of composers (see **biography**), which seek to establish an accurate account of the composer's life, often with some connection to the music. This does not in itself constitute a structuralism, but in Barthes' terms such writing privileges the composer ('author') over the interpreter ('reader'). Other forms of musicology also have an aura of objectivity and a positivistic drive, evident through musicological activities such as the dating of manuscripts, the identification of a composer's **sketch** material and the compilation of editions of musical works (see **historical musicology**).

That musicology in general, and analysis in particular, projects certain parallels with structuralism suggests that they are susceptible to post-structuralist critiques. The first meaningful attempt to do so came from within the discipline, with American musicologist Joseph Kerman providing an account of musicology that was not really post-structuralist in itself but did reflect some of the issues outlined above. His book *Musicology* (*Contemplating Music* in America; Kerman 1985) provides a wide-ranging summary of the discipline, one that contemplates the interaction between musicology and positivism. More significant in this context is Kerman's essay 'How We Got into Analysis, and How to Get Out' (Kerman 1994). Originally published in 1980, this has had a wide impact, and its issues reflect many concepts discussed in this book (see **analysis**, **criticism**, **formalism**). In this context, we can read Kerman's plea for a 'new breadth and flexibility in academic music criticism' (*ibid.*, 30) as reflecting a post-structuralist suspicion of the certainties of structuralism.

In recent years, new formations of musicology (see **critical musicology**, **new musicology**, **postmodernism**) have reflected Kerman's challenge to musicology but have also mirrored the wider contexts of post-structuralism. Post-structuralism, often intertwined with postmodernism, is present in the wide range of issues and subjects now considered by musicology, but, more significantly, it is also present and active in the perspectives that they are viewed from. Effective examples include the work of Susan McClary, whose feminist perspective (see **feminism**, **gender**) on music is charged with a critical suspicion of concepts related to structuralism, primarily that of the autonomous (see **autonomy**) musical work (McClary 1991), and Lawrence Kramer (Kramer 2002), who projects a wide interdisciplinary perspective and critical engagement that admirably reflects Kerman's 'new breadth and flexibility'.

Further reading: Burke 1993; Engh 1993; Kramer 1995; Moriarty 1991; Subotnik 1996

PSYCHOLOGY

Investigations into musical behaviour and experience are wide-ranging and impinge on studies of all aspects of music, including performance, listening, **theory**, **analysis** and composition. In its strictest sense, the psychology of music amounts to scientifically based empirical studies of perception and cognition in listening. Much of this work has centred on psycho-acoustics – studies of the sensory mechanisms responsible for our perception of pitch, loudness and timbre (Seashore 1967; Deutsch 1982). The main conclusion from this work is that the physical and perceptual properties of sound do not map on to one another directly. For example, the perception of rhythm is only accurate over short time spans (Dibben 2002b). However, at the other end of the spectrum is the growing field of social psychology, which investigates the reciprocal relationship between listeners and their context (see Hargreaves and North 1998). This area includes music therapy (see Pavlicevic 2000), **ethnicity** and **gender** studies, composition, and education. Taste (see **value**) has been demonstrated by social psychologists to be influenced to some degree by social context and demographics, as well as having a reciprocal relationship with a person's **identity** formation. Psychologists have also considered how music may affect consumer behaviour.

The link between emotional response and music, for example in relation to specific events or memories, has also been an important consideration for psychologists (see Sloboda 1991), and external features, such as programme notes and music videos, may influence these responses (Cook and Dibben 2001). Another established area of psychological study is performance and musical expression, including research into the role of the **body** (Davidson 1993; Clarke 1995; see also **recording**), and some studies have argued that biological factors are more important than cultural ones, especially in infant learning (Hill 1997).

The subject of music perception is one that has figured prominently in various analytical studies. An early example of this is the analytical language of Arnold Schoenberg, in which traces of the ideas of Austrian psychoanalyst Sigmund Freud can be detected, in particular in Schoenberg's concept of the *Grundgestalt*, or 'basic shape', from which an entire piece may be shown to evolve (see **modernism**, **organicism**). Attempts have been made to synthesize this concept with the ideas of Austrian music theorist Heinrich Schenker (Epstein 1979). Similarly, Leonard Meyer's consideration of melodic, harmonic and rhythmic implications in tonal music led to Eugene Narmour's implication–realization model, which relates music perception to stylistic expectations (Narmour 1992; see **style**). Also of significance is the work of composer Fred Lerdahl and linguist Ray Jackendoff (Lerdahl and Jackendoff 1983). Influenced by linguist Noam Chomsky, their study is an attempt to form a grammar consisting of a set of rules governing the relationship between the physical sounds of tonal music and the way these are organized in a listener's mind – what they have called a generative theory of tonal music. This grammar consists of a hierarchical grouping of events, although it does not consider how such groups are constructed through repeated listening (see Sloboda 1992).

In an attempt to deal with what he saw as deficiencies in traditional music analysis **discourse**, American music theorist David Lewin produced an important investigation into the division between sound events and our interpretation of them in their tonal context by drawing on Edmund Husserl's phenomenological theories of perception (Lewin 1986; for an account of Husserlian phenomenology – a study of our conscious experience, including accounts of perceiving single tones and melodies – see Miller 1984). Lewin illustrates how the perception of music is dependent upon having a 'well-formed context' for sounds. For example, a proper context is necessary for listeners to distinguish between the first and second bars of Beethoven's *Eroica* Symphony (1806) (both E♭ triads), a distinction that would not be perceived if they were played in isolation (Lewin 1986, 337). He also problematizes the distinction that Husserl makes between acoustic and mental objects. In its emphasis on multiple layers of perception, Lewin's model can be seen to reflect ideas inherent in **post-structuralism** (see also Lerdahl 1989; Morris 1993).

Accounts of particular composers and works have also taken psychoanalytical factors into consideration. In some cases, this may reflect interests that composers themselves have declared, such as Michael Tippett's interest in the work of Carl Jung, in particular the idea of 'image', and the possible implications of this for Tippett's conception of musical form (Clarke 2001). However, Wagner is the composer who has most frequently attracted psychoanalytical interpretation (Donington 1984; Wintle 1992; Žižek and Dolar 2002), although pioneering ideas on music and psychology are present in the work of music critic Hans Keller, as reflected in his development of so-called functional analysis, but especially in his interpretations of *Peter Grimes* (1945) and other operas by Benjamin Britten (Keller 2003).

Further reading: Booth Davies 1980; Meyer 1973; Storr 1992

RACE

Race refers to perceived social differences based on biological essences, such as skin, hair and eye colour. The eighteenth-century **Enlightenment** developed theories about race to present a hierarchical view of the world, with white Europeans at its pinnacle. This view was based on the belief that phenotypical (or somatic) differences determined temperament, **culture**, and human capacities of various kinds. The eighteenth century saw the beginnings of a racist **ideology** in modernist discourses (see **discourse**). The kernel of this ideology is present in the work of the German philosophers Immanuel Kant and G.W.F. Hegel (see Kant 1996, Hegel 1991; Gilroy 2000) and the French philosopher Jean-Jacques Rousseau. It amounted to the classification of 'natural races' into categories and the formation of a 'Classical episteme' (Foucault 1972) that incorporated a progressive teleology and naturalist conceptions of difference (see **alterity**). These ideas grew throughout the nineteenth century, when they were especially noticeable in the anti-semitism of Wagner but found their fullest expression in the race laws of Hitler's Germany in the 1930s.

According to twentieth-century developments in the biological sciences, however, physical differences have been demonstrated to have no correlation with genetic variation among humans. Despite this, the term persists both in everyday **discourse** and in the social sciences, informing a collective sense of **identity**. Most often race is associated with populations descended from Africa and is linked to slavery, colonial domination, and political and economic oppression. Although the term grew through its association with resistance, political movements, such as the 1960s Black Power movement in America, have helped to legitimize a concept that was originally conceived by Europeans to label and subvert the non-European Other.

As Steve Fenton has pointed out, there is a high degree of inconsistency in use of the term. South Asian communities in Britain and America at times may be included in the idea of a black race, whereas in India groups are described as communal rather than racial, and in Northern Ireland the troubles are sectarian (Fenton 1999). In academic discourse, the terms race and ethnicity will overlap, as, for example, someone of black race may claim British **ethnicity**. Where ethnicity may be seen to evolve and change, as in the case of black communities in Britain, the idea of race will remain fixed. In view of the scientific discrediting of the term 'race', and the opportunity it affords for racism, Robert Miles has instead suggested the term 'racialization', which refers 'to the historical emergence of the idea of "race" and its subsequent reproduction and application' (Miles 1989, 78). Racial discourse has also been demonstrated to have a defining effect on certain ethnic categories (Sollors 1986; Miles and Brown 2003, 99).

Central to views on race in European concert music, especially in eighteenth- and nineteenth-century opera, is **Orientalism**. This concept amounts to the projection of Western ideas and values on to colonial subjects as a means of conceptualizing and controlling them (Said 1978). In relation to this idea, cultural theorist Homi Bhabha has described racism as the embodiment of desire (Bhabha 1990). Although primarily related to the French Revolution, Orientalism can be traced in earlier music. Matthew Head has suggested that the taste that late eighteenth-century Viennese audiences had for Turkish styles (see **style**) reflects their admiration (and fear) of the neighbouring Ottoman Empire (Head 2000). In *Die Entführung aus dem Serail* (1781), Mozart presents a stereotypical version of a brutal, barbaric Turk (the character Osmin). However, he also shows Osmin more sympathetically, as a character with a propensity for lyrical song, and as someone with a rational side, which indicates the **Enlightenment** image of humanity. This example not only illustrates Orientalism in action on the stage but also suggests that composers (and societies) do not necessarily adopt narrow or singular interpretations of racialized subjects.

A link has also been noted between race and sexuality. This association can be seen at work in Bizet's opera *Carmen* (1873–4), which deliberately casts a female gypsy as its central character, representing a racial and sexual world that existed beyond the boundaries of acceptable bourgeois culture. In this example, as in the context of nineteenth-century opera as a whole, the concept of race was closely linked to a sense of **alterity**, in terms of **gender**, ethnicity and **class**. According to Susan McClary, however, Bizet deployed these themes as a means of critiquing nineteenth-century French society (McClary 1992). Similar arguments are also proposed by Head in relation to Mozart's use of Turkish music (Head 2000).

Narrow conceptions of race have also helped to construct attitudes towards musicians and repertoires. For example, the **reception** of Jimi Hendrix includes his being labelled a 'white nigger' for appearing deliberately to conform to ideas about virile black men in his stage performances, as formed from the perspective of his European audience (Gilroy 1999, 93–5). Conversely, Elvis Presley, from the opposite side of the race line, adopted some of the performing gestures and sounds of black music. The Presley example points to an appropriation of ideas and music that are considered by some to be the racial property of black musicians. This idea is extended by David Brackett in his argument that James Brown reappropriated and revitalized twelve-bar blues forms following the success of rock bands such as the Beatles and Cream, bands that were indebted to black blues musicians (Brackett 2000). However, without denying the importance of these interactions, the question of ownership dissolves when it is considered that the blues originally grew from an interaction between slaves and Europeans in North America (Tagg 1989).

Also linked to race and ethnicity is the idea of **hybridity**, whereby different racial and ethnic groups may share, appropriate and dominate one another's music and other cultural forms (Werbner and Modood 1997).

Further reading: Fanon 1967; Floyd 1995; Malik 1996; Ramsey 2003

RECEPTION

Reception refers to critical responses to art, literature and music in terms of public reviews that appear in written or printed sources such as books, journals, newspapers, letters and diaries. This applies not only to reception that is contemporary with an art work's entrance into the public domain but also to subsequent generations, since interpretations (see **inerpretation**) may change and take on new meanings according to different contexts. The origins of attempts to theorize reception history reside in German literary criticism dating from the 1960s (see Jauss 1982) and forms part of a more widespread move to replace the idea of a single authored text (see

post-structuralism). These ideas began to enter German musicology in the late 1960s and Anglo-American musicology in the 1980s (see Everist 1999). The study of the reception history of specific composers, genres (see **genre**) or works (see **work**) has generated a theory that offers the potential to develop more fine-grained appreciations of the social construction of musical **meaning**, musical **aesthetics**, ideologies (see **ideology**) and philosophies and provides an insight into the processes of cultural evaluation of particular periods (see **value**, **periodization**). It also makes it necessary to reconsider the concept of work. According to Mark Everist:

> Theories of reception move historical enquiry away from questions of production and composition and towards issues related to response, audience, and what Carl Dahlhaus, following Walter Benjamin, called the 'after-life' of musical works.
>
> (Everist 1999, 379; see also Dahlhaus 1983a)

Studies of reception are therefore closely bound to related areas such as **cultural studies**, reader response theory (see post-structuralism), **hermeneutics** and theories of **canon** formation. These theories have informed musicological studies of canon formation, such as Katherine Ellis's revealing analysis of canon in nineteenth-century France, which considers the effect of **nationalism** on music reception (Ellis 1995). Arguably, although such work helps to develop an understanding of past cultures, a sense of the strangeness and Otherness of the past (see **alterity**) should remain in order to bring such accounts to life.

Central to many of the sources that reception history explores is the role of **narrative**, especially in nineteenth-century accounts of musical works. One writer who explores this idea is Scott Burnham in his seminal book *Beethoven Hero* (Burnham 1995). Burnham considers the role that a set of commonly recurring narrative topics have in influencing forms of music **analysis** (see also Krummacher 1994); these topics include the unity of life and work (see **biography**), and the necessity of artistic striving and suffering. However, it can be objected that this approach simply reinstates a fixed set of evaluative criteria and ignores the qualities of the aesthetic work that emerge later in history (Spitzer 1997).

Other issues explored in reception studies include performance, for example the reception of Chopin's piano music (see Methuen-Campbell 1992) and conducting styles (see Knittel 1995). Reception theory has also been used to highlight the role of 'expert listeners' in reception history; an example of this is Sandra McColl's study *Music*

Criticism in Vienna 1896–1897, in which music critics emerge as highly cultured 'guardians of... artistic tradition' (McColl 1996, 223). McColl draws on reception theory to contextualize the music criticism of Eduard Hanslick, the politics of the Brahms–Wagner debates (see **absolute**), and the early theories of Heinrich Schenker. Reception studies have also been produced in relation to **popular music**, for example in studies of fan-based cultures (see Lewis 1992), and Bernard Gendron has skilfully explored shifting responses to the concept of the *avant-garde* in popular music and **jazz** in France and America (Gendron 2002).

To explore how reception theory is 'performed' and to consider its problems and potential further, it is worth considering in some detail Nicholas Cook's study of the performance history of Beethoven's Ninth Symphony (1822–4; Cook 1993). Anticipation of the Ninth Symphony saw a number of reviews that heralded the piece as a standard bearer for fast-disappearing classical values, those associated with Haydn and Mozart. As Cook notes:

> Beethoven's Ninth Symphony was from the very first associated with what in the 1830s and 40s would become a full-blown revivalist movement, the result of which was the establishment of the classical repertory as we know it today – a more or less fixed and unchanging repertory of 'great and immortal works'.
>
> (*ibid.*, 20)

In other words, anticipation of the Ninth Symphony already set out the terms for what is now known as the musical canon.

However, the reception of the first performance in Vienna, on 7 May 1824, points to a creative problem with reception theory. Those who were unsympathetic to modern music, or who championed Italian *risorgimento* opera over domestic symphonies, portrayed the performance as a failure, whereas those who supported Beethoven painted a more sympathetic picture. On the one hand, these differences indicate differing discourses current at the time (see **discourse**), principally those of an older, reactionary conservatism centred on classical values, such as clarity and precision, and a younger, more liberal attitude associated with **Romanticism**. On the other hand, these differences make it hard to decide which versions were more accurate. Some cultural theorists have argued that there is no need to choose between competing versions of an event, arguing instead for a relativistic approach that presents a synchronic, or vertical, view of history that complements a diachronic or evolutionary one (see Smith

1988; see also **postmodernism**). German musicologist Friedhelm Krummacher, on the other hand, has argued that differing versions can be measured against the music itself (Krummacher 1994). Even if the relativistic option is taken, however, the overall impression is of a form of concert performance that differs markedly from those of the later twentieth century, contradicting, in particular, the kind of reverence more recently afforded to Beethoven. There was applause during movements, violinists set their bows down when they reached a passage that they could not play, singers left notes out, the double basses, according to one critic, had 'not the faintest idea what they were supposed to do with the recitatives [and produced] nothing but a gruff rumbling' and Beethoven 'threw himself back and forth like a madman' while the choir and orchestra paid no attention to him but followed the direction of possibly two other conductors (Cook 1993, 22–3). Separating fact from fiction in accounts like these is clearly problematic, but later accounts, including those written by people not present at such events, often betray an even greater tendency towards myth making. However, the reviews do highlight aesthetic tensions that are illuminating (see **aesthetics**). For example, Beethoven's inclusion of Turkish music in the finale was a problem for some, and attempts were made to justify its use by stressing an organic manner of presentation (see **organicism**, **Orientalism**).

It took almost thirty years, modifications in orchestral performance and rehearsal standards, the direction of Berlioz and, perhaps more significantly, a Romantic frame of reference among the critics following the efforts of writers such as A.B. Marx (see **Romanticism**) to finally realize the work in a more satisfactory manner. Subsequently, and still more importantly, came Wagner's interpretations of the work. Increased rehearsals, additions and alterations to parts and a conducting style that introduced rubato and contrasting tempi established a new performance history for the work. These factors enable a consideration of questions of **authenticity** and of traditions of interpretation. However, they do so not in order to argue for a single, original mode of performance but to argue against any attempt to settle the work into a fixed interpretative tradition by drawing attention to its complex performance history. Where conductors such as Arturo Toscanini and, more recently, Roger Norrington and Christopher Hogwood have claimed that their performances restore works to their original contexts, Cook asks which context should be recreated? The first, muddled performance in Vienna, the disastrous English premiere, Berlioz's interpretation, or Wagner's (see also Taruskin 1995, 235–61)?

Cook goes on to trace the work's reception through Wagner's writings – in particular during the 1848–9 revolutions and his attempt to claim the work as the main precedent for his conception of music drama – through the twentieth century, including communist China and late twentieth-century Japan. He also notes the success of the work and the way in which it has been adapted by different cultures to suit very different political or social contexts and so be 'consumed by ideology' (Cook 1993, 105). Cook concludes that while this appears to effectively interpret the piece out of existence, there remain aspects of the work – its incongruities and ironies – that resist totalizing accounts (see **narrative**).

However, it is possible to sense in this conclusion a need to rescue the Ninth Symphony from the vagaries of reception history and to preserve the value of **analysis**. If reception theory contains the possibility of transcending canonical boundaries (Everist 1999, 378), in other words of contributing to the postmodern-influenced approaches of the **new musicology**, this potential remains to be explored in full.

Further reading: Garratt 2002; Holub 1984; Samson 1994

RECORDING

Recording is a concept that has particular relevance to music from the late nineteenth century onwards. The rise of electronic means of recording and reproducing sound has had a significant impact on the study and **analysis** of all non-notated music, including **popular music**, **jazz** (see Eisenberg 1988; Cook 1998b), folk and non-Western music. The existence of recording technology even had an important role in the establishment of ethnomusicology (see **ethnicity**). Recording of all music has political, social and cultural ramifications that have more recently given rise to issues of ownership and copyright (see Attali 1985; Keil and Feld 1994; Hesmondhalgh 2000). The existence of recordings has created the possibility of studying the history of performance (Philip 1998), enabling scholars to reassess the concept of **authenticity** (see Taruskin 1995, 235–61), as well as giving rise to histories of recording (see Chanan 1995). Since the 1940s and 1950s, the studio has been used as a compositional tool leading to new musical forms, genres (see **genre**) and techniques, such as sampling (see Hebdige 1987; Metzer 2003). Certain types of music, such as serialism, have been supported and sustained by broadcast media dependent on recorded sound, a feature that has been effective in influencing audience tastes (Doctor 1999). Recording has led to various types of **hybridity** in music, which can be traced from the infiltration of *avant-garde* techniques into popular music and jazz in the late 1960s. Some musicians, such as the Beatles, abandoned live performance in preference for the recorded format. However, recording has raised a number of problematic theoretical issues, some of which will be outlined below.

The late 1930s gave rise to a debate between German critical theorists Walter Benjamin and Theodor Adorno (see **critical theory**) on the subject of the technology used to reproduce images and sound. Benjamin, in his article 'The Work of Art in the Age of Mechanical Reproduction' (Benjamin 1992), outlined a difference he perceived between film and painting, and subsequent writers have applied these distinctions to music. Where painting was approached with reverence and awe, resulting from the **value** placed on the authenticity of the original art work, in film and photography, Benjamin argued, mechanical reproduction removes the object from contemplative modes of **reception** shaped by traditional **aesthetics**. Benjamin was concerned with what he saw as 'outmoded concepts, such as creativity and **genius**, eternal value and mystery' (*ibid.*, 212). The fact that mechanical reproduction results in a depreciation, or loss, of authenticity and originality (what he termed 'aura') was offset by the possibility it offered of 'a tremendous shattering of tradition' (ibid., 215). The fact that film could reach a wide audience also appealed to Benjamin. However, he noted that in film contemplation is replaced by distraction, by which he meant a form of reception that was open to political manipulation, as occurred in the case of Nazi propaganda (see **ideology**).

Adorno, on the other hand, was more concerned with the ramifications of such questions for recorded music, and his work with the Princeton University Radio Project in the late 1930s led to an interest in the influence of sound recording on the formation of different types of listening and listener (see Leppert 2002, 228–9). In his article 'The Fetish-Character of Music and the Regression of Listening' (Adorno 2002), he outlined his concern that records will become commodity items and that capitalist modes of production (what he terms 'standardization') will have a regressive effect on listening habits, not least by making classical music appear easy to listen to (see **culture industry**). As John Mowitt comments, 'Adorno preferred the peculiarly classical isolation of the avant-garde to Benjamin's proletarianized public' (Mowitt 1987, 188). Adorno also suggested that recording preserves music as a universal, but petrified, form of text (see

narrative), and that in some cases performances, through a 'barbarism of perfection', may anticipate their recorded status (here he had Italian conductor Arturo Toscanini in mind).

An indication that these issues still have relevance in more recent scholarship is provided by the work of musicologist Adam Krims, who has drawn attention to new modes of musical listening that result from production techniques and repackaging of classical and popular music by recording companies to provide music for different private and public spaces – for example, recordings that add nature sounds to Beethoven for use in 'lifestyle stores' or collections such as 'Mozart for Dinner' and 'Bach for Relaxation': 'What is new and worth noting is the successful cross-marketing of these recordings with interior décor and "lifestyle" accessories, and especially the targeting of classical recordings as an aspect of interior living spaces' (Krims 2001, 352).

In other words, classical recordings may be used to design interior spaces. These recordings do not attempt to resemble live concert experience but are 'made for private, indoor listening and [take] that situation as [their] exemplary location' (*ibid.*, 353). The result of this is music that is used as decoration and also to sell particular places (see **place**) such as shopping centres, bars and dance clubs. The other side of Krims's argument here, that recorded music can change urban spaces and affect consumption of goods and services, is that listener responses are equally susceptible to change: the ubiquity of a pop song may be detrimental to its reception, and it will shape, and be shaped by, a listening subject's sense of **identity** (DeNora 2000).

Further reading: Engh 1999; Gilbert and Pearson 1999; Gronow and Saunio 1998; Kahn and Whitehead 1992

RENAISSANCE

The concept of Renaissance, or 'rebirth', is most commonly associated with art, religion, politics and science between the late fourteenth and early seventeenth centuries, although the term reappeared in Britain in the late nineteenth century, following the apparent rebirth of English music in the works of Hubert Parry, Charles Villiers Stanford and Edward Elgar (see Howes 1966; Hughes and Stradling 2001).

The original concept began to evolve in fourteenth-century Italian writing, notably in the poetry of Petrarch and Boccaccio. The Italian term *rinascita* was subsequently supplanted by the French term *Renaissance* in 1855, and a key work in historicizing (see **historicism**) the concept was German art historian Jacob Burckhardt's *The Civilization of the Renaissance in Italy*, published in 1860 (Burckhardt 1990). The concept is linked to a revival of interest in antiquity, the philosophy, art and politics of ancient Greece and Rome. These pre-Christian texts were especially appealing to societies that were increasingly developing a sense of the secular, as indicated by the emergence of merchant wealth, lay patronage, and the concepts of citizenry and civic rights. Interest in classical texts moved from monasteries to universities and other collections, including ones in Mantua, Florence and Venice. As a result of the invention of printing techniques, translations of these texts were widely disseminated.

In the case of music, there was increased interest in the **theory** and **aesthetics** of ancient Greek and Roman writers such as Boethius and Ptolemy, as well as the discovery of previously unknown works by Aristotle, Plato and Aristoxenus, whose *Harmonics* was first translated in 1562. Although knowledge of the sound of ancient music remained elusive, studies of these authors led to the development of Renaissance music theories, such as those of Joannes Tinctoris, Heinrich Glarean, Gioseffe Zarlino (especially his *Le institutioni harmoniche* of 1558) and Joachim Burmeister, writers who were influenced by developing humanist concerns. These concerns were reflected in a Renaissance belief in the superiority of its own art and artists to those of the preceding medieval period (see **periodization**). This can be seen in the historiographical (see **historiography**) tendency to celebrate individual artists, for example Vasari's *Lives of the Painters* of 1550 (Vasari 1963), which extolled the virtues of Raphael and Michelangelo, and Tinctoris's preface to his counterpoint treatise of 1477, which identified a 'new art' in the music of Dunstable, Dufay and Binchois. The influence of humanism can also be detected in an interest in classical theories of rhetoric (see **language**) – Burmeister, in particular, emphasized music's human, rhetorical character following Quintillian's theories on rhetoric in his *Institutione oratoria*. A stress on the importance of words and text setting emerged in the late sixteenth century, when it sparked a controversy that centred on a search for more expressive styles, as characterized by the *seconda prattica* music of Monteverdi, monody, and the rise of instrumental and vocal virtuosity (see **work**). This debate was contemporary with the development of opera, one of the defining genres (see **genre**) of the Renaissance, alongside the madrigal, the mass and the motet.

Musically, the rise of a Renaissance musical **style** is commonly traced from the emergence of choral polyphony, which German musicologist Manfred F. Bukofzer dates from around 1430 (Bukofzer

1951, 188), a defining moment being the performance of Dufay's motet *Nuper rosarum flores* at the consecration of Florence Cathedral, complete with Brunelleschi's dome, in 1436. As this example indicates, theories concerning the origins of Renaissance music are complicated by the fact that the majority of the important composers first associated with the concept travelled to Italy from Northern Europe. Further complications arise with the consideration of how best to periodize the subject. Howard M. Brown suggests an early period (1420–90), two high periods (1490–1520 and 1520–60) and a late period (1560–1600) (Brown 1976), whereas Reinhardt Strohm separates the Renaissance concept from what he perceives to be a separately emerging stylistic phenomenon in music that he traces from 1380 to 1500 (Strohm 1993). While it is argued that Renaissance values encouraged artists to develop and tailor consciousness of their own identities (see **subjectivity**; see also Greenblatt 1980), similar ideas can be detected in the music of Machaut and others who predate 1380 (see Leach 2003; Dillon 2002).

Although early studies were necessarily more concerned with source materials, dating, and the editing and preparation of complete editions, Renaissance music studies have always shown an awareness of contextual issues, such as humanism (Palisca 1985), **place** (Lowinsky 1941; Wright 1975; Kisby 2001), and social and political concerns (Fenlon 1989). Despite the importance of music **theory** to considerations of Renaissance music (see Berger 1987; Judd 2000), until recently the subject has largely resisted **analysis**. Consideration of concepts such as imitation, emulation and parody (see Lockwood 1966; Brown 1982) continues to be important, but attention is increasingly being given to compositional process (Owens 1997) and music analysis (Judd 1998).

Although Renaissance scholars have been slower to respond to the changes introduced through **new musicology**, there are notable exceptions. One important example is Gary Tomlinson's study *Music in Renaissance Magic* (Tomlinson 1993b). Influenced by the new **historicism**, Tomlinson seeks to explore Renaissance music not in terms of musical style or a composer's intentions but through an examination of the cultural discourses (see **discourse**) surrounding music at the time, what he calls 'the forces beyond individual agency that have conspired in shaping music histories' (*ibid.*, 246). The intention is to develop an understanding of music as perceived by writers at the time, but also in terms of its intersection with overlapping cultural concerns, such as belief in magic and the supernatural. This method, which is influenced by French cultural anthropologist and theorist Michel

Foucault, Tomlinson calls 'musical archeology'. It emphasizes the gap between our experience of Renaissance music and the subjective experiences of it in its own time. This results in a perception of the difference (see **alterity**) of the music, rather than its familiarity, in terms of what fits neatly into established accounts of musical evolution. Although Tomlinson's book is short on concrete observations, it does provide a valuable alternative to existing accounts, an attempt to move around the highly prescriptive methodologies that have arisen in relation to Renaissance music.

Further reading: Blume 1967; McClary 1991

RHETORIC *see* **language**

ROMANTICISM

Romanticism is a concept that is generally applied to music from the nineteenth century, although exact dates for its inception and culmination vary. While there is a tendency to relate the concept to music composed during the so-called Romantic period (see **periodization**), the term can be seen to embrace a number of philosophical and aesthetic concerns that are not necessarily confined to music or other arts from the nineteenth century. The beginnings of a Romantic artistic sensibility can be linked to the French Revolution and the rise of the **Enlightenment**, especially the work of German Romantic poet Novalis and German writer and critic K.W.F. von Schlegel. These writers emphasized the importance of re-imagining the familiar and the ordinary as alternative worlds, and the concepts of the sublime and the infinite – how the magnitude of nature points to the limitations of human understanding – ideas that are related to the work of German philosophers Immanuel Kant, J.G. Fichte and G.W.F. Hegel. Of particular significance are Kant's ideas about disinterested pleasure – enjoyment in the act of contemplation – which is developed through Romanticism's cult of 'serious listening' and the idea of an 'art for art's sake' (see **aesthetics**). Hegel's claim that music, like any individual art form, is engaged in a dynamic struggle to master its materials is cultivated through Romanticism's belief in progress and evolution through artistic striving, resulting in more complex compositional techniques (see **sketch**) and the image of the heroic individual artist (see **subjectivity**). This idea has been especially well investigated in a study of Beethoven by American musicologist Scott Burnham (Burnham 1995). Following a loss of religious certainties, Romanticism saw a move towards a human **subjectivity** the philosophies of Arthur Schopenhauer and Friedrich Nietzsche.

The first well-documented association of the term Romantic with music was written in 1810 by German music critic E.T.A. Hoffmann (see **criticism**). His article was a review of Beethoven, but he argued that music in general could be considered 'the most romantic of all the arts' (Charlton 1989, 236). However, the association of the Romantic ideal with Beethoven clearly points to a discursive relationship between the so-called Classical period and what followed:

> Romanticism may in essence be a matter of giving increasing emphasis to elements already present in Classicism. But those emphases...are as much a critique of Classicism as a tribute to it. The Romantic period, age or era grew out of, and vigorously away from, Classicism.
>
> (Whittall 1987, 12)

Romanticism is further problematized by the diversity of musical styles (see **style**) and composers that it encompasses, including Verdi, Schumann, Berlioz, Wagner, Brahms, Wolf and Rimsky-Korsakov, although it can be linked to the rise of new genres (see **genre**) such as the symphonic poem, the song cycle and music drama, and an increasing concern for **organicism**, episodic structure, a desire to make music 'speak' programmatically (see **language**), and such technical devices as thematic transformation. It also led directly to a number of other concepts, such as **nationalism**, realism (see Dahlhaus 1985), impressionism and expressionism (see **subjectivity**; see also Samson 1991), some of whose features coexisted with Romantic elements, while others attempted to break away from them. As British musicologist Arnold Whittall points out, 'the challenge for the historian is to determine to what extent that which is non-Romantic is actually *anti*-Romantic' (Whittall 1987, 13). He goes on to stress that while operas such as Bizet's *Carmen* (1873–4) and Mussorgsky's *Boris Godunov* (1868–72) may have been inspired by non-Romantic concerns, such as a desire to portray the realities of (low) life or the true history of a people, the musical styles and techniques deployed are not necessarily non-Romantic but may instead be seen to belong to a set of expressive practices that originated in the early part of the nineteenth century. In other words, there was an overlap between progressive developments in art and literature and older, romantic practices and values (see **value**) in music. By the end of the nineteenth century, music was Romantic in an un-Romantic age (see **modernism**).

A seminal figure concerned with the interpretation of Romanticism in music was German musicologist Carl Dahlhaus, who stated that 'the heart of the "aesthetic religion" of the nineteenth century was the cult of **genius**' (Dahlhaus 1989b, 2; see also Hepokoski 1991). The most obvious example of this is the mythology that developed around Beethoven, Mendelssohn's 'rediscovery' of Bach and his appropriation of the eighteenth-century composer into the cultural and critical value systems of the nineteenth century, as well as the cultivation of the performer genius, most obviously in the forms of Liszt and Paganini and the idea of virtuosity (see Samson 2003). Dahlhaus also noted that Romantic compositions were often fragments of idealized autobiography (Dahlhaus 1989b, 3), an idea supported by such works as Berlioz's *Symphonie Fantastique* (1830) and the trend for composer biographies, notably those on Bach (see **biography**), as well as Berlioz's own *Life of Berlioz*, first published just after his death in 1870 (Berlioz 1903).

According to Dahlhaus, **absolute** music – purely instrumental music that appears to exist without reference to anything beyond itself – became the principal aesthetic paradigm in nineteenth-century German musical **culture**. However, he argues that it is hard to present the case for a unified *Zeitgeist* (spirit of the age) during the nineteenth century, especially in light of the monumental contribution of Wagner in the second part of the century and Wagner's association with a critique of the idea of absolute music, which was chiefly represented by the instrumental music of Brahms (see Chua 1999; Hoeckner 2002). For this reason, the second half of the nineteenth century was labelled the age of Wagner, but Dahlhaus also refers to the term 'neo-Romanticism' (Dahlhaus 1989b), a concept that originated in early nineteenth-century literary theory to distinguish each successive kind of Romanticism from the previous one. Among the various types, Dahlhaus mentions French Romanticism, from 1830 onwards, and a revived Romanticism from around 1900, but of obvious significance to any division of the nineteenth century were the European social and political revolutions of 1848–9, in which Romantic artists took an active role. These events, it has been argued, while signalling a shift from private, privileged music making to more public concerts for the emerging middle classes, lead to new creative directions and a general 'withdrawal, on the part of composers and of artists, from politics to art, from engagement to detachment, from idealism to realism' (Samson 1991, 12).

Recent engagements with the concept of Romanticism include reassessments of music theorists (see **theory**) and the cultural ideas of the nineteenth century, for example Ian Biddle's consideration of F.W.J. Schelling's organicist musical aesthetic and the importance that it attached to corporeal sense (see **body**), and Ian Bent's examination of Friedrich Schleiermacher's theory of **hermeneutics** (Biddle 1994, see also Bent 1996b). Considerations of Romanticism have increasingly located nineteenth-century music in its cultural and aesthetic context, in some cases leading to the practice of what Scott Burnham has described as poetic criticism (Burnham 1999), analogous in certain ways to the hermeneutic criticism of the nineteenth century, while others have informed their analyses of the music with recourse to more recent literary criticism (see **deconstruction**) of Romantic poets and authors (see Kramer 1993b).

Further reading: Bowie 1993; Bowman 1998; Bujić 1988; Dahlhaus 1989c; Garratt 2002; Rosen 1999

SEMIOTICS

Semiotics is a concept that holds that all human communication is effected by means of systems of signs articulated in contexts, such as literature, television, film, music, and art, that may be considered forms of **language** and text (see **narrative**). However, the concept is linked to **analysis** and **structuralism** in the sense that it 'tends to concentrate on pattern rather than content, to seek out structure rather than to interpret meanings' (Monelle 1992, 5). Two important theories of semiotics were developed by Swiss linguist Ferdinand de Saussure (de Saussure 1983) and American philosopher Charles S. Peirce. The former introduced the term 'semiology' (the study of signs) and distinguished between the signifier, such as a word, and the signified, the idea associated with that word. However, many theorists, such as Peirce, have argued that semiotics is more complex than de Saussure's binary model would suggest. There are many different kinds of semiotic theory, but they all illustrate how **meaning** is socially constructed and how the relationship between signifier and signified is essentially arbitrary.

Important musicological studies that draw upon semiotic theory include Kofi Agawu's book concerning the play of musical signs in music from the classical period (Agawu 1991) and Robert Hatten's account of semantic content in Beethoven (Hatten 1994). Agawu's work draws on eighteenth-century theories about rhetoric (see **language**) as well as Leonard Ratner's study of classical expression, form and **style** (Ratner 1980), which identifies twenty-seven musical 'topics', such as Turkish music (see **Orientalism**), pastoral (see **landscape**) and hunt style. Agawu is concerned with ways in which the rhetorical structure of the music (the harmonic and melodic gestures that suggest beginnings, middles and endings, for example) contrasts with the surface pattern of stylistic topics, a feature that is particularly characteristic of Beethoven's late style (see Monelle 1992, 226–32). Hatten's work is indebted to an approach developed by linguist Michael Shapiro and considers ways in which musical events are marked in some way. These narrative tropes, as Hatten calls them, are marked by their context in the music and the extent to which they contradict stylistic expectations.

Other influential work has been published by Finnish musicologist Eero Tarasti, who has used semiotic theory to explore the relationship between myth and music, for example in the music dramas of Wagner (Tarasti 1994). Semiotics has also been applied to **popular music**, most notably by Philip Tagg in his work on Abba's 'Fernando' (1976) and the theme tune to the American television series *Kojak* (Tagg 2000). Tagg's concerns include an awareness that particular chords and melodic ideas may have different semantic functions according to the music's **genre** or style, and the possibility that music may carry a meaning that is at variance with the words it accompanies.

See also: **post-structuralism**

Further reading: Eco 1977; Monelle 1998, 2000; Nattiez 1982; Samuels 1995

SERIALISM *see* **modernism**

SEXUALITY *see* **body, feminism, gender**

SKETCH

In musicology, the concept of sketch implies a visual record of a composer's private and primary thoughts, something that documents a stage of composition that pre-dates a final score. It may contain verbal, musical or purely graphic information (such as a pre-compositional plan), and it may indicate a first step (a melodic fragment or harmonic skeleton). Information added to a composer's 'finished' manuscript, or a draft that is not definitive in the manner of a fair copy, may also be considered under this concept.

Sketch study became an important discipline in musicology following interest in Beethoven manuscripts, in particular through the work of Nottebohm in the second half of the nineteenth century. Consequently, the earliest sketch studies centred on nineteenth- and twentieth-century music, although some material for music before the seventeenth century does exist, as discussed by Owens (Owens 1997). Initially, sketch studies concentrated on developing chronologies of works and an understanding of composers' working practices, and they confined their discoveries to the field of musical **biography**. In the late 1960s and 1970s, however, sketch study developed alongside music **analysis**, and sketches were used both to challenge and to authenticate analytical claims. The latter practice drew criticism, notably from Douglas Johnson (Johnson 1978–9) and Joseph Kerman (Kerman 1982), for appearing to discuss only those aspects of the sketches that supported an applied analytical system (for more on this debate, but in relation to the music of Arnold Schoenberg, see Haimo 1996).

In the twentieth century, in particular through the development of serialism, sketches gained significance as composers' highly individual styles developed in relation to their new techniques. As tonality was abandoned, the form and pitch structures of works became harder to trace from the score alone. This problem reached its apex in such works as Boulez's *Le Marteau sans Maître* (1953–5) and Stockhausen's *Klavierstücke* (1952–7). It therefore became desirable to probe sketch material for clues to the structure of a **work** (see **structuralism**). At the same time, the composer's own conceptions of the act of composition became closely linked to their innovative sketching practices, as in Stockhausen's *Momente* (1965), in which the sketch is effectively the score.

One problem with sketch study is the difficulty of accounting for what Marshall called 'creative processes' (Marshall 1972; see Bent 1984 for a revealing discussion of compositional process in eighteenth-century music). These are the decisions and thoughts that may lie behind a particular sketch but that are not documented, information that must be deduced from the evidence that is available. This is further complicated by the fact that sketches are often incomplete, both in their relation to the finished score and in terms of lost or missing pages. Furthermore, as Kerman points out, sketches may reveal only a series of compositional stages, and 'tentative stages at that' (Kerman 1982, 176).

Sketch studies have been dismissed on the grounds that a composer's intentions are difficult to substantiate or are irrelevant to analytical inquiry. Dai Griffiths has even suggested that sketches are of marginal interest because they are purely conceptual ideas that 'don't exist' in the final work (Griffiths 1997). He has also sounded a word of warning that sketch study may lead to a fetishizing of **genius**. Studies of the genesis of a work are open to criticism if they appear to interpret a composer's alterations as a series of 'failed experiments' in the construction of an organic (see **organicism**) and teleological whole. However, sketch study offers potential as a deconstructive (see **deconstruction**) tool for undermining the idea of a fixed and unitary work; this is particularly the case in studies of opera (see Hall 1996). Sketches may also reveal information that can inform historiographical accounts (see **historiography**), such as Richard Taruskin's consideration of Stravinsky's use of folk material in *The Rite of Spring* (Taruskin 1980), or expose the programmatic origins of a symphony (Frogley 2002).

Further reading: Beard 2001; Brandenburg 1978–9; Haimo 1990; Hall and Sallis 2005; Marston 1995, 2001

STRUCTURALISM

The musicological use of this term implies a preoccupation with structure, often at a deep level, in musical works and the techniques that are applied to uncover that structure. From this perspective, it has a close familial relationship with **analysis** and, through the often casual interchange between form and structure in musicological **discourse**, it has a certain resemblance to **formalism**.

However, the origins of structuralism as a concept are located in linguistics, and its dependence on **language** provides a statement of its nature and application. Structuralism first emerged through the writings of Swiss linguist Ferdinand de Saussure, primarily in his *Course in General Linguistics*, originally published in 1916 (de Saussure 1983). He attempted to construct an understanding of language that could be seen as the study of the structure of relationships in language, conducted with a rigour that assumes the appearance of a scientific objectivity. For de Saussure, language consisted of two elements: *langue* and *parole*. The former refers to language as a recognizable system; the latter concerns the individual utterances within that system. This distinction, along with other relationships, reflects de Saussure's understanding of language as a series of binary oppositions and/or relationships. This is reflected in his most widely cited claim that the linguistic sign consists of two elements, the *signifier* (the actual phonetic sound) and the object to which it refers, which he called the *signified*. These signs also function through relationships of difference (to say what something is is also to say what it is not). This reference to signs and their actions and positions in networks of relationships projects a model of language and its meanings. It also leads towards the concept of **semiotics**, the study of signs, a concept that is coterminous with structuralism. In addition, de Saussure claimed that language could be studied synchronically, in effect as a slice of time, rather than diachronically – how it exists in a temporal continuum. This move helps to add the appearance of scientific scrutiny in that it involves the isolation of the object under consideration. It also in effect de-historicizes both the progression of language and its study.

The development of de Saussure's account of language into what became generally known as structuralism occurred in the 1950s and developed through into the 1970s, with the term being applied to a wide range of contexts and concepts. As Eagleton effectively states: 'Structuralism in general is an attempt to apply this linguistic theory to objects and activities other than language itself. You can view a myth, wrestling match, system of tribal kinship, restaurant menu or oil painting as a system of signs, and a structuralist analysis will try to isolate the underlying set of laws by which these signs are combined into meanings. It will largely ignore what the signs actually "say" and concentrate instead on their internal relations to one another' (Eagleton 1996, 84). The reference to 'tribal kinship' relates to the work of cultural anthropologist Claude Lévi-Strauss, who studied extensively the underlying structures of myth (Lévi-Strauss 1969). The other activities listed by Eagleton suggest the work of French literary theorist Roland Barthes, specifically his book *Mythologies*, originally published in 1957 (Barthes 1973), in which he analyzed a wide range of social and cultural activities. The extension of structuralism into a diverse range of fields is also reflected in the structural repositioning of Marxism by Althusser (Althusser 1996) and Michel Foucault's structural account of the history of knowledge (Foucault 1972).

It is clearly possible to invoke music as an object of structuralist inquiry, and some aspects of musicology parallel and intersect with structuralism. Music is often referred to in terms of its structure, usually represented by certain recognizable formal shapes and outlines (see **analysis**). The act of composition also implies a conscious structuring process, and it is notable that the prominence of structuralist thought coincided with the establishment of a post-Second World War *avant-garde* of composers (Boulez, Stockhausen, Nono) who were preoccupied with new levels of compositional process and structure. However, it is in the activity of analysis that a musicological reflection of structuralism is most readily apparent. The act of analysis is usually constructed as the attempt to reveal deep, perhaps hidden, levels of structure. This activity implies that a structure is present in the music, and the actual processes through which this structure is revealed often assume the appearance of pseudo-scientific rigour and, potentially, a claim of objectivity.

In recent years, the analytical methods associated with Austrian music theorist Heinrich Schenker have emerged as one recognizable manner of analyzing tonal music (Schenker's preoccupation was with what he considered the great Austro-Germanic **tradition** from Bach to Brahms; see **canon**). Schenker's original writings (Schenker 1979) have been codified into a coherent system for analysis. This organization of Schenker is most clearly made in Forte and Gilbert's *Introduction to Schenkerian Analysis* (Forte and Gilbert 1982), which has become the standard textbook in the field. In this construction, we are presented with a series of moves that reduce the music through a series of levels, from foreground to background, at which point a predetermined structural archetype is identified. This process has a clear relationship to wider aspects of structuralist thought through the reduction to an essential (perhaps essentialist) structure. This would also seem to be a process that could be described as synchronic in that it treats the individual musical **work** and its structure as autonomous (see **autonomy**). In other words, the work's content is divorced from any real sense of context. However, in any analysis there is still a sense of the music passing through time, with what has become known as the fundamental line, the structural shape that gravitates towards a conclusion, having its own diachronic identity.

Other forms of analysis also sustain their own structuralism. The study of post-tonal music, for example, has often been bound up with the explication of structure. This relationship emerged via the already mentioned post-war compositional *avant-garde* and its wider influence. Allen Forte, in his book *The Structure of Atonal Music* (Forte 1973), attempted to provide a systematic vocabulary for the understanding of post-tonal (atonal) music that involved the identification of underlying consistencies behind the often distinct, differentiated surfaces of much post-tonal/atonal music. The resulting method, known as pitch-class set theory, has all the appearance of rigour and system, which had become a consistent feature of structuralism.

These and other manifestations of structuralism in musicology have become increasingly susceptible to criticism, with musicology again providing certain parallels with wider shifts from structuralism to **post-structuralism**. A structuralist musicology would seem to privilege structure/form over other, equally significant, musical parameters. The claimed distinction between content and context is difficult to sustain, since analysis usually involves the application of a **theory** such as Schenkerian or set theory, and theory always brings its own issues of context and perspective. Ultimately, the identification of a given structural model for any musical work is an act of **interpretation**, and as such it is always loaded with its own issues of **subjectivity** and **ideology**.

Further reading: Clarke 1996; Dosse 1997; Hawkes 1977; Williams 2001

STYLE

The concept of style refers to a manner or mode of expression, the way in which musical gestures are articulated. In this sense, it can be seen to relate to the concept of **identity**. In music, style requires a consideration of technical features, such as melody, texture, rhythm and harmony, and it concerns ways in which these features operate independently or in conjunction, or as categories, such as counterpoint. In its broadest sense, style may refer to music as a style of art, while in its narrowest sense it can apply to a single note, which may have stylistic characteristics determined by tone, dynamic, timbre and so on. Style may determine historical **periodization**, and it exercises a reflexive relationship with the form, function and **genre** of a **work**. The term emerged from the categorizing impulses of the **Enlightenment**, which are reflected in the work of German music theorists such as Athanasius Kircher and Johann Mattheson. Kircher, in his *Musurgia universalis* of 1650, and Mattheson, in *Der Vollkommene Capellmeister* of 1739 (see Harriss 1981), both spoke of national styles (see Ratner 1980; see also **nationalism**). As a greater interest in theorizing music arose (see **theory**), so in turn did a desire to determine theories based on common practice.

Studies of music of the eighteenth century and earlier tend to define style in terms of a common practice, for example Charles Rosen's *The Classical Style* (Rosen 1971), which explores the music of Haydn, Mozart and Beethoven in terms of a shared **language**. At an even broader level, it is still possible to speak of a classical style, in the sense of concert music, as opposed to folk or popular styles. Although, at first sight, there may appear to be significant problems with such generalizations, as Lucy Green points out, '*we must have some knowledge of the style of a piece of music in order to experience inherent meanings as distinct from non-musically meaningful sound*' (Green 1988, 34; italics in original). In other words, listeners require some conception of musical style, however broad, in order to orient themselves and begin to find meaning in the sounds they hear.

Style can be applied to the work of individual composers, to define a synthesis of styles, such as Verdi's operatic style, or to indicate those aspects of a composer's entire output that are consistent from one work to another. This suggests that there may be an element of personality to style, and a sense of an evolving personality may be expressed through a detection of stages in a composer's career, as with the idea of early, middle and late Beethoven styles. Aspects of one composer's style may be detected in the work of another, which suggests a form of stylistic **intertextuality**. Alternatively, as in the case of the neoclassical works of Stravinsky (see **modernism**), older styles may be adapted and integrated into a more contemporary musical language (see Messing 1996).

The fact that composers, from Mozart to Stravinsky, have used many styles points once again to the idea that a style is something that a composer may adopt, as an actor may put on a mask; it exists independently from anything a composer may bring to it. This view is expressed by art historians Alois Riegl and Arnold Hauser (see Hauser 1982), whose work directly influenced one of the earliest musicologists, Guido Adler (see **historical musicology**). In his *Der Stil in der Musik* (1911), Adler described the history of music as the history of style, an approach that found its culmination in Donald J. Grout's *History of Western Music* (Grout and Palisca 2001).

However, the view that style exists as an entirely autonomous entity excludes the fact that a composer can bring something to an existing style. American music theorist Leonard Meyer has argued that style results from a set of choices that composers make, within the constraints of social, cultural and technical knowledge that has been learned or assimilated (Meyer 1989). Such knowledge will be specific to geographical location and historical period. Accordingly, it is style that generates evolution in music, as composers make choices that challenge and possibly overturn existing genres, or a composer's own earlier music.

In her essay 'Adorno's Diagnosis of Beethoven's Late Style', American musicologist Rose Rosengard Subotnik explores these issues of choice and artistic development through the writings of German critical theorist Theodor Adorno (Subotnik 1991; see **critical theory**). Adorno's views on these matters reflect his **interpretation** of the dialectics of G.W.F. Hegel, **Marxism** and Arnold Schoenberg's writings on composition, for example his essay 'New Music, Outmoded Music, Style and Idea', first published in 1946 (Schoenberg 1975). Adorno believed that a crystallization of reason and self-consciousness had taken place in music at the time of Monteverdi, when the term style first entered musical vocabulary. This led to what Immanuel Kant later defined as the individual's right to freedom, through the exercise of moral choice. Adorno felt that Beethoven's middle period came close to achieving a Hegelian synthesis of the individual and the social. It did so by developing, in musical terms, a dialectic between the apparent opposites of objective form and subjective freedom (see **subjectivity**).

However, Adorno argues that this synthesis proved impossible, and that Beethoven's third, or late-period style, recognized this reality and achieved a more authentic expression, both a truer reflection of the condition of society and of the artist as autonomous subject. In this sense, Adorno sees the late-period style as a critique of the second: if this change had not taken place, Adorno argues, Beethoven's music would have become **ideology**, its surface hiding a more negative reality. The result is a negative dialectic, a music that articulates form and freedom as irreconcilable opposites, suggesting the impossibility of art itself. This leads to an exaggeration of conventional stylistic features, such as trills and ornaments, and a removal of more subjective elements, such as sharply defined sonata or fugal subjects. An example of this would be the *Missa Solemnis* (1824), in which Beethoven adopts a range of older stylistic practices that create an archaic surface behind which his more subjective humanistic ideas reside. While such observations are potentially illuminating, it could be argued that both Adorno and Subotnik are primarily concerned with a history of German thought rather than with the specific social or practical realities of Beethoven's time.

In recent musicology, the term style is less frequently encountered, perhaps because it has been extensively and consistently researched by German and Anglo-American musicologists. However, ethnomusicologists, such as Philip Bohlman, have developed our understanding that the social, shared dimension of style is crucial to its construction and recognition (Bohlman 1988). **Popular music**, and social and **cultural studies** also point to the important role of non-musical styles, such as clothing, cover art, image, music video and other aspects of commercial promotion (see Hebdige 1979).

Further reading: Lippman 1977; Moore 2001b

SUBJECTIVITY

Subjectivity emerged as an important concept during the late eighteenth and early nineteenth centuries, especially in the work of British Romantic poets such as Keats, Coleridge, Wordsworth, Byron and Burns, and German writers and philosophers such as Kant, Hegel, Fichte, Schiller, Goethe, Novalis, Schleiermacher, Schelling and Hölderlin (see **Romanticism**). Literary works by some of these authors focused on such topics as the subjective feelings of the isolated artist, introspection and *Weltschmerz* (anguished feeling) (see Bowie 1993).

In his *Critique of Judgement* of 1790, Immanuel Kant developed a notion of beauty in art and nature that recognized the function both of objectivity and subjectivity (see **aesthetics**). According to Wayne D. Bowman:

> There must be, Kant concludes, a 'subjective principle' of beauty: one we see exemplified in beauty's purposive and seemingly rational designs; one whose manifestations we rightly presume all others can similarly see . . . one whose appeal is to the distinctive feeling which is aesthetic experience.
>
> (Bowman 1998, 80)

Kant believed that judgements of beauty are not wholly objective but that they 'may provide "knowledge" of a sort inaccessible to the rational or practical mind' (*ibid.*, 80).

Lawrence Kramer has suggested that music, in conjunction with what he calls the project of Romantic individualism, was an appropriate medium for exploring 'aesthetic, psychical, and sexual' subjectivities, arguing that they were cultivated and constrained in a process that reflected contemporary social values (Kramer 1998, 2; see also

value). Musicologist Scott Burnham has also argued that nineteenth-century German ideas about subjectivity have been crucial in constructing interpretations (see **interpretation**) of Beethoven. In particular, he refers to the so-called *Goethezeit*, the age of Goethe, Kant and Hegel, as 'an age characterized by the centrality of the Self' (Burnham 1995, 113), in which narratives (see **narrative**) concerning the evolution of the self, 'such as birth and death, personal freedom and destiny, self-consciousness [see **identity**], and self-overcoming' (*ibid.*, 112), shaped the meaning and interpretation of aesthetic texts (see **work**):

> The hero of German classical literature... both enacts and sees himself enacting, and thus bears the weighted wrap of self-consciousness, *the* human condition which was to become fundamental to German Idealism's concept of reality and its history.
>
> (*ibid.*, 116–17)

In his study of sexuality, subjectivity and song in Schubert, however, Lawrence Kramer argues that the early nineteenth-century Viennese composer challenged such normative expectations and explored alternative models of subjectivity:

> Schubert tends to reconstruct subjectivity in song....On the one hand, he writes songs that ally themselves with the norm by projecting an image of virile strength and confidence....In most such songs, however, Schubert qualifies the virile ideal by relaxing its rigour at a crucial point, putting the text in dialogue with musical intimations of self-doubt, dependency, and passive, even masochistic, desires....On the other hand, Schubert writes songs that openly explore alternative subjectivities, a process Susan McClary has also found at work in certain instrumental pieces, notably the 'Unfinished' Symphony [1822].
>
> (Kramer 1998, 3; see also McClary 1994)

The contrast between these two accounts of subjectivity in nineteenth-century music could be summarized as a shift from a public network of social relations to a private interiority.

Kramer has also explored the problem of where to locate the musical subject, pointing out that many, including French **Enlightenment** theorist Jean-Jacques Rousseau and German philosopher

G.W.F. Hegel, have associated it with melody. One person who has considered this issue in some detail is German critical theorist (see **critical theory**) Theodor Adorno, who was especially concerned with subjectivity and its relationship to social practices as mediated in musical form. In the highly developmental thematic processes in Beethoven's late period (see **periodization**), for example, Adorno sensed an expression of (an individual) subjectivity that is withdrawn from the material world and in conflict with the (social) confines of musical form (see also **style**). According to Adorno, this situation was advanced by Brahms, in whose music the idea of continual thematic development 'took possession of the sonata as a whole. Subjectification and objectification are intertwined. Brahms's technique unites both tendencies' (Adorno 1973, 56–7). Through a dialectical process, Schoenberg then develops the tendencies of Beethoven and Brahms. At first this is embodied in expressionism – a movement in painting, literature and music around 1900–18, concerned with direct expression of an artist's subjective will, alienation and psychological anguish. In musical expressionism, traditional forms are apparently abandoned:

> With the liberation of musical material, there arose the possibility of mastering it technically. It is as if music had thrown off that alleged force of nature [tonality] which its subject-matter exercises upon it, and would now be able to assume command over this subject-matter freely, consciously, and openly. The composer has emancipated himself along with his sounds.
>
> (*ibid.*, 52)

Adorno's view of expressionism, with its emphasis on the composer assuming command over subject matter, clearly contrasts with other interpretations, some of which would hold that 'the progress of music towards total freedom of the subject would appear to be completely irrational insofar as . . . it by-and-large dissolves the easily comprehensible logic of superficial organisation' (*ibid.*, 136; see also Crawford and Crawford 1993). Adorno argued that two incompatible approaches emerged as a consequence of this problem. One was represented by Schoenberg's serial technique, in which the alienated modern subject immersed itself in form and technique. The other was the objectified music of Stravinsky, which presented an impoverished version of subjectivity, mechanistic and dehumanized:

> The convincing force which [Stravinsky's music] exerts is due, on the one hand, to the self-suppression of the subject, and on

the other to the musical language, which has been especially contrived for authoritarian effects. This is most obvious in the emphatic, strikingly dictatorial instrumentation, which unites brevity and vehemence.

(*ibid.*, 202)

While this account has provided musicologists with a model for historicizing (see **historicism**) musical **modernism**, it nonetheless exposes a clear prejudice for a German musical **tradition** and a dislike of the music of Stravinsky. Other composers whose work has been examined in terms of subjectivity include Mahler (Johnson 1994), Webern (Griffiths 1996) and Britten (Rupprecht 2001). Johnson observes a Romantic subjective straining for closure in Mahler's Ninth Symphony (1908–9) set alongside alternative, plural strategies that are 'essentially modern' (Johnson 1994, 120), and Britten's opera *Death in Venice* (1971–4) provides an example of a musical portrayal of obsessive mental breakdown, one that is inextricably linked to a sense of **place**.

Subjectivity is often used to refer to an artist, listener or performer's sense of self. In this sense, the concept has particular relevance to **popular music**, whose artists can provide insight into subjective experience. For example, Sheila Whiteley has explored a range of female performers, examining ways in which their music 'is about love or rape, sexual desire or sexual assault, childbirth, miscarriage or abortion . . . or simply having fun' (Whiteley 2000, 1). Subjectivity and music will also arise at the level of audience **reception**; for example, Maria Pini has explored club cultures in terms of female experiences of clubbing in an attempt to rescue consideration of this music from exclusively male perspectives (Pini 2001; see **gender**, **feminism**). Consideration of subjectivity inevitably brings musicologists around to an acknowledgement that musical experience is profoundly individual. As with identity, however, the relationship is reciprocal, and music will inform and construct a sense of the self in the process. The listening experience will involve a sense of being in the perhaps timeless presence and place of a piece. The experience may be 'both thoroughly other and fully [the listener's]' (Kramer 2001, 153; see **alterity**). However, Kramer locates a 'limit of listening', where music makes too many technical and stylistic demands and assumes too much knowledge. By extension, he notes that **analysis** 'in the narrow sense depersonalises or desubjectivises the musical work in the sense of bracketing or at least temporarily voiding its subject positions' (*ibid.*, 170). However, he concludes that this tendency of analysis to desubjectivize may be used to consider alternative subject positions (see **subject position**) in a work, moving away from the one provided by the composer.

Further reading: Kramer 2002

SUBJECT POSITION

Subject position is a concept that arose in film studies and media theory but has recently been applied to **popular music**, Romantic lieder and opera. The term conveys an inherent problem, since it need not refer to an individual subject. Instead, it implies a notion that is roughly equivalent to 'viewpoint', more specifically, the viewpoint that a film encourages a viewer to adopt towards its content. Determining a subject position ideally combines a structuralist approach (see **structuralism**) – a search for **meaning** in the form (see **analysis**) of a text (see **narrative**) – with a consideration of how a film relates to social codes and generic expectations (see **genre**) that reside outside itself. Sheila Johnston, who introduced the concept in relation to film theory, refers to a subject position 'soliciting' and 'demanding' a 'certain closely circumscribed response from the reader by means of its own formal operations' (Johnston 1985, 245). She also suggests that 'it promises a method which avoids the infinite pluralism which posits as many readings as there are readers, and an essentialism which asserts a single "true" meaning' (*ibid.*, 245). In other words, subject position attempts to steer a middle course between determinism – the insistence on a single meaning – and the pluralism of reader response theory (see **post-structuralism**).

A key distinction that it is necessary to make when determining the subject position of a film is that between subject matter (the content of the film) and subject position (the attitude that the film takes towards that content). Musicologist Eric Clarke makes the point that in cinema it is possible to distinguish clearly between the narrative content of a film and the way in which the 'formal devices of film-making solicit or demand a certain kind of attitude to the events of the film...the manner in which we as viewers are allowed or invited to know about [the] narrative' (Clarke 1999, 352). The question is this: can the same idea be applied to music? Clarke suggests that in music the distinction to be made is between musical content (its subject matter) – in terms of **style**, form and technique – and the attitude the music, or musicians, adopt towards that content (its subject position), again traceable in terms of style, genre and parody techniques.

The most likely place to find subject position in music is in works that combine music and words, especially examples that contain more than one narrative voice, since this will potentially include multiple identities (see **identity**) and viewpoints. Lawrence Kramer, who believes that 'the basic work of culture is to construct subject positions' (Kramer 2001, 156), has suggested that 'a song will typically seek to manage the interplay of text, voice and musical technique in order to privilege one of the available positions' (Kramer 1995, 147). Some more detailed examples are provided by Clarke in his discussion of songs by Frank Zappa and P.J. Harvey (Clarke 1999). In his analysis of Zappa's 'Magdalena' (1972), whose narrative voice is that of a father who has abused his daughter, Clarke illustrates the separation of subject matter and subject position at a moment when the father appeals to his daughter to trust him and feel sympathy for him, while the music, which shifts to a Broadway show style, indicates that what the father is singing is fake: 'It is Zappa's use of ironised, exaggerated and ridiculed musical styles, and the cultural values that each style specifies, together with a number of aspects of the vocal delivery, that articulates the music's subject-position' (Clarke 1999, 357).

However, at the end of his investigation, Clarke concludes:

We are not allowed the easy comfort of a clear ideological perspective: the song is neither a crushing and serious-minded indictment of abuse, nor a simple indulgence in the smutty humour that is a part of the violence and abuse that are described.

(*ibid.*, 362)

In other words, the subject position overall is not clear, since the critique entails an element of complicity – pointing to the listener's own involvement in the problem – and the range of responses from listeners will vary widely as a result. In this instance, the examination of subject position has avoided presenting a single meaning. In the case of P.J. Harvey's song 'Taut' (1996), however, which deals with the theme of sexual abuse as narrated by the victim, Clarke argues that the subject position is far less ambivalent. In contrast to the constant shifts of style in 'Magdalena', 'Taut' is remarkably consistent and confrontational, drawing the listener into a direct identification with the singer and protagonist. This manufacturing of an authentic (see **authenticity**) expression can be traced back to early **Romanticism** (Bloomfield 1993, 27).

A further point to emerge from Clarke's study is its emphasis on the sound-based elements of a song, rather than the aspects that can be notated. It also draws attention, in the Zappa song, to techniques that undermine a sense of authorial authenticity. In this sense, it can be seen as part of a wider project to reassess the **work** concept. By extension, a consideration of subject position may extend to production techniques, promotional materials, artist interviews, music videos, the role of the media, performance details and other non-score-based factors (see Dibben 2001).

Clarke further suggests that subject position may, potentially, be revealed in instrumental music in the way in which a conventional form, genre or style is treated by a composer. He suggests that 'the separation between matter and position comes about often by an awareness of surplus, excess or disjunction of one sort or another' (Clarke 1999, 371). This idea is similar to Kramer's notion of a 'hermeneutic window' (see hermeneutics). Such questions have also informed studies of opera. Philip Rupprecht has considered how subject position may be encoded instrumentally through what he terms 'voice placement' – the textural disposition of orchestra and singers at specific moments (Rupprecht 2001). This may amount to differing timbres in the instrumental support for certain characters, instrumental enactments of attitudes, and echoes of certain utterances. For example, the following description of a passage in Britten's opera *Billy Budd* (1950–1), which presents the viewpoints of three different characters: '[against Billy's stammer trill] Vere's order to "answer!" is advanced with bright trumpet support, while string octaves draw out rising-fifth intervals as echoes of the direct accusation Claggart has just made' (*ibid.*, 116).

However, the question that this example raises is what is the subject position of the opera at this point? How is the music inviting us to interpret the scene? In some cases, it is difficult to tell where enactments of situations end and orchestral commentaries begin, and Rupprecht acknowledges that hearing unambiguous signs of narrative distance in opera is 'tricky'.

Even though the degree of insistence of a subject position may vary from demanding to inviting a particular interpretation, and despite the claim by Clarke that it 'does not imply a kind of authorial determinism' (Clarke 1999, 354), it is difficult to see how describing subject position can avoid the charge of determinism that is often levelled against other forms of analysis. However, a way around this problem is suggested by certain arguments concerning Strauss's operas *Salome* (1905) and *Elektra* (1909). In these works, it has been argued, the orchestra's viewpoint has been constructed in such a way that it may be said to parody and satirize contemporary patriarchal views (Gilman 1988; Kramer 1990, 1993c). In other words, the next step to describing a work's subject position may be to subject that position to further **interpretation**.

Further reading: Dibben 1999

SUBLIME

While the concept of the sublime came into clearest focus through the **aesthetics** of the eighteenth century, and it has been reconfigured through the contemporary context of **postmodernism**, it does have a long history stretching back to antiquity. However, it is through Immanuel Kant and his *Critique of Judgement*, published in 1790 (Kant 1987), that the sublime is fully conceptualized. Kant defines the sublime as 'that which makes everything else seem small in comparison with it' (le Huray and Day 1981, 224). On this account, the definition of something as sublime adds a heightened sense of **value**; the sublime object becomes that which overshadows all that surrounds it. Kant offers a subdivision of the sublime into the mathematically and the dynamically sublime. The mathematical sublime conveys the impression of largeness, or magnitude, the scale of which we are unable to understand through the construction of any concept. In other words, it goes beyond our normative conceptual framework. In contrast, the dynamically sublime represents force, as represented through the phenomena of nature for example, that cannot be contained or restricted by any existing concept. Music can often be written about in ways that reflect these two models of the sublime, with the overwhelming impression made by some music seeming to meet with incomprehension (see **reception**).

Kant uses beauty as a point of comparison to the sublime. However, this comparison had already been made by Edmund Burke in his *Philosophical Enquiry into the Origin of our Ideas of the Sublime and Beautiful*, published in 1757 (Burke 1998). According to Burke:

> sublime objects are vast in their dimensions, beautiful ones comparatively small: beauty should be smooth and polished; the great, rugged and negligent; beauty should shun the right line yet deviate from it insensibly; the great in many cases loves

the right line; and when it deviates, it often makes a strong deviation: beauty should not be obscure; the great ought to be dark and gloomy: beauty should be light and delicate; the great ought to be solid and even massive. They are indeed ideas of a very different nature, one being founded on pain, the other on pleasure.

(le Huray and Day 1981, 70–1)

This comparison, and the equating of sublime with great, emphasizes again the vastness of the concept. This comparison can also be given a musical resonance, with the heroic image of Beethoven constructed through the reception of **Romanticism**, for example, reflecting Burke's description of the sublime. The music of Haydn, a composer whose work was contemporary with the **aesthetics** of the **Enlightenment**, is often referred to in terms of the sublime. Gustav Schilling, writing in the nineteenth century, connects Haydn's oratorio *The Creation* (1797–8) to the sublime:

the concept of the sublime transcends all physical reality and if religious faith in miracles ultimately stems from the same source as aesthetic feelings for the sublime, then in music too the sublime achieves its most perfect expression and greatest power when it links the finite and phenomenal, so to speak, with the infinite and divine, thereby clothing the sublime with a miraculous radiance. Thus there is still no music of greater sublimity than the passage, 'and there was Light' which follows 'and God said' in Haydn's *Creation*.

(*ibid.*, 474)

The description of specific musical moments as sublime can also relate to instrumental music (see **absolute**). James Webster retrospectively refers to the introductions to Haydn's late symphonies, commenting on 'an avoidance of symmetrical melodies and regular periods (except, perhaps at the beginning), in favour of short, contrasting, irregularly-phrased motives, juxtaposed in unexpected or apparently incommensurable ways' (see symphonies nos. 97 (1792) and 102 (1794–5)). Webster concludes: 'The aesthetic result was nothing less than an invocation of the sublime – a transfer, towards the end of the eighteenth century, of this concept from the domains of poetry and aesthetics, as represented by writers such as Burke and Kant, to that of instrumental music' (Webster 1991, 163).

The sublime has resurfaced through the context of postmodernism, with theorists as diverse as Jameson, Lyotard and Žižek all making reference to the concept (see Hartley 2003). This specific context has not yet made an impact on musicology, as the exploration of the musical potential of postmodernism and its related concepts has not as yet been fully developed.

Further reading: Brown 1996; Taruskin 1995

THEORY

The concept of theory in music concerns the measurement and description of sound properties and the abstract and syntactical components of musical **language**, for example its tones, intervals, scales, rhythms, timbres and key signatures. Such investigation has led to pedagogical guides designed to teach harmony, counterpoint, orchestration and composition. However, music theory may also refer to the quasi-scientific consideration of the components of music in relation to the mathematical and physical sciences; this can be dated back to Aristotle and, later, the quadrivium, which saw music taught alongside arithmetic, geometry and astronomy during the Middle Ages. Theoretical insights may also be related to music **analysis** and broader aesthetic concerns (see **aesthetics**), such as the desire, active since the **Renaissance**, to understand how music is related to nature (see Clark and Rehding 2001).

As this account indicates, considerations of music's physical and abstract properties have changed through history, notably with the move towards tonality around 1600 and then away from tonality around 1900. Initially, the idea that music was divine – a gift from God – was foremost, leading to the belief that the laws of nature should also be the laws of music (such thinking is prevalent even in the twentieth century, for example in arguments that serial music is degenerate, or unnatural; see Potter 1998). But with the encroachment of acoustic science in the seventeenth century, music was gradually reduced to quantifiable sound and a viewpoint best summed up by German physicist and physiologist Hermann von Helmholtz (see **positivism**): 'The construction of scales and harmonic tissues is a product of artistic invention and by no means furnished by the natural formation or natural function of our ear, as has been hitherto most generally asserted' (Helmholtz 1954, 365).

An example of such 'invented' practice was the correction of the 'laws in nature' by the Florentine Camerata, who championed the use of tempered tuning around 1600 (see Chua 2001). These changes led, ultimately, to the widespread use of equal temperament and the cycle of fifths – the foundations of modern tonality. The eighteenth century saw the rise of formal analysis, which was directly linked to a greater understanding of the structural potential inherent in the tonal system. Recent critical work has investigated theories from this period in terms of **gender**, especially in the context of thematic processes and key signatures in sonata form (Burnham 1996), **hermeneutics** (Bent 1994) and the link between theory, **sketch** study and compositional process (*ibid.*). In the nineteenth and twentieth centuries, a number of music theorists, including Hugo Riemann and Heinrich Schenker, further refined techniques of tonal analysis and the associated ideas of musical unity and coherence (see **analysis**, **organicism**). Linked to the concept of musical unity was the development of a surface/ depth **metaphor** – a hierarchical division between surface detail and a reduced, deeper structural level, with high **value** being placed on the presence of connection and direction at the deeper structural level. (For a critical and cultural evaluation of the surface/depth metaphor, see Fink 1999.) Both as a result of advances in mathematics and linguistics and their influence on recent music theory, and following the rise of a plurality of musical styles and techniques in the twentieth century, music theory currently forms a discipline on its own terms.

In this more developed theoretical context, a number of contrasting approaches exist. One of the central debates associated with music theory is what American musicologist Scott Burnham calls 'the continued tension between musical practice and intellectual model' (Burnham 1993, 77). In some instances, this has led to a desire to relate music theory to aural perception (Cook 1987). Other trends include approaches influenced by developments in **psychology** (Lerdahl and Jackendoff 1983), theories based on melodic and rhythmic contour (Morris 1993), pitch–class set theory (Forte 1973), and theories based on the study of systems of tonal functions and relationships (Lewin 1982, 1995). This last example has developed into so-called neo-Riemannian theory, which builds on Riemann's ideas about the relationships between triads in tonal music. American music theorist Richard Cohn has pointed out that neo-Riemannian theory has arisen as part of an evolving post-structuralist critical practice (see **post-structuralism**). In particular, it is a response to analytical problems formed by chromatic music 'that is triadic but not altogether tonally unified' (Cohn, 1998, 167; see also Lewin 1982). This theory concerns music in which the use of triads persists but in a more lightly chromatic context, for example in music by Wagner and Liszt. Schubert has also attracted much theoretical attention owing to a longstanding view of him as a composer who disrupts or inflects Classical form and harmonic syntax. One scholar who has brought a combination of musical and multidisciplinary theory to bear on a reconsideration of Schubert's music is Lawrence Kramer (Kramer 1998). However, Kramer has been criticized by Suzannah Clark for failing to examine the Schenkerian theory he applies to the same extent as the literary theories he draws on. The result, according to Clark, is that '[Schubert's] harmonic predilection and formal inclinations – identified as symbols of deviance – [are] subordinated to the norm' (Clark 2002, 237). Similar charges have been levelled at Susan McClary and Carolyn Abbate for their work on harmonic disjunctions in Mozart and Mahler, respectively (Agawu 1993a, 94–7).

Another recent trend in theoretical work is the application of apparently anachronistic analytical and theoretical models to musical works (see **work**) in order to challenge embedded notions about how music from certain periods functions. For example, Mozart has been examined using pitch-class set theory, and Webern's serial music has been explored in terms of tertian (triadic) harmonies (Phipps 1993). By extension, Burnham makes the point that studies of music theorists should not essentialize their work by measuring it in terms of whether it ultimately proved right or wrong. Instead, he argues:

> our present theoretical prejudices can start a dialogue with the earlier theory, in the manner of a hermeneutic [see **herme-neutics**] exchange. Such an exchange would take the shape of a questioning, starting... with those aspects of earlier theory which seem to stand in greatest contradiction to our own views.... Every test of an earlier theorist's assumptions is thus at the same time a test of our own assumptions. The result would be a more integrated view of ourselves as historical beings.
>
> (Burnham 1993, 79)

Burnham then pursues an illuminating examination of aspects of the harmonic theory of French music theorist and composer Jean-Philippe Rameau. Burnham illustrates not only how aspects of Rameau's theories were the product of the **Enlightenment** thought of his time but also how subsequent interpretations of Rameau, notably by Riemann and Schenker, were heavily conditioned by historical and cultural ideas following the First World War, linked to philosophical notions of German intellectual supremacy dating back to the poetry and philosophy of Friedrich Schiller and Johann Wolfgang von Goethe. Such considerations may be summarized as considerations of 'the inherently cultural dimension of music-theoretical claims' (Clark and Rehding 2001, 8; see also Bent 1996a; Judd 2000; Rehding 2003).

Increasingly, theoretical work has come under close scrutiny, the most obvious example being the search for unity and **organicism** and the association of these features with coherence, value and **genius**. American musicologist Fred Everett Maus has identified three principal ways in which the concept of unity has been questioned: calls for a more explicit or accurate account (Cohn and Dempster, 1992); a consideration of other valuable qualities in music and an account of these other qualities in relation to unity (Kerman 1994); and a more radical questioning of whether the search for unity is 'ever appropriate as a critical or scholarly aim' (Maus 1999, 173). Although he dismisses the third question as inappropriate, on the grounds that it does not concur with his personal experience of music, Maus does pursue an investigation into the existence of different types of unity.

While considerations of music theory developed in the past are increasingly entering into a reflexive relationship with the present, and the tension between model and practice continues to feature in current studies, the gap that has always existed between the work of music theorists and composers contemporary with them continues to grow, although ideally the activities of one will continue to inform the other.

See also: **critical theory**, **cultural studies**, **deconstruction**, **ideology**, **structuralism**

Further reading: Bent and Drabkin 1987; Brown *et al.* 1997; Klumpenhouwer 1998; Littlefield and Neumeyer 1998

TRADITION

Music is closely bound by a concept of tradition, which may be commonly understood as sets of beliefs and practices that are transmitted across generations to form a context that then becomes a framework for subsequent cultural activity (see **culture**) and **interpretation**.

Musicology reflects upon specific traditions of music and is defined and shaped by its own contexts and agendas, which could be conceived as forming part of a tradition. Specific cultural traditions are often represented through the discourses (see **discourse**) of ethno-musicology (see **ethnicity**). Tradition, or traditions, can be presented as a context in which to understand the work of a specific composer (Taruskin 1996) or as a part of a wide-ranging historical perspective (Abraham 1974). Musical **style** and **genre** are often closely inter-twined with a concept of tradition, as both generate continuities and form models and points of reference.

Throughout many different intellectual contexts, how tradition is defined is open to debate. Poet and critic T.S. Eliot, in a highly influential and widely cited essay titled 'Tradition and the Individual Talent' (originally published in 1919), suggested that tradition 'involves, in the first place, the historical sense, which we may call nearly indispensable to anyone who would continue to be a poet beyond his twenty-fifth year; and the historical sense involves a per-ception, not only of the pastness of the past, but of its presence' (Eliot 1975, 38). For Eliot, then, tradition involves an awareness of the past, a sense of historical precedent, which becomes an active force in the present. This view could be readily relatable to music, with the creative act of composition and the role of the interpreter reflecting the awareness of precedents and precursors. Eliot goes on:

> the historical sense compels a man to write not merely with his own generation in his bones, but with a feeling that the whole of the literature of Europe from Homer and within it the whole of the literature of his own country has a simultaneous existence and composes a simultaneous order.

> (*ibid.*, 38)

Eliot now suggests an essentially conservative view of the past through a construction of 'order'. It is also notable that he makes reference only to a European tradition, by implication excluding non-European traditions, and through the proposition of the 'whole' indicates that this tradition is now available only as a totality. This perspective is further enhanced by the positioning of Homer as the starting point, a strategy that links tradition to the construction of a **canon** of great figures and works.

While the past as tradition suggests a conservative impulse, this past can positively shape the present and future. This possibility is devel-oped in some detail by American music theorist Joseph Straus in his book *Remaking the Past: Musical Modernism and the Influence of the Tonal Tradition* (Straus 1990). Straus characterizes the musical modernism of composers such as Berg, Bartók, Schoenberg, Stravinsky and Webern through their problematic relationships to the tonal tradition, but he also considers how this tradition is represented in the presence of modernism. He develops his argument through reference to the literary theory of Harold Bloom, which sought to articulate the 'anxiety of influence' (Bloom 1973; see also **influence**).

If tradition is read as a representation of the past, it also suggests a certain context, a point of location or reference, but this need not be a fixed conception. According to philosopher Hans-Georg Gadamer: 'Tradition is not simply a permanent precondition; rather, we produce it ourselves inasmuch as we understand, participate in the evolution of tradition, and hence further determine it ourselves' (Gadamer 2003, 283). This version of tradition embraces fluidity, the past as process, to which we contribute and determine. Gadamer's conception of tradition is invoked by jazz scholar David Ake in his discussion of jazz cultures (Ake 2002) through reference to recordings by Wynton Marsalis (*Marsalis Standard Time Vol. 2: Intimacy Calling*, 1991) and Bill Frissell (*Have a Little Faith*, 1993). The Marsalis recording revisits standard material from the past played in a style that seeks to respect and represent a jazz tradition. The Frissell recording also uses past material, but from an eclectic range of sources (including Madonna, Bob Dylan, Copland and Ives). Both, then, revisit past music, but different traditions are viewed in different ways. Marsalis attempts to position himself within a tradition that reflects a neoclassical orientation (see **modernism**) but also betrays a certain postmodern nostalgia (see **postmodernism**). In contrast, Frissell stands outside various traditions and does not seek to perpetuate any single tradition but instead articulates a postmodern **hybridity**. For Ake, this comparison suggests a multiplicity of traditions: 'each of these albums . . . presents only one way of understanding and presenting jazz, not *the* way. In a sense, multiple jazz traditions are – and always have been – "the tradition"' (Ake 2002, 175). This proposal of multiple jazz traditions can be readily transferred to other musical contexts, with a plural rather than singular concept of tradition reflecting the diversity of contemporary musical and musicological experiences.

Further reading: Pickering 1999; Whittall 2003

VALUE

Musicology operates its own systems of values. The decisions taken concerning which composers, periods, works and contexts are studied might reflect personal preferences or ideological positions (see **ideology**). They may also reflect mechanisms of value as defined by the status and legacy of the **canon**.

Questions of value also resonate through the context of **aesthetics**, in which the judgements associated with value form a core issue. The central text in debates surrounding the question of value is Immanuel Kant's *Critique of Judgement*, originally published in 1790 (Kant 1987). In this work, Kant sought to consider the essence of judgement and the aesthetic issues of value. For Kant, a distinction was made between the pleasure that could be derived from art, through the designation of value in the form of beauty, and a more functional sense of enjoyment from what were conceived of as more mundane social pleasures. This distinction, through the claim of an aesthetic purity, leads to a view of aesthetic value as essentially autonomous (see **autonomy**), a view that has been subjected to much critical scrutiny.

It is evident that much musicological work has assumed a sense of aesthetic value through a preoccupation with the internal functions of musical works (see **analysis**, **formalism**), the focus on the composer as **genius** and the historical development of individual styles (see **style**) and genres (see **genre**). All these factors could be seen to suggest the operation of autonomous value systems that are bound by their own self-legitimization and freed from context. The claimed distinction between an aesthetic realm and that which by implication fails to reach this condition has reflections in the study of classical music, but it raises even more accentuated problems for the **interpretation** of **popular music**.

Popular music is a context loaded with issues of value. It is a music disseminated through a commercial market, which confers its own sense of value upon the music (see **culture industry**). This is evident by economic measurements such as charts and the tracking of record sales. It is also reflected in the popular media and its historicization of popular music through the consideration of 'great', 'classic' albums (see **canon**). Popular music scholar Simon Frith has written extensively on the questions of value judgements in relation to popular music, seeking to go beyond commercial value to consider the possibility of an aesthetic value in relation to the social discourses (see **discourse**) that coalesce around the music: 'Part of the pleasure of popular culture is talking about it; part of its meaning is this talk, talk which is run through with value judgements. To be engaged with popular culture is to be discriminating' (Frith 1996, 4). But how do we move from a scenario based around a discourse of like/dislike into a more constructive framework? According to Frith, 'aesthetic arguments are possible only when they take place within a shared critical discourse' (*ibid.*, 10). In other words, for a meaningful dialogue to take place concerning different values and judgements, it is essential for some common ground to be established. From this, we may deduce that classical and popular music inhabit different territories and speak different critical languages. It is also possible to suggest that with the increasing pluralization of popular music and its attendant styles and subcultures (see **culture**), there may be such a vast distance between some popular music styles that no shared critical discourse is readily available. However, the actual process of formulating value judgements may betray some underlying similarities. With reference to the critical distance between classical ('high') and popular ('low') culture, Frith claims that 'in responding to high and low art forms, in assessing them, finding them beautiful or moving or repulsive, people are employing the same evaluative principles. The differences lie in the objects at issue (what is culturally interesting to us is socially structured), in the discourses in which judgements are cast, and to the circumstances in which they are made' (*ibid.*, 19). However, any shift from consideration of individual responses and the values that they indicate to a larger theoretical understanding of the issues remains problematic and available for further research within the broad context of music aesthetics.

See also: **work**

Further reading: Dahlhaus 1983b; Kieran 2001

WORK

The concept of a musical work can be dated back at least as far as the fifteenth century, when composers such as Dunstable and Dufay were increasingly identified on musical sources; there is also evidence of the concept in writings by **Renaissance** humanists (see Strohm 1993). However, from the late eighteenth century onwards musical works became the basic unit of artistic production and consumption, largely as a result of increased links between music and state institutions and wider access of the public to 'art' music. Subsequently, through German **Romanticism**, a new concept of an autonomous (see **autonomy**) often purely instrumental work (see **absolute**) arose, along with determining criteria such as structure, unity (see **organicism**, **analysis**), wholeness, coherence and **genius**. However, the work concept developed in dialogue with other tendencies, such as programme music, which promoted the idea that music's **meaning** lay beyond itself, in a set of musico-poetic images, and the rise of the virtuoso performer-composer, which often led to a sense that the 'performance exceeded the work' (Samson 2003, 4). Certain technical practices have also existed in a critical relationship to the concept of the musical work, including borrowing, quotation (see **intertextuality**), re-composition, arrangement and transcription.

Recently, the concept of the musical work has come under increasing scrutiny, most notably by philosopher Lydia Goehr, who has been concerned with the philosophical problem of the ontological status of a work (Goehr 1992). Goehr's central claim is that the work concept has directly shaped modern musical attitudes since its emergence around 1800, in particular by helping to construct a **canon** of works that are deemed more important than others (see **value**), a system that is still in place today (see Strohm 2000; Goehr 2000).

Central to Western conceptions of the musical work is the existence of a published score. The purpose of a score is primarily to preserve music, but it also facilitates its reproduction, and this is clearly central to the continued existence of a work, ensuring that it has an afterlife. However, it has been contested that the musical score is a very imprecise medium (Boorman 1999, 413), and in many cases, such as nineteenth-century keyboard improvisations, they have merely provided a starting point for performance. In some musical periods (see **periodization**), performers have been required to embellish a score, a fact that composers such as Machaut, Josquin and Handel would have appreciated. Conversely, more verbal instruction, as in the scores of Debussy, and precise notation, in the case of Ferneyhough, have opened the space between the score and its realization in performance even more, either because directions in words leave too much to the imagination, or because an overload of graphic information is difficult to reproduce exactly. A score is therefore only one possible version of a work. Even the concept of an *Urtext* – an 'authorized' edition of a composer's work, based on original manuscripts – can be undermined by editorial misreading.

Implicit in the idea of the musical work has been the assumption that what is composed, performed and received by an audience is the same fixed, unchanging object (Talbot 2000). However, this assumption can easily be disproved, especially in relation to changing performance and conducting traditions (see **authenticity**, **reception**). As works enter different social and historical contexts, so their meanings (see **meaning**) will change, while some composers have a habit of revising their works during their own lifetimes. Throughout history, different ways of listening have also been developed. Nineteenth-century music critics, such as A.B. Marx, encouraged far more 'informed' listening habits in audiences and emphasized the importance of an awareness of structural matters. However, set against this mode of listening would have been a well-established cultural consciousness of the multiple aspects of a work, the contrasting styles, genres (see **style**, **genre**) and references to traditional folk and popular musical forms.

Another question that arises from the work concept is one of authorship. To whom is the work attributable? Is there a single author, or, as in opera, is the work a collaboration (see Petrobelli 1994)? Questions of authorship intersect with the associated concept of text, which can be applied in the sense of a written or published object, but it can also apply to any form of cultural material from which social, historical and aesthetic meaning can be read. A musical score would be one representation of text. Another would be the existence of manuscript or **sketch** material that pre-dates the final published work.

Much critical work has tended to stress the role of the author (composer) over interpreter (reader, critic). However, in the 1950s, a number of American literary scholars, so-called 'new critics', separated authors from texts in order to clear the way for their structuralist readings (see **structuralism**; see also Wimsatt and Beardsley 1954; Pease 1990). The separation of author and text was subsequently developed in a different way by various post-structuralists (see **deconstruction**, **post-structuralism**), notably French philosopher Jacques Derrida and French literary theorist Roland Barthes. Through their insistence on the multiplicity of meanings inherent in any text, the sense of a literary work as fixed and immutable was seriously undermined. Barthes argued for **interpretation** ('the birth of the reader') as the site of meaning in a literary text (Barthes 1977, 142–8). The resulting reader response theory has been adapted to music, for example in the work of Gary Tomlinson (Tomlinson 1984) and Carolyn Abbate (Abbate 1991, 1993). These musicologists consider the musical work in its wider, intertextual context, as the site of intersecting cultural texts. In this move, the concept of text is applied in its broadest sense, embracing cultural topics as expressed in a range of forms, including painting, **cultural studies**, poetry and literature. Following these developments, Stanley Boorman has concluded:

> The notated text is no longer the definer of a musical composition as we understand it... it is no more than a definer of a

specific moment in the evolving history of the composition: it presents only those elements that a copyist, printer, or performer felt were important.

(Boorman 1999, 420)

More recently, the musical *avant-garde*, active since the 1950s, has further undermined the status of the score, either by overloading it with notation too complex to perform naturally or by introducing chance techniques and offering choice to performers, thereby distancing themselves from the musical work, composing 'in ignorance' of the final result. These experiments deepen a nineteenth-century belief that the musical score is an imperfect realization of a composer's idea and the performance an even less perfect stage in the act of interpretation.

The centrality of the work concept found in recent classical traditions is not precisely replicated in **popular music** and **jazz**, which generally eschew the idea of work. However, Richard Middleton has pointed out that these forms are not entirely free of work-centred thinking (Middleton 2000b). Frequently, a **recording** will take on the status of text. Although ethnomusicologists and popular music scholars have contributed much to undermining the idea of a fixed, stable, unitary work, they have had to study closely the impact of recording technology, a principal means by which the idea of a musical work has been sustained and disseminated. A remnant of the work concept is also contained in, but simultaneously problematized by, the prevalence of the **cover version**. Further evidence of the persistence of work-centred thinking in popular music is provided by the 'greatest hits' compilations and '100 greatest' lists of albums, songs and artists in magazines and television documentaries, as well as the continued use of the term 'classic' when referring to songs or artists of seminal status in pop or jazz history (see **canon**). Middleton has also noted the existence of networks of printed and performed songs in popular music that vary but are demonstrably related to one another. He describes these groups as tune families, a feature that is illustrated by African and Afro-diasporic practices such as dubbing and remixing in reggae (Middleton 2000b; see also Hebdige 1987). Middleton, following the literary theory of Henry Louis Gates Jr, argues that these practices define culture 'as the continual paradigmatic transformation, inter- or intra-textual, of given material, the repetition and varying of stock elements, the aesthetic of a "changing same"' (Middleton 2000b, 73).

Further reading: Davies 1988; Ingarden 1986; Tagg 2000.

BIBLIOGRAPHY

Abbate, C. (1991) *Unsung Voices: Opera and Musical Narrative in the Nineteenth Century*, Princeton, NJ, Princeton University Press.
—— (1993) 'Opera; or, the Envoicing of Women', in R. Solie (ed.), *Musicology and Difference: Gender and Sexuality in Music Scholarship*, Berkeley and London, University of California Press.
—— (2001) *In Search of Opera*, Princeton, NJ, Princeton University Press.
Abraham, G. (1974) *The Tradition of Western Music*, Berkeley and London, University of California Press.
Adler, G. (1885) 'Umfang, Methode und Ziel der Musikwissenschaft', *Vierteljahrsschrift für Musikwissenschaft* 1, 5–20 [extracts published in English translation in Bujić 1988, 348–55].
Adlington, R. (2003) 'Moving Beyond Motion: Metaphors for Changing Sound', *Journal of the Royal Musical Association* 128/2, 297–318.
Adorno, T. (1973) *Philosophy of Modern Music*, trans. A.G. Mitchell and W.V. Bloomster, London, Sheed and Ward.
—— (1976) *Introduction to the Sociology of Music*, trans. E.B. Ashton, New York, Seabury Press.
—— (1991a) *Alban Berg: Master of the Smallest Link*, trans. J. Brand and C. Hailey, Cambridge, Cambridge University Press.
—— (1991b) *In Search of Wagner*, trans. R. Livingstone, London and New York, Verso.
—— (1991c) *The Culture Industry: Selected Essays on Mass Culture*, ed. J.M. Bernstein, London and New York, Routledge.
—— (1992a) *Mahler: A Musical Physiognomy*, trans. E. Jephcott, Chicago and London, University of Chicago Press.
—— (1992b) *Quasi una Fantasia: Essays on Modern Music*, trans. R. Livingstone, London and New York.
——(1994) 'On Popular Music', in J. Story (ed.), *Cultural Theory and Popular Culture: A Reader*, Hemel Hempstead, Harvester Wheatsheaf.
—— (1997) *Aesthetic Theory*, trans. R. Hullot-Kentor, eds G. Adorno and R. Tiedemann, London, Athlone Press.
—— (1998) *Beethoven: The Philosophy of Music*, trans. E. Jephcott, ed. R. Tiedemann, Cambridge, Polity Press.
—— (2002) *Essays on Music*, trans. S.H. Gillespie. ed. R. Leppert, Berkeley and London, University of California Press.

Adorno, T. and Horkheimer, M. (1979) *Dialectic of Enlightenment*, trans. J. Cumming, London and New York, Verso.

Agawu, K. (1991) *Playing with Signs: A Semiotic Interpretation of Classic Music*, Princeton, NJ, Princeton University Press.

—— (1993a) 'Does Music Theory Need Musicology?' *Current Musicology* 53, 89–98.

—— (1993b) 'Schubert's Sexuality: A Prescription for Analysis?', *Nineteenth Century Music* 17/1, 79–88.

—— (1997) 'Analyzing Music under the New Musicological Regime', *Journal of Musicology* 15/3, 297–307.

Ake, D. (2002) *Jazz Cultures*, Berkeley and London, University of California Press.

Alcoff, L.M. and Mendieta, E. (eds) (2003) *Identities: Race, Class, Gender, and Nationality*, Oxford, Basil Blackwell.

Althusser, L. (1994) 'Ideology and Ideological State Apparatuses', in J. Storey (ed.) *Cultural Theory and Popular Culture: A Reader*, Hemel Hempstead, Harvester Wheatsheaf.

—— (1996) *For Marx*, trans. B. Brewster, London and New York, Verso.

Amico, S. (2001) '"I Want Muscles": House Music, Homosexuality and Masculine Signification', *Popular Music* 20/3, 359–78.

Anderson, B. (1983) *Imagined Communities: Reflections on the Origin and Spread of Nationalism*, London and New York, Verso.

Applegate, C. (1992) 'What is German music? Reflections on the Role of Art in the Creation of the Nation', *German Studies Review* 15, 21–32.

Armstrong, J. (1982) *Nations Before Nationalism*, Chapel Hill, NC, University of Carolina Press.

Arrighi, G. (1994) *The Long Twentieth Century: Money, Power, and the Origins of our Times*, London and New York, Verso.

Ashcroft, B., Griffiths, G. and Tiffin, H. (2002) *The Empire Writes Back: Theory and Practice in Post-Colonial Literatures*, London and New York, Routledge.

Attali, J. (1985) *Noise: The Political Economy of Music*, trans. B. Massumi, Minneapolis, University of Minnesota Press.

Auner, J. (2003) '"Sing it for Me": Posthuman Ventriloquism in Recent Popular Music', *Journal of the Royal Musical Association* 128/1, 98–122.

Ayrey, C. (1994) 'Debussy's Significant Connections: Metaphor and Metonymy in Analytical Method', in A. Pople (ed.), *Theory, Analysis and Meaning in Music*, Cambridge, Cambridge University Press.

—— (1998) 'Universe of Particulars: Subotnik, Deconstruction and Chopin', *Music Analysis* 17/3, 339–81.

Babbitt, M. (1984) 'The Composer As Specialist', in P. Weiss and R. Taruskin (eds), *Music in the Western World*, New York, Schirmer.

Baker, J. (1986) *The Music of Alexander Scriabin*, New Haven, Conn., and London, Yale University Press.

Baker, N.K. and Christensen, T. (eds) (1995) *Aesthetics and the Art of Musical Composition in the German Enlightenment: Selected Writings of Johann Georg Sulzer and Heinrich Christoph Koch*, Cambridge, Cambridge University Press.

Bakhtin, M.M. (2000) *The Dialogic Imagination: Four Essays*, trans. C. Emerson and M. Holquist, ed. M. Holquist, Austin, University of Texas Press.

Banks, P. (1991) 'Fin-de-siècle Vienna: Politics and Modernism', in J. Samson (ed.), *The Late Romantic Era: From the mid-19th century to World War 1*, London, Macmillan.

Barker, A. (ed.) (1989) *Greek Musical Writings: I The Musician and his Art*, Cambridge, Cambridge University Press.

Barkin, E. and Hamessley, L. (eds) (1999) *Audible Traces: Gender, Identity, and Music*, Zürich, Carciofoli Verlagshaus.

Barrell, J. (1980) *The Dark Side of the Landscape: The Rural Poor in English Painting 1730–1840*, Cambridge, Cambridge University Press.

Barthes, R. (1973) *Mythologies*, trans. A. Lavers, London, Paladin.

—— (1977) *Image – Music – Text*, trans. S. Heath, London, Fontana.

—— (1985) *The Responsibility of Forms: Critical Essays on Music, Art, and Representation*, trans. R. Howard, Oxford, Basil Blackwell.

—— (1990a) *The Pleasure of the Text*, trans. R. Miller, Oxford, Basil Blackwell.

—— (1990b) *S/Z*, trans. R. Miller, Oxford, Basil Blackwell.

—— (1990c) *A Lover's Discourse: Fragments*, trans. R. Howard, London, Penguin.

Bauman, R. (1992) 'Genre', in R. Bauman (ed.), *Folklore, Cultural Performances, and Popular Entertainments*, Oxford and New York, Oxford University Press.

Baumgarten, A.G. (1954) *Reflections on Poetry*, trans. K. Aschenbrenner and W.B. Holther, Berkeley and London, University of California Press.

Beach, D. (ed.) (1983) *Aspects of Schenkerian Theory*, New Haven, Conn., and London, Yale University Press.

Beard, D. (2001) '"From the Mechanical to the Magical": Birtwistle's Pre-Compositional Plan for *Carmen Arcadiae Mechanicae Perpetuum*', *Mitteilungen der Paul Sacher Stiftung* 14, 29–33.

Beckerman, M. (1986) 'In Search of Czechness in Music', *Nineteenth-Century Music* 10/1, 61–73.

Bellman, J. (1998a) 'The Hungarian Gypsies and the Poetics of Exclusion', in J. Bellman (ed.) *The Exotic in Western Music*, Boston, Northeastern University Press.

—— (ed.) (1998b) *The Exotic in Western Music*, Boston, Northeastern University Press.

Benjamin, W. (1992) 'The Work of Art in the Age of Mechanical Reproduction', in H. Arendt (ed.), *Illuminations*, London, Fontana.

Bennett, A. (2000) *Popular Music and Youth Culture: Music, Identity and Place*, London, Macmillan.

Bent, I. (1984) 'The "Compositional Process" in Music Theory 1713–1850', *Music Analysis* 3/1, 29–55.

—— (ed.) (1994) *Music Analysis in the Nineteenth Century: Hermeneutic Approaches*, Cambridge, Cambridge University Press.

—— (ed.) (1996a) *Music Theory in the Age of Romanticism*, Cambridge, Cambridge University Press.

—— (1996b) 'Plato–Beethoven: A Hermeneutics for Nineteenth-Century Music?' in I. Bent (ed.), *Music Theory in the Age of Romanticism*, Cambridge, Cambridge University Press, 105–24.

Bent, I. with Drabkin, W. (1987) *The New Grove Handbooks in Music: Analysis*, London, Macmillan.

Berger, K. (1987) *Musica Ficta: Theories of Accidental Inflections in Vocal Polyphony from Marchetto da Padova to Gioseffo Zarlino*, Cambridge, Cambridge University Press.

Bergeron, K. and Bohlman, P. (eds) (1992) *Disciplining Music: Musicology and Its Canons*, Chicago and London, University of Chicago Press.

Berliner, P. (1994) *Thinking in Jazz: The Infinite Art of Improvisation*, Chicago and London, University of Chicago Press.

Berlioz, H. (1903) *Life of Berlioz*, ed. K.F. Boult, London, Dent.

Bernard, J. (2000) 'The Musical World(s?) of Frank Zappa: Some Observations of His "Crossover" Pieces', in W. Everett (ed.), *Expression in Pop-Rock Music: A Collection of Critical and Analytical Essays*, New York and London, Garland.

Bertens, H. (1995) *The Idea of the Postmodern: A History*, London and New York, Routledge.

Bhabha, H. (1990) *Nation and Narration*, London and New York, Routledge.

—— (1994) *The Location of Culture*, London and New York, Routledge.

Biddle, I. (1996) 'F.W.J. Schelling's *Philosophie der Kunst*: An Emergent Semiology of Music', in I. Bent (ed.), *Music Theory in the Age of Romanticism*, Cambridge, Cambridge University Press.

Bloom, H. (1973) *The Anxiety of Influence: A Theory of Poetry*, Oxford and New York, Oxford University Press.

—— (1995) *The Western Canon: The Books and School of the Ages*, London, Macmillan.

Bloomfield, T. (1993) 'Resisting Songs: Negative Dialectics in Pop', *Popular Music* 12/1, 13–31.

Blume, F. (1967) 'The Idea of "Renaissance"', in *Renaissance and Baroque Music: A Comprehensive Survey*, trans. M.D. Herter, New York and London, W.W. Norton.

Bohlman, P.V. (1988) *The Study of Folk Music in the Modern World*, Bloomington, Indiana University Press.

—— (1992) 'Ethnomusicology's Challenge to the Canon: The Canon's Challenge to Ethnomusicology', in K. Bergeron and P.V. Bohlman (eds), *Disciplining Music: Musicology and Its Canons*, London and Chicago, University of Chicago Press.

—— (1993) 'Musicology as a Political Act', *Journal of Musicology* 11/4, 411–36.

—— (2004) *Music of European Nationalism: Cultural Identity and Modern History*, Oxford, ABC-Clio.

Bonds, M.E. (1991) *Wordless Rhetoric: Musical Form and the Metaphor of the Oration*, Cambridge, Mass., and London, Harvard University Press.

Boorman, S. (1999) 'The Musical Text', in N. Cook and M. Everist (eds), *Rethinking Music*, Oxford and New York, Oxford University Press.

Booth Davies, J. (1980) *The Psychology of Music*, London and Melbourne, Hutchinson.

Borio, G. (1993) *Musikalische Avantgarde um 1960: Entwurf einer Theorie der informellen Musik*, Laaber, Laaber-Verlag.

Born, G. (1995) *Rationalizing Culture: IRCAM, Boulez, and the Institutionalization of the Musical Avant-Garde*, Berkeley and London, University of California Press.

Born, G. and Hesmondhalgh, D. (eds) (2000) *Western Music and its Others: Difference, Representation, and Appropriation in Music*, Berkeley and London, University of California Press.

Bottomore, T. (ed.) (1991) *A Dictionary of Marxist Thought*, Oxford, Basil Blackwell.

Boulez, P. (1968) 'Opera Houses? Blow Them Up!' *Opera* 19/6, 440–50.

—— (1993) *The Boulez–Cage Correspondence*, trans. R. Samuels, ed. J.-J. Nattiez, Cambridge, Cambridge University Press.

Bowie, A. (1993) *Aesthetics and Subjectivity: From Kant to Nietzsche*, Manchester, Manchester University Press.

Bowman, W.D. (1998) *Philosophical Perspectives on Music*, Oxford and New York, Oxford University Press.

Boyd, M. (1983) *Bach*, London, Dent.

Brace, C. (2002) *Landscape, Place and Identity*, London, Sage.

Brackett, D. (2000) *Interpreting Popular Music*, Berkeley and London, University of California Press.

Bradbury, M. and McFarlane, J. (eds) (1976) *Modernism: A Guide to European Literature 1890–1930*, London, Penguin.

Bradby, B. (1993) 'Sampling Sexuality: Gender, Technology and the Body in Dance Music', *Popular Music* 12/2, 155–76.

Brah, A. and Coombes, A.E. (2000) *Hybridity and its Discontents: Politics, Science, Culture*, London and New York, Routledge.

Brandenburg, S. (1978–79), 'Viewpoint: On Beethoven Scholars and Beethoven's Sketches', *Nineteenth Century Music* 2/3, 270–4.

Brett, P. (1977) 'Britten and Grimes', *The Musical Times* 118, 955–1000.

—— (1993) 'Britten's Dream', in R. Solie (ed.), *Musicology and Difference: Gender and Sexuality in Music Scholarship*, Berkeley and London, University of California Press.

—— (1994) 'Musicality, Essentialism, and the Closet, in P. Brett, E. Wood and G.C. Thomas (eds), *Queering the Pitch: The New Gay and Lesbian Musicology*, London and New York, Routledge.

Brett, P., Wood, E. and Thomas, G.C. (eds) (1994) *Queering the Pitch: The New Gay and Lesbian Musicology*, London and New York, Routledge.

Brindle, R.S. (1975) *The New Music: The Avant-Garde Since 1945*, Oxford and New York, Oxford University Press.

Brown, A.P. (1996) 'The Sublime, the Beautiful and the Ornamental: English Aesthetic Currents and Haydn's London Symphonies', in O. Bibba and D.W. Jones (eds), *Studies in Music History: Presented to H.C. Robbins Landon on his 70th Birthday*, London, Thames & Hudson.

Brown, H.M. (1976) *Music in the Renaissance*, Englewood Cliffs, NJ, Prentice Hall.

—— (1982) 'Emulation, Competition, and Homage: Imitation and Theories of Imitation in the Renaissance', *Journal of the American Musicological Society* 35/1, 1–48.

Brown, J. (2000) 'Bartók, the Gypsies, and Hybridity in Music', in G. Born and D. Hesmondhalgh (eds), *Western Music and its Others: Difference, Representation, and Appropriation in Music*, Berkeley and London, University of California Press.

Brown, M. (1997) '"Little Wing": A Study in Musical Cognition', in J. Covach and G.M. Boone (eds), *Understanding Rock: Essays in Musical Analysis*, New York and Oxford, Oxford University Press.

Brown, M., Dempster, D. and Headlam, D. (1997) 'Testing the Limits of Schenker's Theory of Tonality', *Music Theory Spectrum* 19/2, 155–83.

Bujić, B. (ed.) (1988) *Music in European Thought: 1851–1912*, Cambridge, Cambridge University Press.

Bukofzer, M.F. (1951) *Studies in Medieval and Renaissance Music*, London, Dent.

Burckhardt, J. (1990) *The Civilization of the Renaissance in Italy*, London, Penguin Classics.

Bürger, P. (1984) *Theory of the Avant-Garde*, trans. M. Shaw, Manchester, Manchester University Press.

Burke, E. (1998) *A Philosophical Enquiry into the Origin of Our Ideas of the Sublime and Beautiful*, ed. A. Phillips, Oxford and New York, Oxford University Press.

Burke, S. (1993) *The Death and Return of the Author: Criticism and Subjectivity in Barthes, Foucault, and Derrida*, Edinburgh, Edinburgh University Press.

Burney, C. (1957) *A General History of Music from the Earliest Ages to the Present Period*, New York, Dover.

Burnham, S. (1993) 'Musical and Intellectual Values: Interpreting the History of Tonal Theory', *Current Musicology* 53, 76–88.

—— (1995) *Beethoven Hero*, Princeton, NJ, Princeton University Press.

—— (1996) 'A.B. Marx and the Gendering of Sonata Form', in I. Bent (ed.) *Music Theory in the Age of Romanticism*, Cambridge, Cambridge University Press.

—— (1999) 'How Music Matters: Poetic Content Revisited', in N. Cook and M. Everist (eds), *Rethinking Music*, Oxford and New York, Oxford University Press.

Butler, C. (1980) *After the Wake: An Essay on the Contemporary Avant-Garde*, Oxford and New York, Oxford University Press.

—— (1994) *Early Modernism: Literature, Music and Painting in Europe 1900–1916*, Oxford and New York, Oxford University Press.

Butler, J. (1990) *Gender Trouble: Feminism and the Subversion of Identity*, London and New York, Routledge.

—— (1993) *Bodies That Matter: On the Discursive Limits of 'Sex'*, London and New York, Routledge.

Cahoone, L. (ed.) (1996) *From Modernism to Postmodernism: An Anthology*, Oxford, Basil Blackwell.

Caldwell, J. (1991) *The Oxford History of English Music Vol. 1, From the Beginnings to c. 1715*, Oxford and New York, Oxford University Press.

Carroll, M. (2003) *Music and Ideology in Cold War Europe*, Cambridge, Cambridge University Press.

Chanan, M. (1995) *Repeated Takes: A Short History of Recording and its Effects on Music*, London and New York, Verso.

Charlton, D. (1989) *E.T.A. Hoffmann's Musical Writings*, Cambridge, Cambridge University Press.

Chua, D. (1999) *Absolute Music and the Construction of Meaning*, Cambridge, Cambridge University Press.

—— (2001) 'Vincenzo Galilei, Modernity and the Division of Nature', in S. Clark and A. Rehding (eds), *Music Theory and Natural Order: From the Renaissance to the Early Twentieth Century*, Cambridge, Cambridge University Press.

Citron, M. (1993) *Gender and the Musical Canon*, Cambridge, Cambridge University Press.

Clark, S. (2002) 'Schubert, Theory and Analysis', *Music Analysis* 21/2, 209–44.

Clark, S. and Rehding, A. (eds) (2001) *Music Theory and Natural Order: From the Renaissance to the Early Twentieth Century*, Cambridge, Cambridge University Press.

Clarke, D. (1996) 'Language Games', *The Musical Times* 137, 5–10.

—— (2001) *The Music and Thought of Michael Tippett: Modern Times and Metaphysics*, Cambridge, Cambridge University Press.

Clarke, E.F. (1995) 'Expression in Performance: Generativity, Perception, Semiosis', in J. Rink (ed.), *The Practice of Performance*, Cambridge, Cambridge University Press.

—— (1999) 'Subject-Position and the Specification of Invariants in Music by Frank Zappa and P.J. Harvey', *Music Analysis* 18/3, 347–74.

Clément, C. (1988) *Opera, or the Undoing of Women*, trans. B. Wing, Minneapolis, University of Minnesota Press.

Clifford, J. (1988) 'On Orientalism', in *The Predicament of Culture: Twentieth-Century Ethnography, Literature and Art*, Cambridge, Mass., and London, Harvard University Press.

Cohen, S. (1991) *Rock Culture in Liverpool: Popular Music in the Making*, Oxford and New York, Oxford University Press.

Cohn, R. (1998) 'Introduction to Neo-Riemannian Theory: A Survey and Historical Perspective', *Journal of Music Theory* 42/2, 167–80.

Cohn, R. and Dempster, D. (1992) 'Hierarchical Unity, Plural Unities: Toward a Reconciliation', in K. Bergeron and P. Bohlman (eds), *Disciplining Music: Musicology and its Canons*, Chicago and London, University of Chicago Press.

Cone, E.T. (1974) *The Composer's Voice*, Berkeley and London, University of California Press.

Cook, N. (1987) 'The Perception of Large-Scale Tonal Closure', *Music Perception* 5/1, 197–205.

—— (1993) *Beethoven: Symphony No. 9*, Cambridge, Cambridge University Press.

—— (1998a) *Music: A Very Short Introduction*, Oxford and New York, Oxford University Press.

—— (1998b) *Analysing Musical Multimedia*, Oxford and New York, Oxford University Press.

—— (2001) 'Theorizing Musical Meaning', *Music Theory Spectrum* 23/2, 170–95.

Cook, N. and Dibben, N. (2001) 'Musicological Perspectives', in P. Juslin and J.A. Sloboda (eds) *Music and Emotion: Theory and Research*, Oxford and New York, Oxford University Press.

Cook, N. and Everist, M. (1999) *Rethinking Music*, Oxford and New York, Oxford University Press.

Cook, N. and Pople, A. (eds) (2004) *The Cambridge History of Twentieth Century Music*, Cambridge, Cambridge University Press.

Cooke, D. (1959) *The Language of Music*, Oxford and New York, Oxford University Press.

Corbett, J. (2000) 'Experimental Oriental: New Music and Other Others' in G. Born and D. Hesmondhalgh (eds), *Western Music and Its Others*, Berkeley and London, University of California Press.

Covach, J. (1997) 'Jazz-Rock, "Close to the Edge", and the Boundaries of Style', in J. Covach and G.M. Boone (eds), *Understanding Rock: Essays in Musical Analysis*, Oxford and New York, Oxford University Press.

—— (2000) 'Jazz-Rock? Rock-Jazz? Stylistic Crossover in Late-1970s American Progressive Rock', in W. Everett (ed.), *Expression in Pop-Rock Music: A Collection of Critical and Analytical Essays*, New York and London, Garland.

Coyle, M. (2002) 'Hijacked Hits and Antic Authenticity', in R. Beebe, D. Fulbrook and B. Saunders (eds), *Rock Over the Edge: Transformations in Popular Music Culture*, Durham, NC, and London, Duke University Press.

Crawford, J.C. and Crawford, D.L. (1993) *Expressionism in Twentieth-Century Music*, Bloomington, Indiana University Press.

Crozier, R. (1998) 'Music and Social Influence', in D.J. Hargreaves and A.C. North (eds), *The Social Psychology of Music*, Oxford and New York, Oxford University Press.

Culler, J. (1983) *On Deconstruction: Theory and Criticism after Structuralism*, London and New York, Routledge.

Cumming, N. (1994) 'Metaphor in Roger Scruton's Aesthetics of Music' in A. Pople (ed.), *Theory, Analysis and Meaning in Music*, Cambridge, Cambridge University Press.

Cusick, S.G. (1993) 'Gendering Modern Music: Thoughts on the Monteverdi–Artusi Controversy', *Journal of the American Musicological Society* 46/1, 1–25.

—— (1999a) 'On Musical Performances of Gender and Sex', in E. Barkin and L. Hamessley (eds), *Audible Traces: Gender, Identity, and Music*, Zürich, Carciofoli Verlagshaus.

—— (1999b) 'Gender, Musicology, and Feminism', in N. Cook and M. Everist (eds), *Rethinking Music*, Oxford and New York, Oxford University Press.

Dahlhaus, C. (1982) *Esthetics of Music*, trans. W. Austin, Cambridge, Cambridge University Press.

—— (1983a) *Foundations of Music History*, trans. J.B. Robinson, Cambridge, Cambridge University Press.

—— (1983b) *Analysis and Value Judgement*, trans. S. Levarie, New York, Pendragon Press.

—— (1985) *Realism in Nineteenth Century Music*, trans. M. Whittall, Cambridge, Cambridge University Press.

—— (1987) 'New Music and the Problem of Musical Genre', in *Schoenberg and the New Music*, trans. D. Puffett and A. Clayton, Cambridge, Cambridge University Press.

—— (1989a) *The Idea of Absolute Music*, trans. J.B. Robinson, Cambridge, Cambridge University Press.

—— (1989b) *Between Romanticism and Modernism*, trans. M. Whittall, Berkeley and London, University of California Press.

—— (1989c) *Nineteenth Century Music*, trans. J.B. Robinson, Berkeley and London, University of California Press.

Dale, C. (2003) *Music Analysis in Britain in the Nineteenth and Early Twentieth Centuries*, Aldershot, Ashgate.

Dame, J. (1994) 'Unveiled Voices: Sexual Difference and the Castrato', in P. Brett, E. Wood and, G.C. Thomas (eds), *Queering the Pitch: The New Gay and Lesbian Musicology*, London and New York, Routledge.

Dart, T. (1967) *The Interpretation of Music*, London, Hutchinson.

Davidson, J.W. (1993) 'Visual Perception of Performance Manner in the Movements of Solo Musicians', *Psychology of Music* 21, 103–13.

Davies, S. (1988) 'Transcription, Authenticity and Performance', *British Journal of Aesthetics* 28, 216–27.

Davison, A. (2004) *Hollywood Theory, Non-Hollywood Practice: Cinema Soundtracks in the 1980s and 1990s*, Aldershot, Ashgate.

Day, G. (2001) *Class*, London and New York, Routledge.

Deathridge, J. (1991) 'Germany: The "Special Path"', in J. Samson (ed.), *The Late Romantic Era: From the Mid-19th Century to World War I*, London, Macmillan.

Denning, M. (2004) *Culture in the Age of Three Worlds*, London and New York, Verso.

Dennis, D.B. (1996) *Beethoven in German Politics, 1870–1989*, New Haven, Conn., and London, Yale University Press.

DeNora, T. (1997) *Beethoven and the Construction of Genius: Musical Politics in Vienna, 1792–1803*, Berkeley and London, University of California Press.

—— (2000) *Music in Everyday Life*, Cambridge, Cambridge University Press.

Derrida, J. (1976) *Of Grammatology*, trans. G.C. Spivak, Baltimore, Johns Hopkins University Press.

—— (1978) *Writing and Difference*, trans. A. Bass, London and New York, Routledge.

—— (1981) *Positions*, trans. A. Bass, Chicago and London, University of Chicago Press.

de Saussure, F. (1983) *Course in General Linguistics*, trans. R. Harris, eds C. Bally and A. Sechehaye, London, Duckworth.

Deutsch, D. (ed.) (1982) *The Psychology of Music*, New York and London, Academic Press.

DeVeaux, S. (1997) *The Birth of Bebop: A Social and Musical History*, Berkeley and London, University of California Press.

Dibben, N. (1999) 'Representations of Femininity in Popular Music', *Popular Music* 18/3, 331–55.

—— (2001) 'Pulp, Pornography and Spectatorship: Subject Matter and Subject Position in Pulp's *This is Hardcore*', *Journal of the Royal Musical Association* 126/1, 83–106.

—— (2002a) 'Gender Identity and Music', in R. MacDonald, D. Hargreaves and D. Miell (eds), *Musical Identities*, Oxford and New York, Oxford University Press.

—— (2002b) 'Psychology of Music', in A. Latham (ed.) *The Oxford Companion to Music*, Oxford and New York, Oxford University Press.

Dibelius, U. (1966) *Moderne Musik I: 1945–65*, Munich, Piper.

—— (1988) *Moderne Musik II: 1965–85*, Munich, Piper.

Dillon, E. (2002) *Medieval Music-making and the Roman De Fauvel*, Cambridge, Cambridge University Press.

Doctor, J.R. (1999) *The BBC and Ultra-Modern Music, 1922–1936: Shaping a Nation's Tastes*, Cambridge, Cambridge University Press.

Donington, R. (1984) *Wagner's 'Ring' and its Symbols*, London, Faber and Faber.

Dosse, F. (1997) *History of Structuralism Vol. 1: The Rising Sign, 1945–1966*, trans. D. Glassman, Minneapolis, University of Minnesota Press.

Doty, A. (1993) *Making Things Perfectly Queer: Interpreting Mass Culture*, Minneapolis, University of Minnesota Press.

Dunsby, J. and Whittall, A. (1988) *Music Analysis in Theory and Practice*, London, Faber and Faber.

During, S. (ed.) (1993) *The Cultural Studies Reader*, London and New York, Routledge.

Eagleton, T. (1991) *Ideology: An Introduction*, London and New York, Verso.

—— (1996) *Literary Theory*, Oxford, Basil Blackwell.

—— (2000) *The Idea of Culture*, Oxford, Basil Blackwell.

Eagleton, T. and Milne D. (eds) (1996) *Marxist Literary Theory*, Oxford, Basil Blackwell.

Eco, U. (1977) *A Theory of Semiotics*, London, Macmillan.

—— (1985) *Reflections on the Name of the Rose*, trans. W. Weaver, London, Secker & Warburg.

—— (1989) *The Open Work*, trans. A. Cancosni, Cambridge, Mass., Harvard University Press.

—— (1992) *Interpretation and Overinterpretation*, Cambridge, Cambridge University Press.

—— (1994) *The Limits of Interpretation*, Bloomington, Indiana University Press.

Eisenberg, E. (1988) *The Recording Angel: Music, Records and Culture from Aristotle to Zappa*, London, Pan Books.

Eliot, T.S. (1975) *Selected Prose of T.S. Eliot*, ed. F. Kermode, London, Faber and Faber.

Ellis, K. (1995) *Music Criticism in Nineteenth-Century France: La Revue et Gazette Musicale de Paris, 1834–1880*, Cambridge, Cambridge University Press.

Engh, B. (1993) 'Loving It: Music and Criticism in Roland Barthes', in R. Solie (ed.), *Musicology and Difference: Gender and Sexuality in Music Scholarship*, Berkeley and London, University of California Press.

—— (1999) 'After "His Master's Voice"', *New Formations* 38, 54–63.

Epstein, D. (1979) *Beyond Orpheus: Studies in Musical Structure*, Cambridge, Mass., MIT Press.

Eriksen, T.H. (1993) *Ethnicity and Nationalism: Anthropological Perspectives*, London, Pluto Press.

Erikson, E. (1968) *Identity: Youth and Crisis* London, Faber and Faber.

Everett., W. (1985) 'Text-Painting in the Foreground and Middleground of Paul McCartney's Beatles Song "She's Leaving Home": A Musical Study of Psychological Conflict', *In Theory Only* 9, 5–13.

Everist, M. (1996) 'Meyerbeer's *Il crociato in Egitto*: *mélodrame*, Opera, Orientalism', *Cambridge Opera Journal* 8/3, 215–50.

—— (1999) 'Reception Theories, Canonic Discourses, and Musical Value', in N. Cook and M. Everist (eds), *Rethinking Music*, Oxford and New York, Oxford University Press.

Fabbri, F. (1982) 'A Theory of Musical Genres: Two Applications', in D. Horn and P. Tagg (eds), *Popular Music Perspectives*, Exeter, International Association for the Study of Popular Music.

Fanon, F. (1967) *Black Skin, White Masks*, New York, Grove Press.

Fenlon, I. (ed.) (1989) *The Renaissance: From the 1470s to the End of the 16th Century*, London, Macmillan.

Fenton, S. (1999) *Ethnicity: Racism, Class and Culture*, Basingstoke, Macmillan.

Fink, R. (1999) 'Going Flat: Post-Hierarchical Music Theory and the Musical Surface', in N. Cook and M. Everist (eds), *Rethinking Music*, Oxford and New York, Oxford University Press.

Flinn, C. (1992) *Strains of Utopia: Gender, Nostalgia, and Hollywood Film Music*, Princeton, NJ, Princeton University Press.

Floyd, S.A. (1995) *The Power of Black Music: Interpreting its History from Africa to the United States*, Oxford and New York, Oxford University Press.

Forman, M. (2002) '"Keeping it Real"?: African Youth Identities, and Hip Hop', in R. Young (ed.), *Critical Studies 19: Music, Popular Culture, Identities*, Amsterdam and New York, Rodopi.

Fornäs, J. (1995a) 'The Future of Rock: Discourses that Struggle to Define a Genre', *Popular Music* 14/1, 111–27.

—— (1995b) *Cultural Theory and Late Modernity*, London and California, Sage.

Forte, A. (1973) *The Structure of Atonal Music*, New Haven, Conn., and London, Yale University Press.

—— (1978) *The Harmonic Organization of 'The Rite of Spring'*, New Haven, Conn., Yale University Press.

—— (1986) 'Letter to the Editor in Reply to Richard Taruskin from Allan Forte', *Music Analysis* 5/2–3, 321–37.

—— (1996) *The American Popular Ballad of the Golden Era, 1924–50: A Study in Musical Design*, Princeton, NJ, Princeton University Press.

Forte, A. and Gilbert S. (1982) *Introduction to Schenkerian Analysis*, New York, W.W. Norton.

Foucault, M. (1972) *The Archeology of Knowledge*, trans. A.M. Sheridan Smith, London and New York, Routledge.

Franklin, P. (1997a) *The Life Of Mahler*, Cambridge, Cambridge University Press.

—— (1997b) 'Kullervo's Problem – Kullervo's Story', in T. Jackson and V. Murtomäki (eds) *Sibelius Studies*, Cambridge, Cambridge University Press.

—— (2000) 'Modernism, Deception, and Musical Others: Los Angeles circa 1940', in G. Born and D. Hesmondhalgh (eds), *Western Music and Its Others: Differences, Representation and Appropriation in Music*, Berkeley and London, University of California Press.

Frigyesi, J. (1998) *Béla Bartók and Turn-of-the-Century Budapest*, Berkeley and London, University of California Press.

Frisch, W. (1984) *Brahms and the Principle of Developing Variation*, Berkeley and London, University of California Press.

Frith, S. (1996) *Performing Rites: On the Value of Popular Music*, Oxford and New York, Oxford University Press.

—— (2000) 'The Discourse of World Music', in G. Born and D. Hesmondhalgh (eds), *Western Music and Its Others: Differences, Representation and Appropriation in Music*, Berkeley and London, University of California Press.

Frith, S. and McRobbie, A. (1990) 'Rock and Sexuality', in S. Frith and A. Goodwin (eds) *On Record: Rock, Pop and the Written Word*, London and New York, Routledge.

Frogley, A. (1996) 'Constructing Englishness in Music: National Character and the Reception of Ralph Vaughan Williams', in A. Frogley (ed.), *Vaughan Williams Studies*, Cambridge, Cambridge University Press.

—— (1997) 'Getting its History Wrong: English Nationalism and the Reception of Ralph Vaughan Williams', in T. Mäkelä (ed.), *Music and Nationalism in 20th-Century Great Britain and Finland*, Hamburg, von Bockel Verlag.

—— (2002) 'Salisbury, Hardy, and Bunyan: The Programmatic Origins of the Symphony', in *Vaughan Williams's Ninth Symphony*, Oxford and New York, Oxford University Press.

Fry, A. (2003) 'Beyond Le Boeuf: Interdisciplinary Rereadings of Jazz in France', *Journal of the Royal Musical Association* 128/1, 137–53.

Fuller, S. (1994) *The Pandora Guide to Women Composers – Britain and the United States, 1629–present*, London, Pandora.

Gabbard, K. (2002) 'The Word Jazz', in M. Cooke and D. Horne (eds), *The Cambridge Companion to Jazz*, Cambridge, Cambridge University Press.

Gadamer, H. (2003) *Truth and Method*, trans. J. Weinsheimer and D.G. Marshall, New York and London, Continuum.

Garratt, J. (2002) *Palestrina and the German Romantic Imagination*, Cambridge, Cambridge University Press.

Gates, H.L., Jr (1984) 'The Blackness of Blackness: A Critique of the Sign and the Signifying Monkey', in H.L. Gates Jr (ed.), *Black Literature and Literary Theory*, New York, Methuen.

—— (1988) *The Signifying Monkey: A Theory of Afro-American Literary Criticism*, Oxford and New York, Oxford University Press.

Gebhardt, N. (2001) *Going for Jazz: Musical Practices and American Ideology*, Chicago and London, University of Chicago Press.

Gendron, B. (1986) 'Theodor Adorno Meets the Cadillacs', in T. Modelski (ed.), *Studies in Entertainment: Critical Approaches to Mass Culture*, Minneapolis, University of Minnesota Press.

—— (2002) *Between Montmartre and the Mudd Club: Popular Music and the Avant-Garde*, Chicago and London, University of Chicago Press.

Gilbert J. and Pearson E. (1999) *Discographies: Dance Music, Culture and the Politics of Sound*, London and New York, Routledge.

Gill, J. (1995) *Queer Noises: Male and Female Homosexuality in Twentieth-Century Music*, London, Cassell.

Gillett, C. (1983) *The Sound of the City*, London, Souvenir Press.

Gilman, S.L. (1988) 'Strauss and the Pervert', in A. Groos and R. Parker (eds), *Reading Opera*, Princeton, NJ, Princeton University Press.

Gilroy, P. (1999) *The Black Atlantic: Modernity and Double Consciousness*, London and New York, Verso.

—— (2000) *Between Camps: Nations, Cultures and the Allure of Race*, London, Penguin.

Gloag, K. (1998) 'All You Need is Theory? The Beatles' Sgt. Pepper', *Music and Letters*, 79/4, 577–83.

—— (1999a) *Tippett. A Child of Our Time*, Cambridge, Cambridge University Press.

—— (1999b) 'Tippett's Second Symphony, Stravinsky and the Language of Neoclassicism: Towards a Critical Framework', in D. Clarke (ed.), *Tippett Studies*, Cambridge, Cambridge University Press.

—— (2001) Situating the 1960s: Popular Music – Postmodernism – History', *Rethinking History* 5/3, 397–410.

Goehr, L. (1992) *The Imaginary Museum of Musical Works: An Essay in the Philosophy of Music*, Oxford and New York, Oxford University Press.

—— (2000) 'On the Problems of Dating or Looking Backward and Forward with Strohm', in M. Talbot (ed.), *The Musical Work: Reality or Invention?* Liverpool, Liverpool University Press.

Goodwin, A. (1994) 'Popular Music and Postmodern Theory', in J. Storey (ed.), *Cultural Theory and Popular Culture*, Hemel Hempstead, Harvester Wheatsheaf.

Gossett, P. (1990) 'Becoming a Citizen: the Chorus in Risorgimento Opera', *Cambridge Opera Journal* 2/1, 41–64.

Gramsci, A. (1971) *Selections from the Prison Notebooks*, eds and trans. Q. Hoare and G. Nowell Smith, London, Lawrence & Wishart.

Grant, M.J. (2001) *Serial Music, Serial Aesthetics: Compositional Theory in Post-War Europe*, Cambridge, Cambridge University Press.

Green, L. (1988) *Music on Deaf Ears: Musical Meaning, Ideology, Education*, Manchester, Manchester University Press.

—— (1997) *Music, Gender, Education*, Cambridge, Cambridge University Press.

—— (2001) *How Popular Musicians Learn: A Way Ahead for Music Education*, Aldershot, Ashgate.

Greenblatt, S. (1980) *Renaissance Self-Fashioning from More to Shakespeare*, Chicago and London, University of Chicago Press.

—— (ed.) (1982) *The Power of Forms in the English Renaissance*, Norman, Okla., Pilgrim Books.

Grey, T. (1995) *Wagner's Musical Prose: Texts and Contexts*, Cambridge, Cambridge University Press.

Griffiths, D. (1996) 'So Who Are You? Webern's Op. 3 No. 1', in C. Ayrey and M. Everist (eds), *Analytical Strategies and Musical Interpretation: Essays on Nineteenth- and Twentieth-Century Music*, Cambridge, Cambridge University Press.

—— (1997) Review of Schreffler, A.C. (1994) *Webern and the Lyric Impulse: Songs and Fragments on Poems of Georg Trakl*, Oxford and New York, Oxford University Press, *Music Analysis* 16/1, 144–54.

—— (1999) 'The High Analysis of Low Music', *Music Analysis* 18/3, 389–435.

—— (2000) 'On Grammar Schoolboy Music', in D. Scott (ed.), *Music, Culture and Society*, Oxford and New York, Oxford University Press.

—— (2002) 'Cover Versions and the Sound of Identity in Motion', in D. Hesmondhalgh and K. Negus (eds), *Popular Music Studies*, London, Arnold.

Griffiths, P. (1995) *Modern Music and After: Directions Since 1945*, Oxford and New York, Oxford University Press.

Grimley, D. and Rushton, J. (2005) *The Cambridge Companion to Elgar*, Cambridge, Cambridge University Press.

Gronow, P. and Saunio, I. (1998) *An International History of the Recording Industry*, trans. C. Moseley, London and New York, Cassell.

Grossberg, L. (1993) 'The Media Economy of Rock Culture: Cinema, Post-modernity and Authenticity', in S. Frith, A. Goodwin and L. Grossberg (eds), *Sound and Vision: The Music Video Reader*, London and New York, Routledge.

—— (1997a) *Dancing in Spite of Myself: Essays on Popular Culture*, Durham, NC, and London, Duke University Press.

—— (1997b) *Bringing it all Back Home: Essays on Cultural Studies*, Durham, NC, and London, Duke University Press.

Grout, D. and Palisca, C. (2001) *A History of Western Music*, New York and London, W.W. Norton.

Guck, M. (1994) 'Analytical Fictions', *Music Theory Spectrum* 16/1, 217–30.

Habermas, J. (1985) 'Modernity – An Incomplete Project', in H. Foster (ed.), *Postmodern Culture*, London, Pluto Press [originally published in *New German Critique* 22 (1981)].

—— (1990) *The Philosophical Discourse of Modernity*, trans. F. Lawrence, Cambridge, Polity Press.

Haimo, E. (1990) *Schoenberg's Serial Odyssey: The Evolution of his Twelve-Tone Method, 1914–1928*, Oxford and New York, Oxford University Press.

—— (1996) 'Atonality, Analysis and the Intentional Fallacy', *Music Theory Spectrum* 18/2, 167–99.

Hall, P. (1996) *A View of Berg's Lulu Through the Autograph Sources*, Berkeley and London, University of California Press.

Hall, P. and Sallis, F. (eds) (2005) *A Handbook to Twentieth-Century Musical Sketches*, Cambridge, Cambridge University Press.

Hallman, D.R. (2002) *Opera, Liberalism, and Anti-Semitism in Nineteenth-Century France: The Politics of Halévy's 'La Juive'*, Cambridge, Cambridge University Press.

Halstead, J. (1997) *The Woman Composer: Creativity and the Gendered Politics of Musical Composition*, Aldershot, Ashgate.

Hamilton, P. (1996) *Historicism*, London and New York, Routledge.

Hanks, W. (1987) 'Discourse Genres in a Theory of Practice', *American Ethnologist* 14, 666–92.

Hanslick, E. (1986) *On the Musically Beautiful*, trans. G. Payzant, Indianapolis, Hackett.

Haraway, D. (2003) 'A Manifesto for Cyborgs: Science, Technology, and Socialist Feminism in the 1980s', in L.M. Alcoff and E. Mendieta (eds), *Identities: Race, Class, Gender, and Nationality*, Oxford, Basil Blackwell.

Hardt, M. and Negri, A. (2000) *Empire*, Cambridge, Mass., and London, Harvard University Press.

Hargreaves, D.J. and North, A.C. (eds) (1998) *The Social Psychology of Music*, Oxford and New York, Oxford University Press.

Harrison, C. and Wood, P. (eds) (2003) *Art in Theory 1900–1990: An Anthology of Changing Ideas*, Oxford, Basil Blackwell.

Harriss, E.C. (1981) *Johann Matheson's Der Volkommene Capellmeister, A Revised Translation with Critical Commentary*, Ann Arbor, Mich., UMI Research Press.

Hartley, G. (2003) *The Abyss of Representation: Marxism and the Postmodern Sublime*, Durham, NC, and London, Duke University Press.

Harvey, D. (1990) *The Condition of Postmodernity*, Oxford, Basil Blackwell.

—— (2003) *The New Imperialism*, Oxford and New York, Oxford University Press.

Hatten, R. (1994) *Musical Meaning in Beethoven: Markedness, Correlation, and Interpretation*, Bloomington, Indiana University Press.

Hauser, A. (1982) *The Sociology of Art*, trans. K.J. Northcott, London and New York, Routledge.

Hawkes, T. (1977) *Structuralism and Semiotics*, London, Methuen.

Hawkins, S. (2002) *Settling the Pop Score: Pop Texts and Identity Politics* Aldershot, Ashgate.

Head, M. (2000) *Orientalism, Masquerade and Mozart's Turkish Music*, London, Royal Music Association.

—— (2002) 'Schubert, Kramer and Musical Meaning', *Music and Letters* 83/3, 426–40.

Headlam, D. (1995) 'Does the Song Remain the Same? Questions of Authorship and Identification in the Music of Led Zeppelin', in M.E. West and R. Hermann (eds), *Concert Music, Rock and Jazz since 1945: Essays and Analytical Studies*, Rochester, NY, University of Rochester Press.

Heartz, D. (1995) *Haydn, Mozart, and the Viennese School, 1740–1780*, New York and London, W.W. Norton.

Hebdige, D. (1979) *Subculture: The Meaning of Style*, London, Methuen.

—— (1987) *Cut 'n' Mix: Culture, Identity and Caribbean Music*, London and New York, Routledge.

Hegel, G.W.F. (1991) *The Philosophy of History*, trans. J. Sibree, Buffalo, NY, Prometheus Books.

—— (1993) *Introductory Lectures on Aesthetics*, trans. B. Bosanquet, ed. M. Inwood, London, Penguin.

Helbe, A. (2000) *Landing on the Wrong Note: Jazz, Dissonance and Critical Practice*, London and New York, Routledge.

Held, D. (1980) *Introduction to Critical Theory: Horkheimer to Habermas*, Cambridge, Polity Press.

Helmholtz, H. von (1954) *On the Sensations of Tone*, trans. A.J. Ellis, New York, Dover.

Hepokoski, J. (1991) 'The Dahlhaus Project and Its Extra-Musicological Sources', *Nineteenth Century Music* 14/3, 221–46.

Hesmondhalgh, D. (2000) 'International Times: Fusions, Exoticism, and Antiracism in Electronic Dance Music', in G. Born and D. Hesmondhalgh (eds) *Western Music and Its Others*, Berkeley and London, University of California Press.

Hill, D. (1997) 'The Origins of Music Perception and Cognition: A Developmental Perspective', in I. Deliège and J. Sloboda (eds) *Perception and Cognition of Music*, Hove, Psychology.

Hobsbawm, E. (1992) *Nations and Nationalism since 1780: Programme, Myth, Reality*, Cambridge, Cambridge University Press.

—— (1995) *Age of Extremes: The Short Twentieth Century 1914–1991*, London, Abacus.

Hoeckner, B. (2002) *Programming the Absolute: Nineteenth Century German Music and the Hermeneutics of the Moment*, Princeton NJ, Princeton University Press.

Holub, R.C. (1984) *Reception Theory: A Critical Introduction*, London, Methuen.

Horkheimer, M. (1972) *Critical Theory: Selected Essays*, trans. M.J. O'Connell, New York, Herder and Herder.

Howes, F. (1966) *The English Musical Renaissance*, London, Secker & Warburg.

Hughes, M. and Stradling, R. (2001) *The English Musical Renaissance, 1860–1940: Constructing a National Music*, 2nd edn, Manchester, Manchester University Press.

Hutcheon, L. (1989) *The Politics of Postmodernism*, London and New York, Routledge.

Hutnyk, J. (1997) 'Adorno at WOMAD: South Asian Crossovers and the Limits of Hybridity Talk', in P. Werbner and T. Modood (eds) *Debating Cultural Hybridity: Multi-Cultural Identities and the Politics of Anti-Racism*, London and Atlantic Highlands, NJ, Zed Books.

—— (2000) *Critique of Exotica: Music, Politics, and the Culture Industry*, London, Pluto Press.

Hyder, R. (2004) *Brimful of Asia: Negotiating Ethnicity on the UK Music Scene*, Aldershot, Ashgate.

Ingarden, R. (1986) *The Work of Music and the Problem of its Identity*, trans. A. Czerniawski, ed. J.G. Harrell, Berkeley and London, University of California Press.

Inge, J. (2003) *A Christian Theology of Place*, Aldershot, Ashgate.

Inglis, F. (1993) *Cultural Studies*, Oxford, Basil Blackwell.

Iwabuchi, K. (2002) *Recentering Globalization: Popular Culture and Japanese Transnationalism*, Durham, NC, and London, Duke University Press.

Jackson, T. (1995) 'Aspects of Sexuality and Structure in the Later Symphonies of Tchaikovsky', *Music Analysis* 14/1, 3–25.

—— (2001) 'Observations on Crystallization and Entropy in the Music of Sibelius and other Composers , in T. Jackson and V. Murtomäki (eds), *Sibelius Studies*, Cambridge, Cambridge University Press.

Jackson, T.L. and Hawkshaw, P. (eds) (1997) *Bruckner Studies*, Cambridge, Cambridge University Press.

Jahn, O. (1891) *The Life of Mozart*, trans. P.D. Townsend, London, Novello, Ewer & Co.

Jameson, F. (1981) *The Political Unconscious: Narrative as a Socially Symbolic Act*, London, Methuen.

—— (1988) 'Periodizing the 1960s', in *The Ideologies of Theory: Essays 1971–1986. Vol. 2: Syntax as History*, London and New York, Routledge.

—— (1991) *Postmodernism, or, the Cultural Logic of Late Capitalism*, London and New York, Verso.

—— (1998) 'Notes on Globalization as a Philosophical Issue', in F. Jameson and M. Miyoshi (eds), *The Cultures of Globalization*, Durham, NC, and London, Duke University Press.

Jauss, H.R. (1982) *Towards an Aesthetic of Reception*, Minneapolis, University of Minnesota Press.

Jay, M. (1973) *The Dialectical Imagination: A History of the Frankfurt School and the Institute of Social Research 1923–1950*, Berkeley and London, University of California Press.

Joe, J. and Theresa A. (eds) (2002) *Between Opera and Cinema*, London and New York, Routledge.

Johnson, D. (1978–9) 'Beethoven Scholars and Beethoven's Sketches' *Nineteenth Century Music* 2/1, 3–17.

Johnson, J. (1994) 'The Status of the Subject in Mahler's Ninth Symphony', *Nineteenth Century Music* 18/2, 108–20.

Johnston, S. (1985) 'Film Narrative and the Structuralism Controversy', in P. Cook (ed.), *The Cinema Book*, London, British Film Institute.

Judd, C.C. (ed.) (1998) *Tonal Structures in Early Music*, New York and London, Garland.

—— (2000) *Reading Renaissance Music Theory: Hearing with the Eyes*, Cambridge, Cambridge University Press.

Kahn, A. (2000) *Kind of Blue: The Making of Miles Davis's Masterpiece*, London, Granta.

Kahn, D. and Whitehead, G. (eds) (1992) *Wireless Imagination: Sound, Radio and the Avant-Garde*, Cambridge, Mass., and London, MIT Press.

Kalinak, K. (1992) *Settling the Score: Music and the Classical Hollywood Film*, Madison, University of Wisconsin Press.

Kallberg, J. (1987) 'Understanding Genre: A Reinterpretation of the Early Piano Nocturne', *International Musicological Society: Conference Report 14, Bologna*, 775–9.

—— (1987–88) 'The Rhetoric of Genre: Chopin's Nocturne in G minor', *Nineteenth Century Music* 11/3, 238–61.

Kant, I. (1987) *Critique of Judgement*, trans. W.S. Pluhar, Indianapolis, Hackett.

—— (1996) *Anthropology From a Pragmatic Point of View*, trans. V.L. Dowdell, Illinois, Southern Illinois University Press.

Karl, G. (1997) 'Structuralism and Musical Plot', *Music Theory Spectrum* 19/1, 13–34.

Kassabian A. (2001) *Hearing Film: Tracking Identifications in Contemporary Film Music*, London and New York, Routledge.

Keil, C. (1966) *Urban Blues*, Chicago and London, University of Chicago Press.

Keil, C. and Feld, S. (1994) *Music Grooves: Essays and Dialogues*, Chicago and London, University of Chicago Press.

Keller, H. (2003) *Music and Psychology: From Vienna to London, 1939–52*, eds C. Wintle and A. Garnham, London, Plumbago Books.

Keller, H. and Mitchell, D. (eds) (1952) *Benjamin Britten: A Commentary On His Works from a Group of Specialists*, London, Rockliff.

Kellner, D. (2002) 'Theorizing Globalization', *Sociological Theory* 20/3, 285–305.

Kelly, M. (ed) (1998) *Encyclopedia of Aesthetics*, Oxford and New York, Oxford University Press.

Kenyon, N. (ed.) (1988) *Authenticity and Early Music*, Oxford and New York, Oxford University Press.

Kerman, J. (1982) 'Viewpoint. Sketch Studies' *Nineteenth Century Music* 6/2, 174–80.

—— (1985) *Musicology* [published as *Contemplating Music* in the USA], London, Fontana.

—— (1994) 'How We Got into Analysis, and How to Get Out', in *Write all These Down*, Berkeley and London, University of California Press [originally published in *Critical Inquiry* (1980), 7, 311–31].

Kielian-Gilbert, M. (1999) 'On Rebecca Clarke's *Sonata for Viola and Piano*: Feminine Spaces and Metaphors of Reading', in E. Barkin and L. Hamessley (eds) *Audible Traces: Gender, Identity, and Music*, Zürich, Carciofoli Verlagshaus.

Kieran, M. (2001) 'Value of Art', in B. Gaut and D. McIver Lopes (eds), *The Routledge Companion to Aesthetics*, London and New York, Routledge.

Kirkpatrick, J. (ed.) (1973) *Charles E. Ives Memos*, London, Calder and Boyars.

Kisby, F. (ed.) (2001) *Music and Musicians in Renaissance Cities and Towns*, Cambridge, Cambridge University Press.

Kivy, P. (1988) *Osmin's Rage: Philosophical Reflections on Opera, Drama, and Text*, Princeton NJ, University of Princeton Press.

—— (2002) *Introduction to a Philosophy of Music*, Oxford and New York, Oxford University Press.

Klumpenhouwer, H. (1998) 'Commentary: Poststructuralism and Issues of Music Theory', in A. Krims (ed.), *Music/Ideology: Resisting the Aesthetic*, Canada, G & B Arts International.

—— (2001) 'Late Capitalism, Late Marxism and the Study of Music', *Music Analysis* 20/3, 367–405.

Knittel, K.M. (1995) '"Ein hypermoderner Dirigent": Mahler and Anti-Semitism in *Fin-de-siècle* Vienna', *Nineteenth Century Music* 18/3, 257–76.

Kofsky, F. (1970) *Black Nationalism and the Revolution in Music*, New York and London, Pathfinder Press.

Korsyn, K. (1991) 'Towards a New Poetics of Musical Influence', *Music Analysis* 10/1–2, 3–72.

—— (1996) 'Directional Tonality and Intertextuality: Brahms's Quintet Op. 88 and Chopin's Ballade Op. 38', in W. Kinderman and H. Krebs (eds), *The Second Practice of Nineteenth-Century Tonality*, Lincoln and London, University of Nebraska Press.

—— (2003) *Decentering Music: A Critique of Contemporary Musical Research*, Oxford and New York, Oxford University Press.

Kramer, L. (1990) 'The Salome Complex' *Cambridge Opera Journal* 2/3, 269–94.

—— (1992) 'The Musicology of the Future' *Repercussions* 1/1, 5–18.

—— (1993a) 'Music Criticism and the Postmodernist Turn: In Contrary Motion with Gary Tomlinson', *Current Musicology* 53, 25–35.

—— (1993b) *Music as Cultural Practice 1800–1900*, Berkeley and London, University of California Press.

—— (1993c) '*Fin-de-siècle* Fantasies: *Elektra*, Degeneration and Sexual Science', *Cambridge Opera Journal* 5/2, 141–65.

—— (1995) *Classical Music and Postmodern Knowledge*, Berkeley and London, University of California Press.

—— (1998) *Franz Schubert: Sexuality, Subjectivity, Song*, Cambridge, Cambridge University Press.

—— (2001) 'The Mysteries of Animation: History, Analysis and Musical Subjectivity', *Music Analysis* 20/2, 153–78.

—— (2002) *Musical Meaning: Toward a Critical History*, Berkeley and London, University of California Press.

Kramnick, I. (ed.) (1995) *The Portable Enlightenment Reader*, London, Penguin.

Krausz, M. (ed.) (1993) *The Interpretation of Music: Philosophical Essays*, Oxford and New York, Oxford University Press.

Krims, A (1998a) 'Introduction: Postmodern Musical Poetics and the Problem of "Close Reading"', in *Music/Ideology: Resisting the Aesthetic*, Canada, G & B International.

—— (1998b) 'Disciplining Deconstruction (For Music Analysis)', *Nineteenth Century Music* 21/3, 297–324.

—— (2000) *Rap Music and the Poetics of Identity*, Cambridge, Cambridge University Press.

—— (2001) 'Marxism, Urban Geography and Classical Recording: An Alternative to Cultural Studies', *Music Analysis* 20/3, 347–63.

—— (2002) 'Rap, Race, the "Local", and Urban Geography in Amsterdam', in R. Young (ed.), *Critical Studies 19: Music, Popular Culture, Identities*, Amsterdam and New York, Rodopi.

Kristeva, J. (1986) 'Word, Dialogue and Novel', in T. Moi (ed.), *The Kristeva Reader*, Oxford, Basil Blackwell.

Krummacher, F. (1994) 'Reception and Analysis: On the Brahms Quartets, Op. 51, Nos. 1 and 2', *Nineteenth Century Music* 18/1, 24–45.

Lackoff, G. (1993) 'The Contemporary Theory of Metaphor', in A. Ortony (ed.), *Metaphor and Thought*, Cambridge, Cambridge University Press.

Lackoff, G. and Johnson, M. (1980) *Metaphors We Live By*, Chicago and London, University of Chicago Press.

Lawson, C. and Stowell, R. (1999) *The Historical Performance of Music: An Introduction*, Cambridge, Cambridge University Press.

Leach, E.E. (ed.) (2003) *Machaut's Music: New Interpretations*, Boydell Press.

le Huray, P. and Day, J. (1981) *Music and Aesthetics in the Eighteenth and Early-Nineteenth Centuries*, Cambridge, Cambridge University Press.

Leppert, R. (1988) *Music and Image: Domesticity, Ideology and Socio-Cultural Formation in Eighteenth-Century England*, Cambridge, Cambridge University Press.

—— (2002) 'Culture, Technology and Listening', in T. Adorno, *Essays on Music*, trans. S.H. Gillespie, Berkeley and London, University of California Press.

Leppert, R. and Lipsitz, G. (2000) '"Everybody's Lonesome for Somebody": Age, the Body, and Experience in the Music of Hank Williams', in R. Middleton (ed.) *Reading Pop: Approaches to Textual Analysis in Popular Music*, Oxford, Oxford University Press.

Lerdahl, F. (1989) 'Atonal Prolongational Structure', *Contemporary Music Review* 4, 65–87.

Lerdahl, F. and Jackendoff, R. (1983) *A Generative Theory of Tonal Music*, Cambridge, Mass., MIT Press.

Levi, E. (1994) *Music in the Third Reich*, London, Macmillan.

Lévi-Strauss, C. (1969) *The Raw and the Cooked*, trans. J. and D. Weightman, London, Jonathan Cape.

—— (1981) *The Naked Man*, trans. J. and D. Weightman, London, Jonathan Cape.

Lewin, D. (1982) 'A Formal Theory of Generalized Tonal Functions', *Journal of Music Theory* 26/1, 23–60.

—— (1986) 'Music Theory, Phenomenology, and Modes of Perception', *Music Perception* 3/4, 327–92.

—— (1995) 'Generalized Interval Systems', *Music Theory Spectrum* 17/1, 81–118.

Lewis, L.A. (ed.) (1992) *Fan Culture and Popular Media*, London and New York, Routledge.

Leyshon, A., Matless, D. and Revill, G. (eds) (1998) *The Place of Music*, New York and London, Guilford Press.

Lippman, E.A. (1977) *A Humanistic Philosophy of Music*, New York, New York University Press.

—— (1992) *A History of Western Musical Aesthetics*, Lincoln and London, University of Nebraska Press.

Lipsitz, G. (1997) *Dangerous Crossroads: Popular Music, Postmodernism and the Poetics of Place*, London and New York, Verso.

Littlefield, R. and Neumeyer, D. (1998) 'Rewriting Schenker: Narrative – History – Ideology', in A. Krims (ed.), *Music/Ideology: Resisting the Aesthetic* Canada, G & B Arts International.

Lochhead, J. (1999) 'Hearing "Lulu"', in E. Barkin and L. Hamessley (eds) *Audible Traces: Gender, Identity, and Music*, Zürich, Carciofoli Verlagshaus.

Lochhead, J. and Auner J. (eds) (2002) *Postmodern Music/Postmodern Thought*, London and New York, Routledge.

Lockwood, L. (1966) 'On "Parody" as Term and Concept in 16th-Century Music', in J. LaRue (ed.), *Aspects of Medieval and Renaissance Music: A Birthday Offering to Gustave Reese*, New York, W.W. Norton.

Longhurst, B. (1995) *Popular Music and Society*, Cambridge, Polity Press.

Lowinsky, E.E. (1941) 'The Concept of Physical and Musical Space in the Renaissance', *Papers of the American Musicological Society*, 57–84.

Lukcás, G. (1971) *History and Class Consciousness: Studies in Marxist Dialectics*, trans. R. Livingstone, London, Merlin Press.

Lyotard, J.-F. (1992) *The Postmodern Condition: A Report on Knowledge*, trans. G. Bennington and B. Massumi, Manchester, Manchester University Press.

MacDonald, R., Hargreaves, D. and Miell, D. (eds) (2002) *Musical Identities*, Oxford and New York, Oxford University Press.

Macan, E. (1997) *Rocking the Classics: English Progressive Rock and the Counterculture*, Oxford and New York, Oxford University Press.

Macfie, A.L. (2002) *Orientalism*, London, Longman.

Mäkelä, T. (ed) (1997) *Music and Nationalism in 20th-Century Great Britain and Finland*, Hamburg, von Bockel Verlag.

Malik, K. (1996) *The Meaning of Race: Race, History and Culture in Western Society*, Basingstoke, Macmillan.

Marshall, R.L. (1972) *The Compositional Process of J.S. Bach: A Study of the Autograph Scores of the Vocal Works*, Princeton, NJ, Princeton University Press.

Marston, N. (1995) *Beethoven's Piano Sonata in E, Op. 109*, Oxford and New York, Oxford University Press.

—— (2001) 'Sketch', in S. Sadie (ed.), *New Grove Dictionary of Music and Musicians*, Vol. 23, London, Macmillan.

Martin, B. (2002) *Avant Rock: Experimental Music from the Beatles to Björk*, Chicago, Open Court.

Marwick, A. (1998) *The Sixties: Cultural Revolution in Britain, France, Italy, and the United States, c. 1958–1974*, Oxford and New York, Oxford University Press.

Marx, K. and Engels, F. (1998) *The Communist Manifesto*, introduction by E. Hobsbawm, London and New York, Verso.

Matless, D. (1998) *Landscape and Englishness*, London, Reaktion.

Maultsby, P. (1990) 'Africanisms in African-American Music', in J.E. Holloway (ed.), *Africanisms in American Culture*, Bloomington, Indiana University Press.

Maus, F.E. (1999) 'Concepts of Musical Unity', in N. Cook and M. Everist *Rethinking Music*, Oxford, Oxford University Press.

—— (2001) 'Glamour and Evasion: The Fabulous Ambivalence of the Pet Shop Boys', *Popular Music* 20/3, 379–94.

Mazullo, M. (1999) *Authenticity in Rock Music Culture*, unpublished PhD thesis, University of Minnesota.

McCann, S. (1996) 'Why I'll Never Teach Rock 'n' Roll Again', *Radical History Review* 66, 191–202.

McCarney, J. (2000) *Hegel on History*, London and New York, Routledge.

McClary, S. (1989) 'Terminal Prestige: The Case of Avant-Garde Music Composition', *Cultural Critique* 12, 57–81.

—— (1991) *Feminine Endings: Music, Gender and Sexuality*, Minneapolis, University of Minnesota Press.

—— (1992) *Georges Bizet: Carmen*, Cambridge, Cambridge University Press.

—— (1993a) 'Music and Sexuality: On the Steblin/Solomon Debate', *Nineteenth Century Music* 17/1, 83–8.

—— (1993b) 'Narrative Agendas in "Absolute" Music: Identity and Difference in Brahms's Third Symphony', in R. Solie (ed.), *Musicology and Difference*, Berkeley and London, University of California Press.

—— (1994) 'Constructions of Subjectivity in Schubert's Music', in P. Brett, E. Wood and G. Thomas (eds), *Queering the Pitch: The New Gay and Lesbian Musicology*, London and New York, Routledge.

—— (2000) *Conventional Wisdom: The Content of Musical Form*, Berkeley and London, University of California Press.

McClatchie, S. (1998) *Analyzing Wagner's Operas: Alfred Lorenz and German Nationalist Ideology*, Rochester, NY, University of Rochester Press.

McClellan, D. (ed.) (2000) *Karl Marx: Selected Writings*, Oxford and New York, Oxford University Press.

McColl, S. (1996) *Music Criticism in Vienna 1896–1897: Critically Moving Forms*, Oxford and New York, Oxford University Press.

McRobbie, A. (1994) *Postmodernism and Popular Culture*, London and New York, Routledge.

Merriam, A.P. (1959) 'African Music', in R. Bascom and, M.J. Herskovits (eds), *Continuity and Change in African Cultures*, Chicago, University of Chicago Press.

Messing, S. (1996) *Neoclassicism in Music: From the Genesis of the Concept Through the Schoenberg/Stravinsky Polemic*, Rochester, NY, University of Rochester Press.

Methuen-Campbell, J. (1992) 'Chopin in Performance', in J. Samson (ed.), *The Cambridge Companion to Chopin*, Cambridge, Cambridge University Press.

Metzer, D. (2003) *Quotation and Cultural Meaning in Twentieth-Century Music*, Cambridge, Cambridge University Press.

Meyer, L.B. (1973) *Explaining Music: Essays and Explorations*, Chicago and London, University of Chicago Press.

—— (1989) *Style and Music: Theory, History and Ideology*, Philadelphia, University of Pennsylvania Press.

Micznik, V. (2001) 'Music and Narrative Revisited: Degrees of Narrativity in Beethoven and Mahler', *Journal of the Royal Musical Association* 126/2, 193–249.

Middleton, R. (1990) *Studying Popular Music*, Milton Keynes, Open University Press.

—— (2000a) 'Musical Belongings: Western Music and Its Low-Other', in G. Born and D. Hesmondhalgh (eds), *Western Music and Its Others*, Berkeley, University of California Press.

—— (2000b) 'Work-in-(g) Practice: Configuration of the Popular Music Intertext', in M. Talbot (ed.), *The Musical Work: Reality or Invention?* Liverpool, Liverpool University Press.

—— (ed.) (2000c) *Reading Pop: Approaches to Textual Analysis in Popular Music*, Oxford and New York, Oxford University Press.

Miles, R. (1989) *Racism*, London and New York, Routledge.

Miles, R. and Brown, M. (2003) *Racism*, 2nd edn, London and New York, Routledge.

Milewski, B. (1999) 'Chopin's Mazurkas and the Myth of the Folk', *Nineteenth-Century Music* 23/2, 113–35.

Miller, I. (1984) *Husserl, Perception, and Temporal Awareness*, Cambridge, Mass., MIT Press.

Miller, S. (ed.) (1993) *The Last Post: Music after Modernism*, Manchester, Manchester University Press.

Mishra, V. and Hodge, B. (1994) 'What is Post(-)colonialism?', in P. Williams and L. Chrisman (eds), *Colonial Discourse and Post-Colonial Theory: A Reader*, New York, Columbia University Press.

Mitchell, W.J.T. (ed.) (1981) *On Narrative*, Chicago and London, University of Chicago Press.

Monelle, R. (1992) *Linguistics and Semiotics in Music*, Chur, Switzerland, and Philadelphia, Harwood Academic Publishers.

—— (1998) *Theorizing Music: Text, Topic, Temporality*, Bloomington, Indiana University Press.

—— (2000) *The Sense of Music: Semiotic Essays*, Princeton, NJ, Princeton University Press.

Monson, I. (1994) 'Doubleness and Jazz Improvisation: Irony, Parody and Doubleness', *Critical Enquiry* 20, 283–313.

—— (1996) *Saying Something: Jazz Improvisation and Interaction*, Chicago and London, University of Chicago Press.

Moore, A. (1997) *Sgt. Pepper's Lonely Hearts Club Band*, Cambridge, Cambridge University Press.

—— (2001a) *Rock: The Primary Text*, Aldershot, Ashgate.

—— (2001b) 'Categorizing Conventions in Music Discourse: Style and Genre', *Music and Letters* 82/3, 432–42.

—— (2002) 'Authenticity as Authentication', *Popular Music* 21/2, 209–23.

—— (ed.) (2003) *Analyzing Popular Music*, Cambridge, Cambridge University Press.

Moore-Gilbert, B. (1997) *Postcolonial Theory: Contexts, Practices, Politics*, London and New York, Verso.

Moriarty, M. (1991) *Roland Barthes*, Cambridge, Polity Press.

Morison, B. (2002) *On Location: Aristotle's Concept of Place*, Oxford and New York, Oxford University Press.

Morris, M. (1999) 'It's Raining Men: The Weather Girls, Gay Subjectivity, and the Erotics of Instability', in E. Barkin and L. Hamessley (eds), *Audible Traces: Gender, Identity, and Music*, Zürich, Carciofoli Verlagshaus.

Morris, R.D. (1993) 'New Directions in the Theory and Analysis of Musical Contour', *Music Theory Spectrum* 15/2, 205–28.

Mowitt, J. (1987) 'The Sound of Music in the Era of its Electronic Reproducibility', in R. Leppert and S. McClary (eds), *Music and Society: The Politics of Composition, Performance and Reception*, Cambridge, Cambridge University Press.

Mulhern, F. (2000) *Culture/Metaculture*, London and New York, Routledge.

Mulvey, L. (1975) 'Visual Pleasure and Narrative Cinema', *Screen* 16/3, 6–18.

Narmour, E. (1992) *The Analysis and Cognition of Melodic Complexity: the Implication–Realization Model*, Chicago and London, University of Chicago Press.

Nattiez, J.-J. (1982) 'Varèse *Density 21.5*: A Study in Semiological Analysis', *Music Analysis* 1/3, 243–340.

—— (1990a) 'Can One Speak of Narrativity in Music?' *Journal of the Royal Musical Association* 115/2, 240–57.

—— (1990b) *Music and Discourse: Toward a Semiology of Music*, trans. C. Abbate, Princeton, NJ, Princeton University Press.

Neale, S. (1980) *Genre*, London, British Film Institute Publishing.

Negus, K. (1999) *Music Genres and Corporate Cultures*, London and New York, Routledge.

Nelson, G. and Grossberg, L. (eds) (1988) *Marxism and the Interpretation of Culture*, Urbana and Chicago, University of Illinois Press.

Nercessian, A. (2002) *Postmodernism and Globalization in Ethnomusicology: An Epistemological Problem*, Lanham, Md, and London, Scarecrow Press.

Neubauer, J. (1986) *The Emancipation of Music from Language*, New Haven, Conn., and London, Yale University Press.

Newcomb, A. (1983–84) '"Once More Between Absolute and Program Music": Schumann's Second Symphony', *Nineteenth-Century Music* 7/3, 233–50.

Nicholls, P. (1995) *Modernisms: A Literary Guide*, London, Macmillan.

Norris, C. (1982) *Deconstruction: Theory and Practice*, London, Methuen.

—— (1990) *What's Wrong With Postmodernism: Critical Theory and the Ends of Philosophy*, Hemel Hempstead, Harvester Wheatsheaf.

—— (1992) *Uncritical Theory: Postmodernism, Intellectuals and the Gulf War*, London, Lawrence & Wishart.

—— (1999) 'Deconstruction, Musicology and Analysis: Some Recent Approaches in Critical Review', *Theses Eleven* 56, 107–18.

Nyman, M. (1999) *Experimental Music: Cage and Beyond*, Cambridge and New York, Cambridge University Press.

Owens, J.A. (1997) *Composers at Work: The Craft of Musical Composition, 1450–1600*, Oxford and New York, Oxford University Press.

Paddison, M. (1991) 'The Language-Character of Music: Some Motifs in Adorno', *Journal of the Royal Musical Association* 116/2, 267–79.

—— (1993) *Adorno's Aesthetics of Music*, Cambridge, Cambridge University Press.

—— (1996) *Adorno, Modernism and Mass Culture: Essays on Critical Theory and Music*, London, Kahn & Averill.

Paley, E. (2000) "'The Voice Which Was My Music": Narrative and Nonnarrative Musical Discourse in Schumann's *Manfred*', *Nineteenth-Century Music* 24/1, 3–20.

Palisca, C. (1985) *Humanism in Italian Renaissance Musical Thought*, New Haven, Conn., and London, Yale University Press.

Palmer, T. (1996) *Dancing in the Street*, London, BBC.

Parker, R. (1997) *Leonora's Last Act: Essays in Verdian Discourse*, Princeton, NJ, Princeton University Press.

Parker, R. and Abbate, C. (eds) (1989) *Analyzing Opera: Verdi and Wagner*, Berkeley and London, University of California Press.

Parry, C.H. (1909) *The Evolution of the Art of Music*, London, Kegan Paul.

Pascall, R. (1989) 'Genre and the Finale of Brahms's Fourth Symphony', *Music Analysis* 8/3, 233–46.

Pasler, J. (2000) 'Race, Orientalism, and Distinction in the Wake of the "Yellow Peril"', in G. Born and D. Hesmondhalgh (eds), *Western Music and Its Others*, Berkeley and London, University of California Press.

Pavlicevic, M. (2000) *Music Therapy in Context: Music, Meaning and Relationship*, London, Jessica Kingsley.

Pease, D.E. (1990) 'Author', in F. Lentricchia and T. McLaughlin (eds), *Critical Terms for Literary Study*, Chicago and London, University of Chicago Press.

Petrobelli, P. (1994) *Music in the Theater: Essays on Verdi and other Composers*, trans. R. Parker, Princeton, NJ, Princeton University Press.

Philip, R. (1998) *Early Recordings and Musical Style: Changing Tastes in Instrumental Performance 1900–1950*, Cambridge, Cambridge University Press.

Phipps, G.H. (1993) 'Harmony as a Determinant of Structure in Webern's Variations for Orchestra', in C. Hatch and D.W. Bernstein (eds), *Music Theory and the Exploration of the Past*, Chicago and London, University of Chicago Press.

Pickering, M. (1999) 'History as Horizon: Gadamer, Tradition and Critique', *Rethinking History* 3/2, 177–95.

Pini, M. (2001) *Club Cultures and Female Subjectivity: The Move from Home to House*, Basingstoke and New York, Palgrave.

Pippin, R.B. (1991) *Modernism as a Philosophical Problem*, Oxford, Basil Blackwell.

Pople, A. (1996) 'Vaughan Williams, Tallis, and the Phantasy Principle', in A. Frogely (ed.), *Vaughan Williams Studies*, Cambridge, Cambridge University Press.

Potter, P. (1998) *Most German of the Arts: Musicology and Society from the Weimar Republic to the End of Hitler's Reich*, New Haven, Conn., and London, Yale University Press.

Propp, V. (1968) *Morphology of the Folktale*, trans. L. Scott, 2nd edn revised and edited with a preface by L.A. Wagner and new introduction by A.D. Dundes, Austin, University of Texas Press.

Radano, R. and Bohlman, P.V. (eds) (2000) *Music and the Racial Imagination*, Chicago and London, University of Chicago Press.

Ramsey, G.P., Jr (2003) *Race Music: Black Cultures from Bebop to Hip-Hop*, Berkeley and London, University of California Press.

Ratner, L.G. (1980) *Classic Music: Expression, Form and Style*, New York, Schirmer Books.

Rehding, A. (2003) *Hugo Riemann and the Birth of Modern Musical Thought*, Cambridge, Cambridge University Press.

Réti, R. (1961) *The Thematic Process in Music*, London, Faber and Faber.
—— (1992) *Thematic Patterns in Sonatas of Beethoven*, New York, Da Capo Press.
Richards, A. (2001) *The Free Fantasia and the Musical Picturesque*, Cambridge, Cambridge University Press.
Ricoeur, P. (1984) *Time and Narrative*, Vol. 1, trans. K. McLaughlin and D. Pellauer, Chicago and London, University of Chicago Press.
Ridenour, R.C. (1981) *Nationalism, Modernism, and Personal Rivalry in Nineteenth-Century Russian Music*, Ann Arbor, Mich., UMI Research Press.
Rink, J. (ed.) (1995) *The Practice of Performance: Studies in Musical Performance*, Cambridge, Cambridge University Press.
Robinson, J. (ed.) (1997) *Music and Meaning*, Ithaca, NY, and London, Cornell University Press.
Robinson, P. (1993) 'Is *Aida* an Orientalist Opera?' *Cambridge Opera Journal* 5/2, 133–40.
Rosen, C. (1971) *The Classical Style: Haydn, Mozart, Beethoven*, London, Faber and Faber.
—— (1980) 'Influence: Plagiarism and Inspiration', *Nineteenth Century Music* 4/2, 87–100.
—— (1999) *The Romantic Generation*, London, Fontana Press.
Rupprecht, P. (2001) *Britten's Musical Language*, Cambridge, Cambridge University Press.
Rutherford, J. (ed.) (1990) *Identity: Community, Culture, Difference*, London, Lawrence & Wishart.
Rycenga, J. (1994) 'Lesbian Compositional Process: One Lover-Composer's Perspective', in P. Brett, E. Wood and G.C. Thomas (eds), *Queering the Pitch: The New Gay and Lesbian Musicology*, London and New York, Routledge.
Sadie, S. (ed.) (2001) *The New Grove Dictionary of Music and Musicians*, 2nd edn, London, Macmillan.
Said, E. (1978) *Orientalism: Western Conceptions of the Orient*, London, Penguin.
—— (1994) *Culture and Imperialism*, London, Vintage Books.
Sakolsky, R. and Ho, W.-H. (eds) (1995) *Sounding Off! Music as Subversion/Resistance/Revolution*, Brooklyn, NY, Autonomedia.
Samson, J. (1989) 'Chopin and Genre', *Music Analysis* 8/3, 213–32.
—— (ed.) (1991) *The Late Romantic Era: from the mid-19th century to World War 1*, London, Macmillan.
—— (1994) 'Chopin Reception: Theory, History, Analysis', in J. Rink and J. Samson (eds), *Chopin Studies 2*, Cambridge, Cambridge University Press.
—— (1999) 'Analysis in Context', in N. Cook and M. Everist (eds), *Rethinking Music*, Oxford and New York, Oxford University Press.
—— (2003) *Virtuosity and the Musical Work: The Transcendental Studies of Liszt*, Cambridge, Cambridge University Press.
Samuels, R. (1995) *Mahler's Sixth Symphony: A Study in Musical Semiotics*, Cambridge, Cambridge University Press.
Savage, J. (1991) *England's Dreaming: Sex Pistols and Punk Rock*, London, Faber and Faber.
Schenker, H. (1921–24) *Der Tonwille*, in 10 volumes, Vienna, Universal Edition.
—— (1979) *Free Composition*, trans. E. Oster, New York and London, Longman.
Schleiermacher, F. (1998) *Hermeneutics and Criticism: And Other Writings*, trans. and ed. A. Bowie, Cambridge, Cambridge University Press.

Schoenberg, A. (1970) *Fundamentals of Musical Composition*, London, Faber and Faber.
—— (1975) *Style and Idea*, trans. L Black, ed. L. Stein, London, Faber and Faber.
—— (1978) *Theory of Harmony*, trans. R. Carter, London, Faber and Faber.
—— (1995) *The Musical Idea and the Logic, Technique and Art of its Presentation*, eds P. Carpenter and S. Neff, New York, Columbia University Press.
Schopenhauer, A. (1995) *The World as Will and Idea*, trans. J. Berman, ed. D. Berman, London, Dent.
Schorske, C. (1981) *Fin-de-siècle Vienna: Politics and Culture*, New York, Vintage Books.
Schuller, G. (1968) *Early Jazz: Its Roots and Musical Development*, Oxford and New York, Oxford University Press.
Schulte-Sasse, J. (1984) Foreword to P. Bürger, *Theory of the Avant-Garde*, trans. M. Shaw, Manchester, Manchester University Press.
Schwarz, B. (1972) *Music and Musical Life in Soviet Russia 1917–1970*, London, Barrie & Jenkin.
Scott, D.B. (1989) *The Singing Bourgeois: Songs of the Victorian Drawing Room and Parlour*, Milton Keynes, Open University Press.
—— (1998) 'Orientalism and Musical Style', *Musical Quarterly* 82/2, 309–35.
—— (ed.) (2000) *Music, Culture, and Society: A Reader*, Oxford and New York, Oxford University Press.
—— (2003) *From the Erotic to the Demonic: On Critical Musicology*, Oxford and New York, Oxford University Press.
Scruton, R. (1999) *The Aesthetics of Music*, Oxford and New York, Oxford University Press.
Seashore, C.E. (1967) *Psychology of Music*, New York, Dover.
Sedgwick, E.K. (1994) *Epistemology of the Closet*, London, Penguin.
—— (ed.) (1997) *Novel Gazing: Queer Reading in Fiction*, Durham, NC, and London, Duke University Press.
Seeger, A. (1987) *Why Suyá Sing: A Musical Anthropology of an Amazonian People*, Cambridge, Cambridge University Press.
Shank, B. (1994) *Dissonant Identities: The Rock'n'Roll Scene in Austin, Texas*, Hanover, NH, Wesleyan University Press.
Sharma, S., Hutnyk, J. and Sharma, A. (eds) (1996) *Dis-Orienting Rhythms: The Politics of the New Asian Dance Music*, London and Atlantic Highlands, NJ, Zed Books.
Shepherd, J. (1991) *Music as Social Text*, Cambridge, Polity Press.
Shipton, A. (2001) *A New History of Jazz*, London and New York, Continuum.
Shuker, R. (1998) *Popular Music: The Key Concepts*, London and New York, Routledge.
Shumway, D. (1999) 'Rock and Roll Soundtracks and the Production of Nostalgia', *Cinema Journal* 38/2, 36–51.
Sitsky, L. (1994) *Music of the Repressed Russian Avant-Garde 1900–1929*, Westport, Conn., Greenwood Press.
Skelton, T. and Valentine, G. (eds) (1998) *Cool Places: Geographies of Youth*, London and New York, Routledge.
Sloboda, J.A. (1991) 'Music Structure and Emotional Response to Music: Some Empirical Findings', *Psychology of Music* 19, 110–20.
—— (1992) 'Psychological Structures in Music: Core Research 1980–1990', in J. Paynter, T. Howell, R. Orton and P. Seymour (eds), *Companion to Contemporary Musical Thought*, London and New York, Routledge.
Smith, A.D. (1986) *The Ethnic Origins of Nations*, Oxford, Basil Blackwell.

Smith, B.H. (1988) *Contingencies of Value: Alternative Perspectives for Critical Theory*, Cambridge, Mass., and London, Harvard University Press.

Soja, E. (1989) *Postmodern Geographies*, London and New York, Verso.

Solie, R. (1980) 'The Living Work: Organicism and Musical Analysis', *Nineteenth Century Music* 4/2, 147–56.

—— (ed.) (1993) *Musicology and Difference: Gender and Sexuality in Music Scholarship*, Berkeley and London, University of California Press.

Sollors, W. (1986) *Beyond Ethnicity: Consent and Descent in American Culture*, New York and Oxford, Oxford University Press.

Solomon, M. (1977) *Beethoven*, New York, Shirmer Books.

—— (1982) 'Thoughts on Biography', *Nineteenth Century Music* 5/3, 268–76.

—— (1989) 'Franz Schubert and the Peacocks of Benvenuto Cellini', *Nineteenth Century Music* 12/3, 193–206.

—— (2003) *Late Beethoven: Music, Thought, Imagination*, Berkeley and London, University of California Press.

Spitta, P. (1884) *Johann Sebastian Bach: His Work and Influence on the Music of Germany 1685–1750*, trans. C. Bell and J.A. Fuller-Maitland, London, Novello, Ewer & Co.

Spitzer, M. (1996) 'The Retransition as Sign: Listener-Orientated Approaches to Tonal Closure in Haydn's Sonata-Form Movements', *Journal of the Royal Musical Association* 121/1, 11–45.

—— (1997) 'Convergences: Criticism, Analysis and Beethoven Reception', *Music Analysis* 16/3, 369–91.

—— (2004) *Metaphor and Musical Thought*, Chicago and London, University of Chicago Press.

Spivak, G.C. (1976) translator's preface to J. Derrida, *Of Grammatology*, Baltimore, Johns Hopkins University Press.

—— (1993) *Outside in the Teaching Machine*, London and New York, Routledge.

—— (1994) 'Can the Subaltern Speak?' in P. Williams and L. Chrisman (eds), *Colonial Discourse and Post-Colonial Theory: A Reader*, New York, Columbia University Press.

—— (1999) *A Critique of Postcolonial Reason: Toward a History of the Vanishing Present*, Cambridge, Mass., and London, Harvard University Press.

Steblin, R. (1993) 'The Peacock's Tale: Schubert's Sexuality Reconsidered', *Nineteenth Century Music* 17/1, 5–33.

Stevens, D. (1980) *Musicology: A Practical Guide*, London, Macdonald.

—— (1987) *Musicology in Practice: Collected Essays by Denis Stevens. Vol. 1: 1948–1970*, ed. T.P. Lewis, London, Kahn and Averill.

Stock, J. (1993) 'The Application of Schenkerian Analysis to Ethnomusicology: Problems and Possibilities', *Music Analysis* 12/2, 215–40.

Stokes, M. (1994) *Ethnicity, Identity, and Music: The Musical Construction of Place*, Oxford, Berg.

Storr, A. (1992) *Music and the Mind*, London, Harper Collins.

Straus, J. (1990) *Remaking the Past: Musical Modernism and the Influence of the Tonal Tradition*, Cambridge, Mass., and London, Harvard University Press.

Stravinsky, I. (1936) *An Autobiography*, New York, Simon & Schuster.

—— (2002) *Memories and Commentaries*, London, Faber and Faber.

Street, A. (1987) 'The Rhetorico-Musical Structure of the "Goldberg" Variations: Bach's *Clavier-übung* IV and the Institutio Oratoria of Quintillian', *Music Analysis* 6/1–2, 89–131.

—— (1989) 'Superior Myths, Dogmatic Allegories: The Resistance to Musical Unity', *Music Analysis* 8/1–2, 77–123.

—— (1994) 'Carnival', *Music Analysis* 13/2–3, 255–98.

—— (2000) '"The Ear of the Other": Style and Identity in Schoenberg's Eight Songs, Op. 6', in C. Cross and R. Berman (eds) *Schoenberg and Words*, New York, Garland.

Strinati, D. (1995) *An Introduction to Theories of Popular Culture*, London and New York, Routledge.

Strohm, R. (1993) *The Rise of European Music, 1380–1500*, Cambridge, Cambridge University Press.

—— (2000) 'Looking Back at Ourselves: The Problem with the Musical Work-Concept', in M. Talbot (ed.), *The Musical Work: Reality or Invention?*, Liverpool, Liverpool University Press.

Subotnik, R.R. (1991) *Developing Variations: Style and Ideology in Western Music*, Minneapolis, University of Minnesota Press.

—— (1996) *Deconstructive Variations: Music and Reason in Western Society*, Minneapolis, University of Minnesota Press.

Sweeney-Turner, S. (1995), 'Speaking Without Tongues', *The Musical Times* 136, 183–6.

Tagg, P. (1989) '"Black Music", "Afro-American Music" and "European Music"', *Popular Music* 8/3, 285–98.

—— (2000) 'Analysing Popular Music: Theory, Method, and Practice', in R. Middleton (ed.), *Reading Pop: Approaches to Textual Analysis in Popular Music*, Oxford and New York, Oxford University Press.

Talbot, M. (2000) 'The Work-Concept and Composer-Centredness', in M. Talbot (ed.), *The Musical Work: Reality or Invention?* Liverpool, Liverpool University Press.

Tarasti, E. (1994) *A Theory of Musical Semiotics*, Bloomington, Indiana University Press.

Taruskin, R. (1980) 'Russian Folk Melodies in *The Rite of Spring*', *Journal of the American Musicological Society* 33/3, 501–43.

—— (1986) 'Letter to the editor from Richard Taruskin', *Music Analysis* 5/2–3, 313–20.

—— (1992) Review of Abbate (1991), *Cambridge Opera Journal* 4/2, 187–97.

—— (1993) 'Revising Revision', *Journal of the American Musicological Society* 46/1, 114–38.

—— (1995) *Text and Act: Essays on Music and Performance*, Oxford and New York, Oxford University Press.

—— (1996) *Stravinsky and the Russian Traditions: A Biography of the Works Through Mavra*, Oxford and New York, Oxford University Press.

—— (1997) *Defining Russia Musically: Historical and Hermeneutical Essays*, Princeton, NJ, Princeton University Press.

—— (2001) 'Nationalism', in S. Sadie (ed.), *New Grove Dictionary of Music and Musicians*, Vol. 17, London, Macmillan.

Taylor, T. (1997) *Global Pop: World Music, World Markets*, New York and London, Routledge.

Thomas, D.A. (1995) *Music and the Origins of Language: Theories from the French Enlightenment*, Cambridge, Cambridge University Press.

Thomas, G.C. (1994) '"Was George Friedrich Handel Gay?" On Closet Questions and Cultural Politics', in P. Brett, E. Wood and G.C. Thomas (eds),

Queering the Pitch: The New Gay and Lesbian Musicology, London and New York, Routledge.

Thornton, S (1995) *Club Cultures: Music, Media and Subcultural Capital*, Cambridge, Polity Press.

Tischler, B.L. (1986) *An American Music: The Search for an American Musical Identity*, Oxford and New York, Oxford University Press.

Tomlinson, G. (1984) 'The Web of Culture: A Context for Musicology', *Nineteenth Century Music* 7/3, 350–62.

—— (1992) 'Cultural Dialogics and Jazz: A White Historian Signifies', in K. Bergeron and P. Bohlman (eds), *Disciplining Music: Musicology and its Canons*, Chicago and London, University of Chicago Press.

—— (1993a) 'Musical Pasts and Postmodern Musicologies: A Response to Lawrence Kramer', *Current Musicology* 53, 18–24.

—— (1993b) *Music in Renaissance Magic: Toward a Historiography of Others*, Chicago and London, University of Chicago Press.

Tomlinson, J. (1999) *Globalization and Culture*, Cambridge, Polity Press.

Tovey, D.F. (2001) *The Classics of Music: Talks, Essays and Other Writing Previously Uncollected*, eds M. Tilmouth, D. Kimbell and R. Savage, Oxford and New York, Oxford University Press.

Trumpener, K. (2000) 'Béla Bartók and the Rise of Comparative Ethnomusicology: Nationalism, Race Purity, and the Legacy of the Austro-Hungarian Empire', in R. Radano and P.V. Bohlman (eds), *Music and the Racial Imagination*, Chicago and London, University of Chicago Press.

Turner, B.S. (1994) *Orientalism, Postmodernism and Globalism*, London and New York, Routledge.

van den Toorn, P.C. (1995) *Music, Politics, and the Academy*, Berkeley and London, University of California Press.

Vasari, G. (1963) *Lives of the Painters, Sculptors and Architects*, trans. A.B. Hinds, ed. W. Gaunt, London, Dent.

Vattimo, G. (1988) *The End of Modernity: Nihilism and Hermeneutics in Post-modern Culture*, trans. J.R. Snyder, Cambridge, Polity Press.

Vaughan Williams, R. (1996) *National Music and Other Essays*, Oxford and New York, Oxford University Press.

Veeser, A. (ed.) (1994) *The New Historicism Reader*, London and New York, Routledge.

Verstraete, G. and Cresswell, T. (eds) (2002) *Mobilizing Place, Placing Mobility: The Politics of Representation in a Globalized World*, Amsterdam, Rodopi.

Walser, R. (1993) *Running with the Devil: Power, Gender, and Madness in Heavy Metal Music*, Hanover, NH, University Press of New England.

—— (1997) '"Out of Notes": Signification, Interpretation and the Problem of Miles Davis', in D. Schwarz, A. Kassabian and D. Siegel (eds), *Keeping Score: Music, Disciplinarity and Culture*, Charlottesville and London, University of Virginia Press.

Weber, W. (1992) *The Rise of Musical Classics in Eighteenth Century England: A Study in Canon, Ritual and Ideology*, Oxford and New York, Oxford University Press.

—— (1999) 'The History of Musical Canon', in N. Cook and M. Everist (eds), *Rethinking Music*, Oxford and New York, Oxford University Press.

Webster, J. (1991) *Haydn's 'Farewell' Symphony and the Idea of the Classical Style*, Cambridge, Cambridge University Press.

—— (2001–02) 'Between Enlightenment and Romanticism in Music History: "First Viennese Modernism" and the Delayed Nineteenth Century', *Nineteenth Century Music* 25/2–3, 108–26.

—— (2004) 'The Eighteenth Century as a Music-Historical Period?' *Eighteenth-Century Music* 1/1, 47–60.

Weiner, M.A. (1995) *Richard Wagner and the Anti-Semitic Imagination*, Lincoln and London, University of Nebraska Press.

Werbner, P. and Modood, T. (eds) (1997) *Debating Cultural Hybridity: Multi-Cultural Identities and the Politics of Anti-Racism*, London and Atlantic Highlands, NJ, Zed Books.

Westrup, J., Abraham, G. *et al.* (1957) *New Oxford History of Music*, Oxford and New York, Oxford University Press.

White, H. (1980) 'The Value of Narrative in the Representation of Reality', in W.J.T. Mitchell (ed.), *On Narrative*, Chicago and London, University of Chicago Press.

White, H. and Murphy, M. (eds) (2001) *Musical Constructions of Nationalism: Essays on the History and Ideology of European Musical Culture, 1800–1945*, Cork, Cork University Press.

Whiteley, S. (2000) *Women and Popular Music: Sexuality, Identity and Subjectivity*, London and New York, Routledge.

Whitesell, L. (1994) 'Men with a Past: Music and the "Anxiety of Influence"', *Nineteenth Century Music* 18/2, 152–98.

Whittall, A. (1982) 'Music Analysis as Human Science? *Le Sacre du Printemps* in Theory and Practice', *Music Analysis* 1/1, 33–53.

—— (1987) *Romantic Music: A Concise History from Schubert to Sibelius*, London, Thames & Hudson.

—— (1991) 'Analysis as Performance', *Atti Del XIV Congresso Della Societa Internazionale Di Musicologica*, Vol. 1, 654–60.

—— (1999) *Musical Composition in the Twentieth Century*, Oxford and New York, Oxford University Press.

—— (2003) *Exploring Twentieth-Century Music: Tradition and Innovation*, Cambridge, Cambridge University Press.

Wicke, P. (1990) *Rock Music: Culture, Aesthetics, and Sociology*, trans. R. Fogg, Cambridge, Cambridge University Press.

Williams, A. (1997) *New Music and the Claims of Modernity*, Aldershot, Ashgate.

—— (2000) 'Musicology and Postmodernism', *Music Analysis* 19/3, 385–407.

—— (2001) *Constructing Musicology*, Aldershot, Ashgate.

Williams, P. (2004) 'Peripheral Visions?' *The Musical Times* 145, 51–67.

Williams, R. (1958) *Culture and Society*, London, Hogarth Press.

—— (1977) *Marxism and Literature,* Oxford and New York, Oxford University Press.

—— (1988) *Keywords: A Vocabulary of Culture and Society*, London, Fontana.

Wilmer, V. (1992) *As Serious as Your Life: John Coltrane and Beyond*, London, Serpent's Tail.

Wimsatt, W.K. and Beardsley, M.C. (1954) *The Verbal Icon: Studies in the Meaning of Poetry*, Lexington, University of Kentucky Press.

Wintle, C. (1992) 'Analysis and Psychoanalysis: Wagner's Musical Metaphors', in J. Paynter, T. Howell, R. Orton and P. Seymour (eds), *Companion to Contemporary Musical Thought*, London and New York, Routledge.

Wojcik, P.R. and Knight, A. (eds) (2001) *Soundtrack Available: Essays on Film and Popular Music*, Durham, NC, and London, Duke University Press.

Wood, E. (1993) 'Lesbian Fugue: Ethel Smyth's Contrapuntal Arts', in R. Solie (ed.), *Musicology and Difference: Gender and Sexuality in Music Scholarship*, Berkeley and London, University of California Press.

Worton, M. and Still, J. (1991) *Intertextuality: Theories and Practices*, Manchester, Manchester University Press.

Wright, C. (1975) 'Dufay at Cambrai: Discoveries and Revisions', *Journal of the American Musicological Society* 28/2, 175–229.

Yegenoglu, M. (1998) *Colonial Fantasies: Towards a Feminist Reading of Orientalism*, Cambridge, Cambridge University Press.

Young, R.J.C. (1995) *Colonial Desire: Hybridity in Theory, Culture and Race*, London and New York, Routledge.

—— (2001) *Postcolonialism: An Historical Introduction*, Oxford, Basil Blackwell.

Žižek, S. (ed.) (1994) *Mapping Ideology*, London and New York, Verso.

Žižek, S. and Dolar, M. (2002) *Opera's Second Death*, London and New York, Routledge.

Zolov, E. (1999) *Refried Elvis: The Rise of the Mexican Counterculture*, Berkeley and London, University of California Press.

Zon, B. (2000) *Music and Metaphor in Nineteenth-Century British Musicology*, Aldershot, Ashgate.

NAME INDEX

SUBJECT INDEX

NOTE: Page numbers in bold indicate the entry for a subject.